MENDING FOR MEMORY

MENDING FOR MEMORY: SEWING IN LOUISIANA
ESSAYS, STORIES, AND POEMS

edited by Lee Meitzen Grue and Susan Tucker

NEW LAUREL REVIEW PRESS
New Orleans, LA
2017

The New Laurel Review Press is an outgrowth of *The New Laurel Review*, an independent non-profit literary journal begun in 1971. Founding editors were Alice Moser Claudel and Calvin André Claudel. Lee Meitzen Grue has been the editor since the 1980s. Editorial and business correspondence should be addressed to the *New Laurel Review*, 828 Lesseps Street, New Orleans, LA 70117.

ISBN: 978-0-692-81146-7

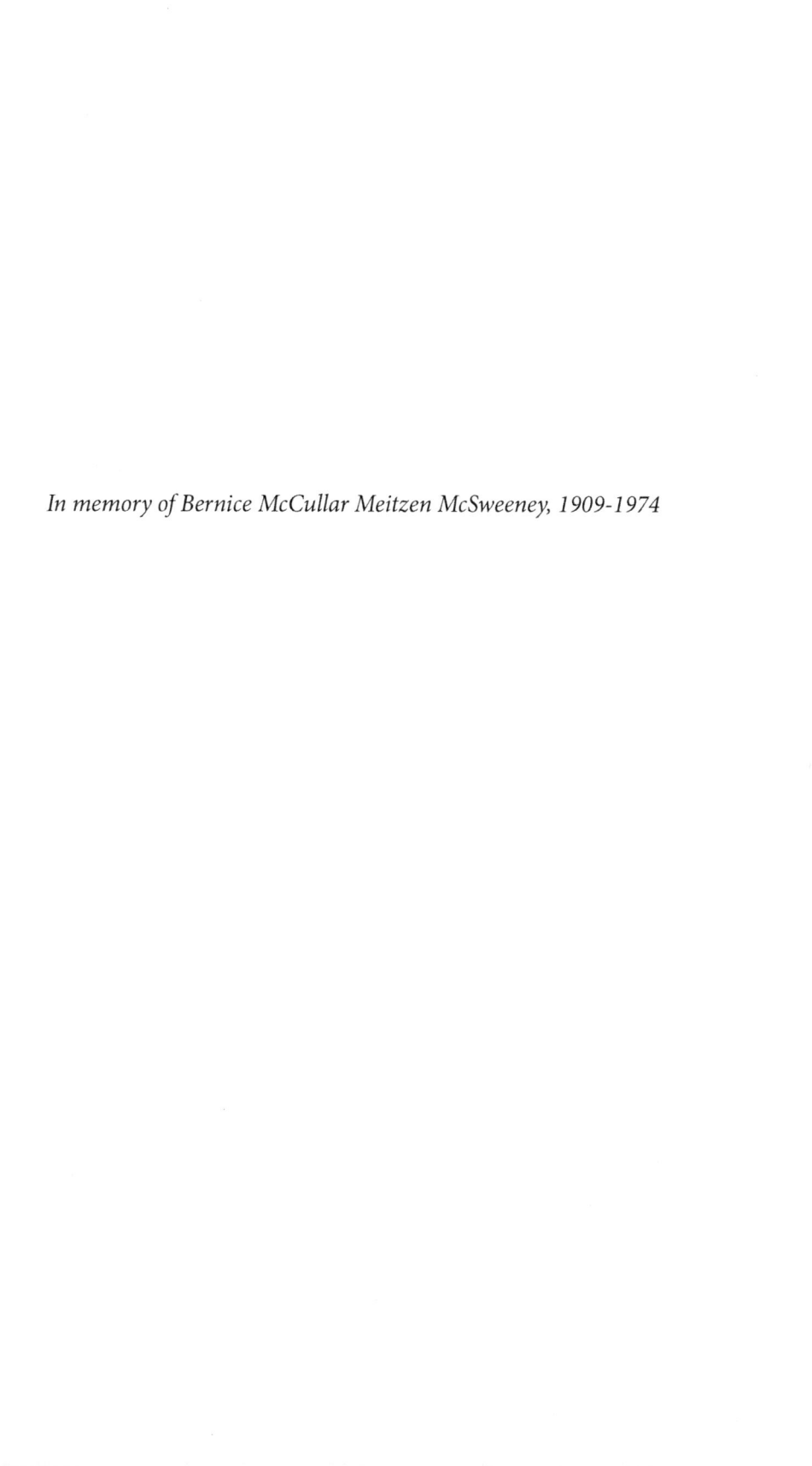

In memory of Bernice McCullar Meitzen McSweeney, 1909-1974

TABLE OF CONTENTS

V. Telling Stories of Cloth, Needle, and Thread

VI. Learning About Ourselves and Others Who Sew

I. Introduction

Figure 1.1. *Her First Lesson in Embroidery*. Unknown Photographer, ca. 1902. Gibbs Manufacturing Company. Courtesy of the Library of Congress, American Memory.

In this book, as contributor Arthur Pfister tells us, the world spins around on "thimbles, pins, needles, tape measures, rulers, ribbons, scissors, spools of thread, yards of material from bolts of fabric of all patterns 'on account' from Mr. Levine (the rag man), zippers, buttons, and notions of all manner and stripes . . . from Krauss, McCrory's, Woolworth's, and Maison Blanche Annex." This is the universe of people who sew, especially those in Louisiana. The contributors (and the depicted seamstresses, tailors, sewers, beaders, knitters, quiltmakers, weavers, and other names used) tell of an exuberance for the stitch, of the knowledge that a lot can be solved by creativity with cloth, and of beneficial skills in general. These people are resourceful in their everyday pursuits, or as another contributor, Martha McFerren, writes, they find sewing and work with cloth in general to be "a useful beauty."

Textiles are also all around us, or, in other words from McFerren, "though transient, factual." From these viewpoints and those of other contributors, and to you readers perhaps, it is both prosaic and academic to say that the world of fiber always has accompanied the journeys of humans to live their lives. Words about cloth in a very real sense allow us to trace humanity. As we compiled this book, these contributors didn't think it at all a leap to remind us that the binding of thin filaments of plants, the carding of various animals' fur, and the weaving and sewing that followed were just as important as fire to the beginning of civilizations.

We hope you also will think about this necessary, happy, and healing trace of needle and thread going in and out of fabric. We hope you will enjoy the thoughts of poets, short story writers, essayists, oral historians, artists, and academics about their placement of pins and their renderings of thread across the landscapes of imagination and history.

We honor here especially Bernice McCullar Meitzen McSweeney. The first essay tells of her life and is written by her daughter, *New Laurel Review* editor and publisher, Lee Meitzen Grue. Celeste Delafosse, Lee's daughter and Bernice McSweeney's granddaughter, also helps us to remember sewing in a poem that appears in the last chapter. And some of McSweeney's creations appear in illustrations.

3

Other mothers and grandmothers figure in additional inclusions. For these writers, women's creations in cloth are both subversive and empowering. Skill with the needle rests upon connections with the past, sets up some contemplative time, necessitates thought and planning, and can be accomplished at home. Almost all girls born before 1960 were taught to sew.

Figure 1.2. *One of the project women making clothes for her family on her new sewing machine, Terrebonne Project, Schriever, Louisiana.* Photograph by Marion Post Wolcott for the U.S. Farm Security Administration, 1937. Courtesy of the Library of Congress, American Memory.

Yet from New Orleans, the contributors tell also of men who sew. Carnival culture especially encourages tailors, as well as others, who take up needles in the creation of clothes for dancing, Carnival masking, second line parades, and processions of Mardi Gras Indians. Some men later sew their daughters' wedding dresses, knit and crochet presents for others, and whip up curtains and slipcovers to match a newly painted room. Like Carnival, sewing alters the social landscape even as it enforces some aspects of daily lives, the hierarchy of domestic tasks, and the types of people who wear those tiaras at balls, those satin pants on parade floats.

Look then to all the entries in the anthology to tell a long history of material culture, to delight by evoking your own memories, and to suggest how the fabric of your own life has been stitched together. As contributor Malaika Favorite advises, "Don't be ashamed to add decorative trims."

Finally, we add this explanation for your consideration. The verb *to mend* means 1. to make something whole, sound, or usable by repairing; 2. to remove or correct defects or errors in; or, 3. to set right. Not much has been written on sewing and fabric in general. They rank low in the world of books. We hope by our writing to change that status. We hope this book is a mending of that status. We hope you carry the memories of sewing and fabrics here to others.

Figure 1.3. *Kevin Dunn, sewing.* Photograph by Judy Cooper, July 31, 2011.

II. Remembering Bernice McCullar Meitzen McSweeney

Figure 2.1. *Sewing Table with Portrait of Bernice McCullar Meitzen McSweeney.* Table manufactured in the 1920s. Photograph by Phyllis Parun, 2013.

My Mother

Lee Meitzen Grue

My mother's name was Bernice, but everyone called her Barney. For much of my life, my mother made our clothes. She was a striking woman. I have pictures of her in the styles of the thirties. With her dark hair worn in a chignon, she looked wonderful in those slender, tailored dresses.

She once told me she learned to sew at the birth of her little brother Claude. He was born at home after their Daddy died during the flu epidemic of 1918. She made Claude's diaper shirts and later little suits.

She was the eldest and became his child nurse to help her mother, Fannie Lee McCullar. Fannie worked as a Practical Nurse for her brother-in-law, Doctor William Grace, who was married to her sister Magdalene. The families lived next door to one another in Plaquemine, a town right on the Mississippi across from Baton Rouge. I remember Fannie as my grandmother, who, I was told, had eight pregnancies before she lost her husband. Only three of these children lived. My mother Bernice, her sister Mercedes (De De), and baby Claude were my grandmother's family, and mine.

My mother made her own dresses and when old enough, worked in Rinato's grocery for eight dollars a week. It was the Depression.

In 1929, when she was nineteen, my father, LeRoy (Mike) Meitzen was passing through on a seismograph crew. He was tall, good looking, and funny. He brought with him the reality of her dream to travel. Before she turned twenty, she had married him and left home. For years they traveled through the little country towns of Louisiana, Mississippi, and Texas exploring for oil for the Independent Exploration Company. Most of the men on the crew were from Germany. They had come to this country with the technology to find oil. My father spoke German; his own grandparents had come to this country through the port of Galveston. The German language helped him get the job when the crew passed through Anahuac, Texas, a few years after Spindletop was discovered in nearby Beaumont.

9

Figure 2.2. Child in dress with appliquéd flowers. Designed and made by Bernice McCullar Meitzen McSweeney, ca. 1970. Photograph by Yuka Petz, 2016.

The men on the crew buried charges of dynamite and exploded them to record the seismic waves on sensitive photographic paper. The waves indicated where they might find oil. My mother had trunks made of the used dynamite boxes to hold the fine handwork she made: monogrammed cutwork sheets and pillow cases, tablecloths embroidered with Chinese silk thread showing dark red flowers and light green silk leaves.

The small, often dirty, new apartments we moved into would be scrubbed and sometimes painted. Our family would live in the apartment for about six months before we moved on. We did this for years. The people on the oil crews lived like theatrical gypsies. The men were hard drinkers with vivid personalities. The women were women who wanted something more exciting than the average small town life. They drank too. They still lived in small towns, but not for long.

I was born in my grandmother's house in Plaquemine, but until the fourth grade I usually traveled on the road with my parents from town to town and school to school. My mother liked to make fine things. I had wonderful costumes and beautiful dresses. While we lived in Plaquemine, I went to the convent for first grade. My teacher was an Irish nun, the famous Sister Mathilda, who taught many generations of Plaquemine children. Once when I went back to Plaquemine for the sixth grade, my mother made me a beautiful red wool coat with a black velveteen collar. I wore it to school for mass one day and a real gypsy child slapped my face. She said, "That's just for being who you are." Sister Boniface said, "It's such a fine coat."

Over the years my father's drinking took hold of him. He suffered from dynamite headaches which came from smelling the fumes of the dynamite charges he worked with. My mother said, "That was the beginning—he drank to sleep." My father was working in Texas and not much of his money came to Plaquemine at my grandmother's house for my mother and me. She made clothes for her relatives and friends. We were poor relations, but I didn't know it.

After my mother and father divorced, I lived with the Meitzens, my father's mother and sisters in Anahuac, Texas, for three years until my mother could afford to take me with her again. I came in the summer twice to visit her in New Orleans. She was living in a

Figure 2.3. Lee Meitzen in dress made by her mother, ca. 1949. Courtesy of Lee Meitzen Grue.

single room on Joseph Street. One time when I came she was working for the Lylian Shop, which made fine clothes for the children of rich families in New Orleans and for the children of movie stars.[1] I once went with her to work in a narrow, long room with a dozen or more Spanish-speaking women at sewing machines. They were all paid very little. I don't know how long she worked there, but I know she later made clothes for Carnival queens.

When I came to live with my mother in New Orleans she was working for a small children's shop called Malinda Jane's Togs for Toddlers. I always saw clearly that my mother turned her sewing into jobs.

Our first apartment in New Orleans was over a drugstore on St. Charles and Milan Street. The shop my mother worked for was across the hall. Our apartment had been vacant for years. She talked the landlord into renting to us. There were three rooms: a kitchen with a sink but no stove, a bedroom, and a bath. We had a hotplate and an icebox that an iceman delivered ice to. We thought it was the iceman who stole my mother's diamond ring. The ring was in her purse in the apartment waiting to be repaired. Mother bought our furniture from the Salvation Army. The only piece I remember was a couch that unfolded to make a bed. She had recovered the couch in burgundy fabric. We slept on it together. My mother had stripped the walls of old wallpaper and painted the whole apartment herself. By the time I got there it looked great. I knew that we had little money, but I never felt poor. I had been spoiled by my aunts and I always had pretty clothes that my mother made for me.

In New Orleans I went to a public high school on nearby Napoleon Avenue called Sophie B. Wright. In those days, most of the high schools were all-girls or all-boys, and were also segregated by race. All the teachers and all the girls at Sophie B. Wright were white, and most of the girls had known one another since childhood. I was an outsider befriended mostly by Jewish girls. In the pecking order that was New Orleans, they were, like me, somewhat outsiders or at least they knew how, in some subtle way, exclusion from Carnival gave them a status not unlike my own:

---

[1] See the essay by Pamela Rabalais-Vinci in this volume.

Figure 2.4. Bernice McCullar Meitzen McSweeney in Africa, ca. 1970. Fourth from left. Courtesy of Lee Meitzen Grue.

someone from "away." All the same, I remember a wonderful teacher by the name of Miss Towles. She taught Civics and we learned about these and other sorts of prejudice. We also knew that until the late 1930s or maybe until World War II, married women were barred from teaching. Even in the late 1940s and early 1950s, most of our teachers were maiden ladies or widows. Most of them had been educated at Normal School or at Newcomb College, so we also learned that some opportunities were open to us.[2]

I graduated in 1951 at seventeen. By this time, my mother was working for Town & Country and Mignon's where she, again, designed and made patterns for custom-made children's clothes. She made my graduation dress. I graduated with 156 girls. We wore white

---

[2] Roberta Towles, sister of Sarah Towles Reed. Both were active in the teacher's union and the initial discussion of the desegregation of the city's schools. Sarah Towles Reed also defied the marriage ban. The sisters were educated at Newcomb College, as were a number of other Sophie Wright teachers such as Fannie Moret.

and carried bouquets of red roses. My dress was copied from the cover of *Vogue* magazine. It was made of imported Swiss Organdy. In excess it had two cummerbunds with sashes. One in blue and one in bright coral, both in silk.

Some years after, when I was out on my own, my mother married a teacher from Delgado College by the name of William J. McSweeney. He was from Boston.

In the late fifties they had the opportunity to live in Uganda, East Africa, where Bill McSweeney taught African students how to do electrical wiring. My mother taught sewing.

They traveled extensively in Uganda, Kenya, and later all over Europe on their way home in 1962. They came home shortly before the British gave Uganda its independence.

In 1961, I went to visit them for a month. With my family, traveling in Bill's old Ford, I saw lions, wildebeests, and zebras in the many great wildlife parks. Near the end of my visit my stepfather hired a small boat to carry us up to Murchison Falls. We traveled up the White Nile with crocodiles by the hundreds slipping off the banks into the water as we passed. The river was full of wonderful pink hippos rising and diving, looking like so much boiled beef. We arrived at the foot of Murchison Falls where we walked off into the bush with the Asian captain and two spear carriers who disappeared when my mother and I were charged by an elephant as she tried to take a picture. But that is another story.

My mother left me a legacy of stories and sewing.

A TRUNK FULL OF PIECE GOODS

Lee Meitzen Grue

Mother, all this material
is hard to use up. Who sews now?
My gift not equal
to yours.

Your trunk
is taking over my house.
Too heavy to move.
I have to sit on top

to close it.
Seersucker pokes out,
dotted swiss
gets torn in the hinges.

I sew hot seams,
too impatient to cast over.
The beauty of what you've made
is aging now.
Impossible to mend.

I've thrown away nothing
seeing it as unfaithful,
lacking in loyalty,
that virtue we consider strong.

Dresses you made
hang in my closet
French seamed, slender,
unworn.

I've gone on.
All your baggage still with me,
overflowing with good stuff
begging to be used.

III. Exploring Sewing Through the Lens of the Academic World

Figure 3.1. Quilt created in the 1930s with annotation from 2014. Courtesy of Maureen Reed Detweiler.

FOR SALE.

A Mulatto Negress, aged 25 years, a first rate house servant and seamstress; she is fully guaranteed. Also, her Son, aged 4 years Apply at the Agency Office.

ju16-22-3t

JOHN WALKER.

Figure 3.2. "For Sale." Slave seamstress advertisement. *New Orleans Daily Picayune*, June 6, 1837.

Figure 3.3. Dressmaker's ledger page, Nov. 14, 1868. RG 68, Historical Center, Louisiana State Museum.

"Each One A Unique Creation": Handsewn Infants' and Children's Garments in Louisiana

Pamela Rabalais-Vinci[1]

According to *The Art of Dressmaking* sewing book published in 1927, "The nicest baby clothes are made entirely by hand." The 1949 *Singer Sewing Book* included the observation, "Many women exclaim regretfully when they see machine stitching on a baby's garment." Both remarks illustrate the long-held consumer preference for handsewn infants' and children's garments as well as a sentiment responsible for what grew to be a large handsewn garment industry in mid-twentieth century South Louisiana.[2]

Retail advertising also documented the popular reputation of Louisiana French women involved in the industry. For example, New Orleans-based company De Lis publicized in its 1920s catalog that its merchandise was locally made by wonderful needlewomen of French descent whose "taste and skill are a matter of inheritance." The French Quarter's Louise Shop, founded by Flora Isaacs Lazard during the same period, also employed Louisiana needlewomen to handsew its infants' and children's wear merchandise. The daughter of Marks Isaacs, a well-known merchant in the city and early partner in the Maison Blanche department store, Lazard did not sew herself but is remembered as having a talent for organizational skills, resulting in a business that continued through three generations of women in the Isaacs family.

To engage seamstresses, Lazard drove to the South Louisiana French-populated countryside every Sunday to different communities, meeting in a home where the host's friends and family were invited to sign up to sew. Packages containing company patterns, instructions, fabrics, laces, and trims were then assembled in the New Orleans shop and mailed to the enlisted sewer's home. The sewer completed the work and mailed it back to New Orleans to be sold in the shop.[3]

---

[1] The author wishes to acknowledge the contributions of Jeannie Downs Baumeister of the "Old Fashion Baby" website in the research and interview process for this essay.

[2] *The Art of Dressmaking* (New York: Butterick Pattern Company, 1927), 229; Mary Brooks Picken, *Singer Sewing Book* (New York: Grosset & Dunlap Publishers, 1949), 159.

[3] "Of Interest to Mothers." *De Lis Catalog* (New Orleans, 1920s), "Introduction"; Leslie Saiewitz Bingham, personal interview

De Lis and the Louise Shop were two of the many New Orleans companies employing Louisiana French women in this cottage industry early in the twentieth century. The old and prominent New Orleans department store, D. H. Holmes, as well as smaller manufacturers and retailers such as Maison Rouf and Isabel, engaged the same group in manufacture of handmade garments. One of these companies provided a rural South Louisiana family, the Berger family of the LeBlanc community just south of Lafayette, with an opportunity for home employment and the development of their needle art skills.[4] Initially involving the one family of five young women, the business arrangement soon engaged others and resulted in community-wide female involvement by mid-century. The few existing sources of information—garments, archival records, and participants' memories recorded in oral interviews—make possible the unique account that follows.

Born in 1855, Louis François Henry Berger is remembered as having the distinction of coming to Louisiana "directly from France" as opposed to being of Acadian descent as his wife and many in the LeBlanc community were. He and eighteen year-old Eugénie Marie Mart Baras married in 1885, with their five daughters born between 1886 and 1903. Céline, Honorine, Anita, Lucy, and Aline are remembered as the first in the LeBlanc community to sew for New Orleans companies. Their father had responded to an advertisement offering such an employment arrangement to supplement the family's income. As Lucy's daughter, Laura Mae Romero, recalls, "They're the ones that started sewing, you know, they ordered that sewing from New Orleans. And the sewing would come and they'd sew and all the people would come and watch them sew." Neighbor involved neighbor, and mother involved daughter. As another community member describes, "All the people was, was sewing. So as I came of age, like fifteen, sixteen years old, my mother would show me. She'd sew.... And she quit and my sister and I took over."[5]

with Pamela P. Rabalais, February 23, 1996, T. Harry Williams Center for Oral History Collection, Louisiana and Lower Mississippi Collections, Louisiana State University, Baton Rouge. Hereafter, all interviews are those by Rabalais now in the Williams Center.

[4] Laura Mae Romero, interview, August 12, 1995; Elsie Hulin LeBlanc, interview, April 4, 1996; Eula Comeaux LeBlanc, interview, August 17, 1995.

[5] Elsie Hulin LeBlanc, interview, August 11, 1995; Eula LeBlanc, interview, August 17, 1995; Elsie LeBlanc, interview, August 11, 1995, April 4, 1996; Laura Mae Romero, interview, April 4, 1996 and August 12, 1995; Elsie Hulin Le Blanc, interview, August 11, 1995.

Although the New Orleans companies continued to provide an outlet throughout the 1930s into the 1940s, another retail channel surfaced and engaged the LeBlanc community needlewomen— the Acadian Handicraft Project. Targeting Acadiana and the preservation of the traditions of its French peoples, the Project began in 1942, sponsored by Louisiana State University's General Extension Division for adult education. The Project was directed and represented solely by Louise Olivier, an Acadian descendant herself. Pledging to promote Acadian crafts by finding a market for them, the Project proposed to furnish an outlet for the self-expression of Acadian women, as well as develop initiative and independence among them.[6]

Project records indicate that by 1946 Olivier had found the LeBlanc community needlewomen, and four of the Berger sisters were sending their samples to her: Mrs. Avery (Anita) Hulin, Mrs. Alphonse (Cécile) LeBlanc, Mrs. Clement (Lucy) LeBlanc, and Mrs. Clet (Aline) LeBlanc. By 1948, the next generations of Berger women were establishing their homes and arranging for their own sewing orders as evidenced by the presence on worker lists of daughters and daughters-in-law of the four sisters. Sisters-in-law of not only daughters but also of daughters-in-law had joined the Project by 1949. Mothers-in-law of daughters were also introduced. Of the seventy infants' and children's wear sewers listed in Project employment records during the course of its activity, sixty can be easily linked to the LeBlanc community, a farming community with a 3-mile radius. As one daughter-in-law remembers her initial involvement, ". . . after I learn well enough, that's when I . . . got me a package of my own and she [Louise Olivier] started me off with diaper shirts."[7]

From its inclusion, the diaper shirt dominated sales in a pre-air conditioning era and developed into forty-five different versions by 1950 with 1,504 shirts sold that year. Over thirty additional infant

[6] Louise Olivier, "Resume Of Louisiana State University French Project Activities 1938-1944," Acadian Handicraft Project Records, Louisiana and Lower Mississippi Valley Collections, LSU Libraries, Louisiana State University, Baton Rouge. Olivier grew up during a period when the use of the Acadian French language was greatly discouraged in schools (before CODOFIL) and the population's traditions were being forgotten. Besides being of Acadian descent herself, she held a fellowship in French at LSU in the 1930s before taking a position in 1938 as "Field Representative" of a project based at LSU with funds obtained from the General Education Board of New York City for "a project directed to the French-speaking people of Louisiana to preserve the language, culture, and traditions of Louisiana's French-speaking people."

[7] Olivier, "Workers 1945 to 1946; Workers July 1, 1947 – July 1, 1948; Workers 1948-49," Acadian Handicraft Project Records; Eula Comeaux LeBlanc, interview, August 17, 1995.

items evolved, from bibs to "snuggers" (gowns with drawstring hems) to "shoulderettes" (burping pads) to christening gowns. The list expanded to include christening bonnets destined for sale in Protestant North Louisiana, which were produced in larger dimensions to fit older children than those produced for the Catholic Louisianians of French descent whose custom was to baptize at birth.[8]

Unlike New Orleans companies' sewers who were sent patterns, Project sewers were encouraged to produce seasonal styles and seek the latest fashions that would appeal to retailers as each sewer competed with fellow workers for orders. As described by one woman, "...if you wanted some new sewing [orders from Olivier], you would have to get on the ball and make something different." Thus, even embroidery work became specific to individual workers, who used personal notebooks to document ownership of their original designs.[9]

Yet, other examples abound of the Project's fostering worker initiative. In correspondence asking Olivier for work, one woman's drive is apparent as she pleads for diaper shirt orders, "I love to make diaper shirt. Everybody say they don't [know] how I can say that. You very seldom hear some body say they like to make them. But for the truth I enjoy making them. The more I make them, the more I pull for them...And lets hope you need more." Another sewer was so anxious to work with the Project that she sent multiple requests for work, each plea using a different alias. However, special problems arose that had to be addressed by these women juggling family life and employment, even employment based in the home. As one sewer remembers, "I had a rocker, which I still do. Put two pillows on it (I had two [children]). And I'd rock with the foot and sew with the hand. You had to learn a way of doing it."[10]

Daily schedules were arranged to include Project sewing as mothers, daughters, and daughters-in-law sewed together. As one woman recalls, "Together as a...I would say, like a company. The mother wanted those girls every afternoon with her. So, they all meet

---

[8] Olivier, "Paper Presented to the Natchitoches Home Demonstration Council," Acadian Handicraft Project Records; Olivier, "Summary of Wholesale and Display Reports, 1955-1958," Acadian Handicraft Project Records.

[9] Laura Mae Romero, interview, August 12, 1995; Elsie LeBlanc, interview, August 11, 1995.

[10] Mrs. Frank Romero, letter to Olivier, Acadian Handicraft Project Records; Olivier, letter to Mrs. Clyde Dutile, Acadian Handicraft Project Records; Eula Comeaux LeBlanc, interview, August 17, 1995.

Figure 3.4. Infant christening bonnet, ca. 1950. White cotton batiste with lace insertion, lace trim, tucks, and satin ribbon. Created by Eula Comeaux LeBlanc. Private collection. Photograph by Mark Kleiner, Digital Imaging by Kevin Duffy.

where the mother was, and they'd do their sewing…Sometimes they eat dinner at 10:30 [a.m.] to get on the ball and sew."[11]

The Acadian Handicraft Project abruptly came to an end in 1962 with the death of Louise Olivier. Two venues offered markets for the LeBlanc community women who continued to sew: Vermilion Parish manufacturer and retailer Flo and New Orleans manufacturer Orleans Product, with a retailing division called the Lylian Shop. Marie Florine Hébert opened Flo's Baby Lane in 1951 in a neighboring community and sold handmade infants' wear and machine-sewn toddler garments, which were finished by hand. Even *House Beautiful* magazine directed its readers traveling through Acadiana to Flo's. Although the shop was sold in 1980 to Flo's first cousin who also operated a furniture business and who changed its name slightly, Earl's Baby Land Shop today advertises in-stock and special-order availability of handsewn merchandise. Its website boasts, "We have two ladies in their eighties who don't plan on stopping anytime soon."[12]

Figure 3.5. Original christening gown design, ca. 1950. Lucy Berger LeBlanc, Artist. Notes attributed to Louise Olivier. Photograph, Courtesy of the Department of Textiles, Apparel Design and Merchandising, Louisiana State University.

---

[11] Eula Comeaux LeBlanc, interview, August 17, 1995.

[12] Marie Florine Hébert, interview with Rabalais, March 1, 1996, All subsequent information about Flo's Baby Lane has been obtained from this source and from Earl's Baby Land, *earlsbabylaand.com*, October 13, 2015.

Figure 3.6. Infant christening gown, 1995. White cotton batiste with lace insertion, lace trim, and tucks. Created by Eula Comeaux LeBlanc. Private collection. Photograph by Mark Kleiner, Digital Imaging by Kevin Duffy.

Orleans Product and its Lylian Shop were the only New Orleans companies involved in manufacturing and retailing handsewn garments as the twenty-first century approached. The sentiment that "the nicest are made by hand" was drawing customers from all over the country to its location on St. Charles Avenue on the streetcar line. Owner Leslie Saiewitz Bingham, the granddaughter of Flora Isaacs Lazard of the 1920s Louise Shop, acknowledged these exceptional needlewomen by not giving them any instructions, just fabric. The

Figure 3.7. Original infant bib design, ca. 1950. Lucy Lange Romero, Artist. Notes attributed to Louise Olivier. Photograph, Courtesy of the Department of Textiles, Apparel Design and Merchandising, Louisiana State University.

results, she reported, were that "...each one is a unique creation, all beautiful works of art." The Lylian Shop closed in 2002, selling the company's handsewn garment business to New Orleans retailer Pippen Lane for its Lylian Collection.[13]

The art is referred to today as French handsewing. Like those sold by the early New Orleans companies, these very special garments incorporate sewing techniques requiring a great deal of "taste and skill" from the very special needlewomen who make them. Every stitch is sewn by hand using a fine thread and needle traditionally

---

[13] Bingham, interview; "Pippen Lane," www.pippenlane.com, last modified 2015, http://www.lylianneworleans.com/.

on high-quality imported cotton batiste, with French lace and Mother-of-Pearl buttons. All seaming is worked using French seams unless joined with *entre deux*, a fine decorative trim that is literally translated as "between two." The garments are embellished, often extensively, with tiny pin-size tucks, hemstitching, and embroidery that includes feather, seed, and *bouillon* (or in English, bullion) stitches. Buttonholes are handworked and hems in infant's garments are most often secured with a running stitch. Christening dresses with matching bonnets are the most elaborate pieces and feature yards of lace insertions sewn onto the fabric.

These works of art are in limited supply since the number of needlewomen has dwindled to a very few. As the twentieth century came to a close, four female sewers who were a part of the Berger needlework network remained in the LeBlanc community. Lucy Lange Romero, the sister-in-law of one of Lucy Berger LeBlanc's daughters, was sewing for the Lylian Shop. Her two daughters-in-law were not sewing. When describing her relationship with the retailer, a business partnership in a modern world, Lucy related a recent transaction with delight, "She [from Orleans Product] paid the postage. And she has a toll-free number."[14]

Eula Comeaux LeBlanc, the daughter-in-law of Aline, had her own business in her home and had contemplated retiring as the 50th anniversary of her needlework approached. Her daughters "work[ed] outside" the home. As a tribute to Anita upon her death in 1989 at age 95, Eula made a burial gown for her aunt-by-marriage's burial. She used the same techniques she employed for christening dresses—handsewn construction, pin tucks, lace insertion, and embroidery. To honor Lucy and Aline whose deaths closely followed, Eula designed a second and third. As a result, Eula's reputation grew to include shrouds for the community.[15]

Elsie Hulin LeBlanc, the daughter of one of Anita's sisters-in-law, did not sew for profit anymore but had carefully saved the pattern for the christening dress, which was her specialty. While debating its donation to Louisiana State University, she commented, "But I know when I'm gone, my daughter won't keep this. She doesn't know what

---

[14] Lucy Lange Romero, interview, August 11, 1995.
[15] Eula Comeaux LeBlanc, interview, August 17, 1995.

to do with it...I might give it to you to bring over there because really it would be stored knowing I have something in that library. Just knowing her mama had things to do...things to do with the library."[16]

Laura Mae Romero, Lucy's daughter, sewed independently, with a sign on the highway that bisected the LeBlanc community, drawing the attention of passing motorists. She prepared examples of her work so that the next generation of community women would know that those before them had "things to do." She confided, "I'm making things and saving them.... I may not be able to sew by the time they [the grandchildren] have children. I make them bonnets and little dresses...different colors and different sizes. Different things...I make a little gown and blanket and [put them in] a Ziploc...those gallon things, and I put a piece of tape on it and I put the date that I made it. They going to have fun one day."[17]

Certainly the LeBlanc community women were sewing to augment family incomes, as was true when Henry Berger responded to the New Orleans's company's advertisement, but they were also sewing for the delightful enjoyment resulting from this creative form of self-expression—different colors, different sizes, and different things—"each one...a unique creation, all beautiful works of art."[18]

[16] Elsie Hulin LeBlanc, interview, April 4, 1996.

[17] Laura Mae Romero, interview, August 12, 1995.

[18] Bingham, interview.

The Liberty Shop and Design in New Orleans (1902–1970)

Wayne Phillips

The Liberty Shop opened in 1902 as a millinery in a second-floor space rented from the Adler family, who began their jewelry business at 722-724 Canal Street four years earlier. Ellen McCann Ragan, a wealthy New Yorker, financed the business, and Emilie Guelton, a native of France, managed the shop's operations.[1]

The Liberty Shop both styled original hats and imported the latest European fashions. Ellen Ragan made annual purchasing trips to Europe, sailing on luxury cruise liners like the *Queen Mary* and the *Mauritania*. As their business grew, the Liberty Shop began executing custom-made garments including gowns for brides, debutantes, and Carnival queens.

To accommodate their expanding enterprise, in 1923 Ragan and Guelton purchased an antebellum home located at 2220 St. Charles Avenue on the edge of the posh Garden District, where many of their clients lived. After overcoming legal battles with the city over their right to operate a commercial venture in a residential property, the Liberty Shop began to flourish as the city's most elegant dressmaking establishment.

Sometime in the 1930s, Helen Clark Warren (1895-1973) came to be one of the regular designers for the shop. Warren was born in Fall River, Massachusetts, a seventeenth-century town south of Boston and a major textile manufacturing hub in the nineteenth and early twentieth centuries. At a young age, Warren moved with her family to New York, where she lived and worked for the rest of her life.

Immediately following high school, Warren enrolled at the prestigious Pratt Institute, a multidisciplinary coeducational art school in New York. In 1915, Warren earned a certificate in Costume and Commercial Illustration after three years of study, which included courses in Freehand Drawing, Life Drawing, Watercolor Painting, and History of Art and Costume.

---

[1] All information in this article comes from material in the Helen Clark Warren Collection, Department of Costumes and Textiles, Louisiana State Museum, New Orleans, LA.

While functioning as the house designer for the Liberty Shop, executing sketches for elegant ladies' daywear and eveningwear from her home in New York City, Warren took on the duties of costume designer for several of the elite Carnival krewes in New Orleans. Counted among the Liberty Shop's clients were the Mistick Krewe of Comus, the High Priests of Mithras, the Mystic Club, and the Prophets of Persia. Warren was likely the first designer of royal costumes for the Krewe of Hermes, founded in 1936 and another Liberty Shop client.

Warren also maintained a successful fashion career in New York City during this time. She offered many clients her expertise in accumulating sophisticated wardrobes. The DuPonts were among her most loyal customers. It is perhaps surprising to know that Warren did not count sewing among her prodigious talents.

After the deaths of Guelton and Ragan in the early 1940s, ownership and operation of the shop fell to longtime employees Hazel Pearson, Louise Buhler, and Camille Henderson. Buhler oversaw the shop's bustling team of twenty to thirty seamstresses, depending on the season.

Business expanded beyond New Orleans. The Queens of the Rose Festival in Tyler, Texas, frequently went to the Liberty Shop for their custom-made gowns, as did women participating in the tradition of Pilgrimage in Natchez, Mississippi.

By 1970, the owners of the shop were no longer able to continue its operation, as shoppers became more accustomed to the convenience of ready-to-wear. In 1972, entrepreneur Bonnie Broel bought the house and located her dressmaking and retail business there, dubbing it the House of Broel. Although the clothing retail side of her enterprise has ended, Broel makes the graceful home at 2220 St. Charles Avenue available year round for private events. In so doing, Broel keeps the spirit of the Liberty Shop alive, making sure that the home's history of operation by a long chain of accomplished businesswomen endures.

Sketch of dress for Veva Ruidi Miller. Queen of Comus. 1939
The dress was cloth of silver embroidered with rhinestones of many sizes.
The dress was designed in Paris, and the cloth of silver woven in France.
The dress was made by The Liberty Shop, St. Charles Avenue, New Orleans. La.

Figure 3.8. Helen Clark Warren, design for gown worn by Veva Miller, the Queen of the Mistick Krewe of Comus, in 1939. Watercolor and graphite on paper, 18 x 15 in. (45.7 x 38.1 cm). Gift of Veva Miller Wood. Courtesy of the Collections of the Louisiana State Museum.

The Christian Woman's Exchange for Woman's Work: "To all needy gentlewomen who desire to help themselves this Exchange has opened a door"

Beth Willinger

> *There is a difference in the variety of work sold through this Exchange, as some of the articles consigned to it differ widely from anything to be found in any other. . . . The hand woven material, made by Acadian women, suitable for outing suits or gentlemen's clothing, the soft heavy goods known as Evangeline cloth, used for portiers [doorway curtains] or draperies of any sort, with the handsome netted fringes for trimming, hand-made by the same women. The baskets made by the Indian women who dwell on the Teche, unlike any others to be found anywhere except in Alaska, but very like them in texture as well as coloring. Most unique and so soon to fail even in our market, there are but two women living who make them and they will not teach the art. The wonderful work of the women of Fayal [of the Azores] and last, though by no means least, the exquisite laces of the Italian women consigned to this Exchange by the Countess di Brazza.[1]*

This entry from the fifteenth annual report of the Christian Woman's Exchange reveals several important, yet subtle, details about women's lives in the late nineteenth century. First, and foremost, it tells of a national movement of women-helping-women that allowed women to make baskets, fabrics, laces, and other products in their own homes, and thus earn a living by turning their domestic skills and unpaid labor into marketable goods for which they would be paid.

In 1881, the New Orleans's Woman's Exchange, called the Christian Woman's Exchange (CWE), was organized when some of New Orleans's "best people" sought a way to lift the city's women out of poverty. Their ideas centered on providing a salesroom, or

---

[1] The Christian Woman's Exchange, Fifteenth Annual Report, 1896. Christian Woman's Exchange records, Manuscripts Collection 257, Louisiana Research Collection, Howard-Tilton Memorial Library, Tulane University, New Orleans, LA (hereafter, CWE).

Exchange, where women could sell the products they made at home. The plan also permitted needy women a level of anonymity so that their financial needs might never be known to others.

The first of the CWE's salesrooms was located in several rented rooms at 41-43 Bourbon Street (today 227 Bourbon Street). The announcement of the CWE's opening appeared in newspapers and circulars reading simply: "The Christian Woman's Exchange for Woman's Work: This Association has opened a saleroom at Nos. 41 and 43 Bourbon Street, where all kinds of plain and fine sewing, ornamental and fancy needlework, will be received and sold."[2]

Success was immediate and within weeks of its founding, the CWE negotiated the rent of the entire building, which included a second floor. The additional space allowed the CWE to advance its training mission by offering instruction in embroidery, sewing, cooking, and painting, explaining, "so that those who are anxious to do, but feel incompetent, may have thorough instruction, for it is this feeling of incompetency that adds to the misery of those who are thrown on their own resources."[3]

Their first instructional effort was the creation of the Artistic Needlework Department, hiring a teacher to provide instruction in Kensington Embroidery, and asserting that "a supply of English Embroidery, Silks, Crewels, Begun Work, etc. will be kept constantly on hand."[4] These materials were purchased from the Society of Decorative Art of New York and were for sale to anyone who desired to purchase them. Other classes offered in the early years included Cutting and Fitting Dresses, and Children's Clothing.

With the additional space, the CWE also opened a lunchroom that was "supplied almost entirely from the entries in the salesroom" including salads, gumbos, breads, "jellies, cakes, rolls, ice cream and other dainties." Soon, too, the CWE offered room rentals "making our building a *Home* for women forced out upon the world to make their own way in it."[5]

---

[2] "The Christian Woman's Exchange for Woman's Work," circular pasted in "Book No. 1 Christian Woman's Exchange April 1881, Record of Correspondence," CWE.

[3] *Daily Picayune*, "Exchange Notes," October 9, 1881.

[4] CWE, Minutes of the Board, November 11, 1881.

[5] *Daily Picayune*, "Exchange Notes," June 10, 1881; July 3, 1881.

An early newspaper article promoting the work of the Exchange gives us some idea of the products made by the women, as well as the fashions popular in the late nineteenth century:

Here can be found fine specimens of needlework, embroidery, knitting, crochet work, and other arts familiar to women's skillful hands...There are numerous articles of worsted work, notably sacques, hoods and mittens...A table cover in cretonne embroidered with silk is very handsome and ornamental. A number of large, well made and comfortable Afghans are offered for sale: one of these is the work of a ten-year-old little lady. The Exchange boasts of an extra fine assortment of pin-cushions, one of tufted work...Two sofa pillows, one a rich Turkish cushion, and the other a satin one with cretonne work being especially noticeable...A large number of mats, contributed by earnest workers ranging from fourteen to seventy-five years of age are displayed. The exhibition of shawls is worthy of special mention. There are some pretty ones of black mohair and gold and blue and silver. Some fascinators, made in what is known as the cloud style, are very attractive. Besides these there are tidies, dolls and doll's clothes...real lace handkerchiefs and shawls, and numerous other fancy articles.[6]

Earnings reported by the CWE speak to the interest and necessity of such an enterprise. For the month of December 1881, after just seven months in operation, salesroom receipts totaled $908.55 (the purchasing power of approximately $21,700 in 2015) and lunchroom receipts added another $754.20 (approximately $18,000 in 2015).[7]

At the close of its first year, 15,988 articles had been entered for sale at the Exchange. Of these, 13,322 were sold. The sales appear to have been divided fairly equally between food products and handiwork with sales in the lunchroom totaling $5,627, while in the "fancy work, etc." department, the sales amounted to $5,932.[8]

---

[6] *Daily Picayune*, "The Woman's Exchange. Great and Deserved Success of this Noble Institution," November 4, 1881.

[7] *Daily Picayune*, "Exchange Notes," January 15, 1882. All 2015 monetary conversions are estimates provided by Lawrence H. Officer and Samuel H. Williamson. "Purchasing Power of Money in the United States from 1774 to the Present," available at http://www.measuringworth.com/.

[8] *Daily Picayune*, "Christian Women's (sic) Exchange; The Annual Meeting-Report of the Good Work Done in the First Year of Its Existence," April 12, 1882. The sales had a purchasing power of approximately $124,000 and $131,000 in 2010.

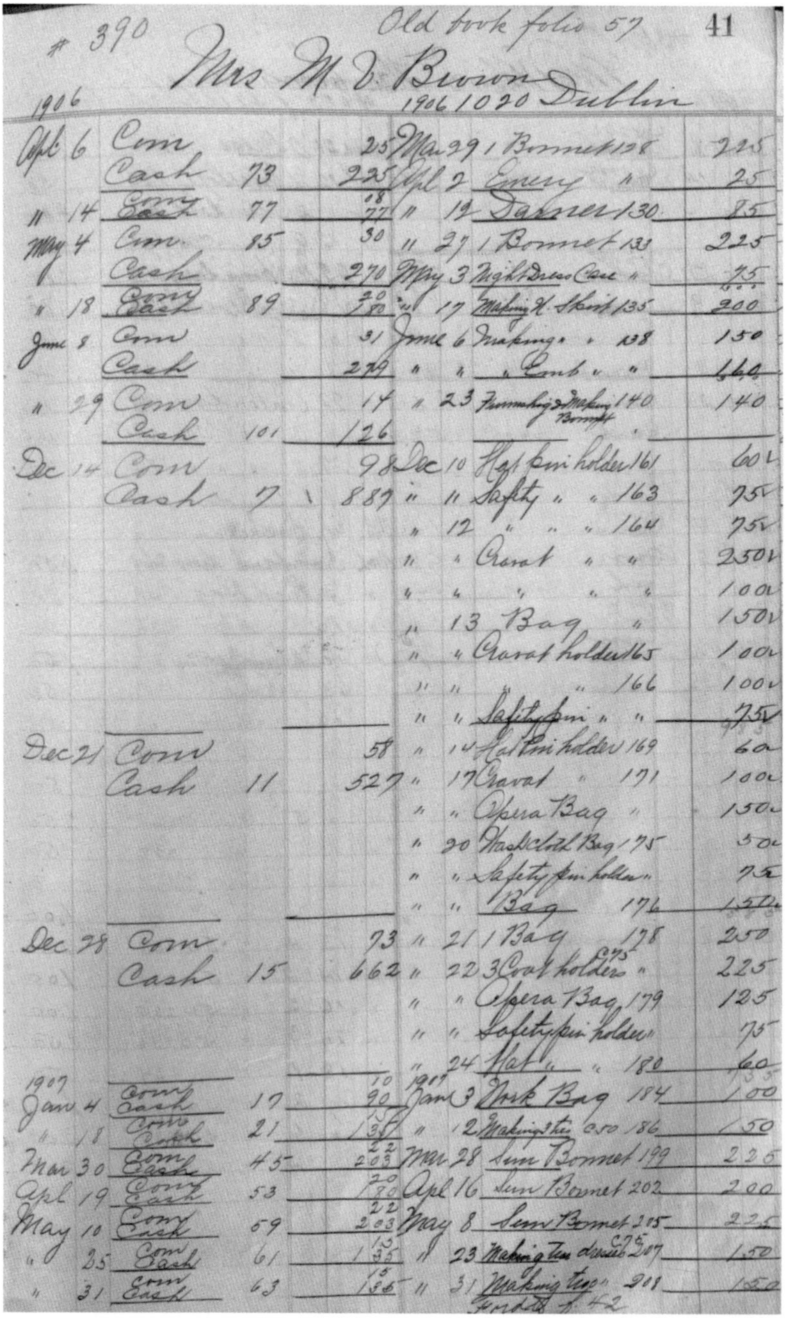

\# 390 Old book folio 57 41

Mrs M. D. Brown Dublin

1906				1906	1020	
Apl 6	Com		25	Mar 29	1 Bonnet 128	225
	Cash	73	225	Apl 2	Emery "	25
" 14	Com / Cash	77	08 / 77	" 19	Darner 130	85
May 4	Com	85	30	" 27	1 Bonnet 133	225
	Cash		270	May 3	Night Dress Case "	75
" 18	Com / Cash	89	20 / 180	" 17	Making H. Skirt 135	200
June 8	Com		31	June 6	Making " 138	150
	Cash		279	" "	" Comb " "	160
" 29	Com		14	" 23	Trimming & Making 140 Bonnet	140
	Cash	101	126			
Dec 14	Com		98	Dec 10	Hat pin holder 161	60
	Cash	7	887	" 11	Safety " " 163	75
				" 12	" " " 164	75
				"	" Cravat " "	250
				"	" " " "	100
				" 13	Bag "	150
				"	" Cravat holder 165	100
				"	" " " 166	100
				"	" Safety pin " "	75
Dec 21	Com		58	" 14	Hat pin holder 169	60
	Cash	11	527	" 17	Cravat " 171	100
				"	" Opera Bag "	150
				" 20	Wash cloth Bag 175	50
				"	" Safety pin holder "	75
				"	" Bag 176	150
Dec 28	Com		73	" 21	1 Bag 178	250
	Cash	15	662	" 22	3 Coat holders "	225
				"	" Opera Bag 179	125
				"	" Safety pin holder "	75
				" 24	Hat " " 180	60
1907				1907		
Jan 4	Com / Cash	17	10 / 90	Jan 3	Work Bag 184	100
" 18	Com / Cash	21	15 / 135	" 12	Making the " 186	150
Mar 30	Com / Cash	45	22 / 203	Mar 28	Sun Bonnet 199	225
Apl 19	Com / Cash	53	20 / 180	Apl 16	Sun Bonnet 202	200
May 10	Com / Cash	59	22 / 203	May 8	Sun Bonnet 205	225
" 25	Com / Cash	61	15 / 135	" 23	Making Tea " 207	150
" 31	Com / Cash	63	15 / 135	" 31	Making Tea " 208	150
					Forward to 42	

Figure 3.9. Page from Consignors' Ledger, Christian Woman's Exchange records, Collection 257, Louisiana Research Collection, Tulane University.

Unfortunately, little is known of the women who made these exquisite products and benefitted from their sale. They were ordinary white women whose day-to-day lives were not likely to have been considered noteworthy. Moreover, the anonymity afforded consignors added a layer of secrecy: their names were not mentioned in the organization's minutes or announced in newspaper descriptions of the Exchange. Here and there, a few stories are recorded about a consignor's need or success. For example, one is quoted as writing: "I am truly grateful for an opportunity of disposing of my work, and if you could only know how very much you help me by selling it, I am sure you would feel repaid for your trouble, for I am needing money badly."[9]

In order for a woman to sell her goods at the Exchange, she was required to have a member of the CWE "sponsor" her. CWE members, those who paid the $5.00 annual membership fee, were given three tickets and "the privilege" of giving the tickets to three "worthy women." The potential consignors could then take their goods with the ticket to the Exchange any weekday at 11:00 a.m. for inspection. Members of the Visiting Committee determined if the products "were up to a certain standard of excellence." Two "failures" by Committee members (an unknown number inspecting) meant the item(s) could not be sold at the Exchange. Consignors whose products were approved were known to all but the Committee only by the number assigned them. Consignors determined the price of each article submitted for sale and when the item sold, they were paid the price, less ten percent commission. Checks were mailed to the consignors twice each month. Theoretically, consignors benefitted both from the sale of their products and the entrepreneurial skills gained by setting their own value for the goods made. Often, though, members of the Visiting Committee suggested lowering the price to promote the sale, or raising the price when it would undercut the value of other similar items.

It's unclear how CWE members identified the "needy," "worthy women," or women whom they desired to aid when giving out tickets to enter work at the Exchange. Notably, CWE members made assumptions of worthiness based on race. After a lengthy "discussion

[9] CWE, Fourth Annual Report, 1885.

in regard to applicants for tickets," a motion that "any member shall be permitted to assist anyone in distress without regard to color" was "finally withdrawn." The CWE, like Exchanges nationally, tended to identify as "worthy" women, white middle- and working-class women who had fallen on hard times, were too old to work, or were once prosperous widows. They were women who members might have known through their churchwork or other charitable activities. However, shortly after organizing, the CWE passed a resolution requesting that members with "no applicant" leave their tickets at the Exchange for "discretionary distribution by the Visiting Committee."[10]

Announcements to this effect frequently went out from the Board of Managers suggesting either that women in need of assistance were not known to members, or that a number of potential consignors brought their goods directly to the Exchange upon hearing about the opportunity through advertisements or word of mouth. Several years after the founding of the Exchange, women unable to afford the full membership fee of $5.00 were able to pay $2.00 and receive one consignor's ticket, good for entering work for one year.[11] Although unstated, this was a way for a consignor to enter her own work without the sponsorship of a CWE member. Eventually, all consignors were required to pay an annual fee of $2.00 to enter their products for the year. Mrs. Walmsley, the longtime president of the CWE, addressed the issue of the "needy" in a paper read to the New Orleans City Council around 1898. She remarked, "We have frequently been asked what we did about receiving work from women in comfortable circumstances, who desire to sell the work of their hands for the purpose of increasing their pocket money. We can reply very promptly to such a question, that we have had no such applications."[12] By 1887, 1,243 names had been recorded as consignors.[13]

As noted above, the Exchange philosophy was not unique to New Orleans. Modeled after the New York Exchange for Women's Work, founded in 1878, the CWE was the first Exchange formed in

---

[10] CWE, Minutes of the Board, April 18, 1881; CWE, Minutes of the Board, May 4, 1881.

[11] CWE, Seventh Annual Report, 1887-88.

[12] CWE, reprinted in The Christian Women's Exchange, Nineteenth Annual Report, 1899-1900.

[13] CWE, Seventh Annual Report, 1887-88.

the South and the twelfth in the United States.[14] However, the CWE's intent was always to be a service for "women of every state." Besides towns in Mississippi, Alabama, and Arkansas, women sent goods from Broomfield, MA; Pasadena, CA; Cincinnati, OH; and Norwich, CT and other places. It was thought that some women entered their goods at several Exchanges around the country. As would be expected, however, there was always more interest in local products, or at least in those having a local connection, such as the yards of lace, lace collars, tablecloths, and napkins consigned by Countess di Brazza.

Figure 3.10. Cover page to *A Guide to Old and New Lace in Italy*. Pamphlet of exhibition items sent to the Woman's Pavilion of the World's Columbian Exposition, held in Chicago in 1893.

Countess di Brazza was born in New Orleans and her aunt was a strong supporter of the local Exchange where women could sell handiwork. Di Brazza remained attached to New Orleans through the Exchange, sending lace from Italian women to be sold. Di Brazza and the Christian Woman's Exchange members saw skills with the needle as an economic resource.

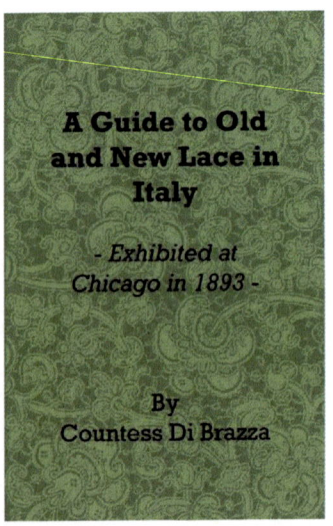

A Guide to Old and New Lace in Italy

- Exhibited at Chicago in 1893 -

By Countess Di Brazza

Countess di Brazza had been an annual member of the Exchange from at least 1887, allowing her to give three tickets annually to worthy women, and allowing her also to participate in the life of her hometown though she lived most of the year in Italy. Born Cora Ann Slocomb, the Countess was the niece of Ida Richardson, the longtime chairwoman of the CWE Finance Committee and purportedly the wealthiest woman in New Orleans. The Countess was known for her keen interest and promotion of lace production and history, as well as women's rights. In 1893, she had charge of the Italian Lace Exhibit

[14] Kathleen Waters Sander, *The Business of Charity: The Woman's Exchange Movement, 1832-1900* (Urbana and Chicago: University of Illinois Press, 1998), 121-23.

on display at the World's Columbian Exposition in Chicago, which was comprised largely of Italy's queen Marghuerita's collection of laces valued at more than $100,000 (approximately two and a half million dollars in 2010). That same year, the New Orleans-born countess opened her own lace school at her villa in Friuli. Her purpose in doing so was both to make Italian lace known in the United States and thereby establish a trade with this country, and to provide Italian peasant girls with an alternative means of earning a livelihood.[15] The laces consigned by Countess di Brazza, apparently made by the lace makers from her villa, comprised a large number of articles available in the salesroom. The 1908-1910 record book of consignments shows she was owed $236 (approximately $5,830 in 2010) "c/o Mrs. T. Richardson," the largest amount recorded.

Other consignors in this period included No. 24, Miss A. W. Creevy, who, between April 1906 and June 2007, sold some eighty Indian baskets of varying sizes and prices, ranging from 15 cents to $2.50 for a hamper; No. 200, Miss M. L. Witherspoon, who from 1909 through 1910, sold thirty-three rag dolls, ranging in price from $1.10 to $2.75, with the majority selling for the lower price; No. 16 Mrs. C. Charles who in 1908 sold some thirty articles including baby dolls, dusting bags, needle cases, calendars, and pin cushions ranging in price from 25 cents for a pin cushion to $3.50 for a doll; and No. 390, Mrs. M. V. Brown at 1020 Dublin Street who made sun bonnets, opera bags, and holders for flat pins, safety pins, and cravats, among other items.

In 1889, the CWE purchased their own home and headquarters at the corner of South and Camp Streets on Lafayette Square. To this very large residence, the CWE moved the Exchange shop, lunchroom, and classrooms, and increased the number of room rentals. Despite these many other undertakings, the Exchange shop remained the CWE's *raison d'être*.

From its very beginning, the CWE Board of Managers used a variety of methods to promote the sale of items at the Exchange shop.

---

[15] Countess di Braza promoted women in various ways, including her defense of an Italian immigrant woman accused of murder. See Idanna Pucci, *The Trials of Maria Barbella: The True Story of a 19th Century Crime of Passion* (NY: Vintage Press, 1997). See also for interests on lace, Countess di Brazza, *A Guide to Old and New Lace in Italy, Exhibited in Chicago in 1893* (Chicago: W. B. Conkey Co., 1893); H. D. Northrop, *The World's Fair as Seen in One Hundred Days* (Philadelphia: Ariel Book Co., 1893).

Ads were regularly placed in the city's daily and Sunday newspapers; pre-printed letters were given to CWE members with the request that they mail them to their personal friends; and advertising cards and circulars were frequently distributed to "various hotels, steamboats, car lines, and other public places" for distribution to "strangers" in the city. Mention was often made in the organization's minutes concerning the artistic display of products and the efforts made by various CWE members to arrange the items in the salesrooms and sales cases in a manner that attracted the eye and promoted purchases. A 1925 handwritten report by one of the saleswomen describes her marketing strategy: "I decided to **create** a demand for black lace shawls—telephoned several people—we had some lovely ones—remarkably cheap—shoulder capes—ranging from 10.00 to 20.00—they were **all sold**."

Their marketing benefitted particularly from the backing of Eliza Jane Nicholson, editor of the New Orleans *Daily Picayune* and the first woman publisher of a daily metropolitan newspaper in the country. Nicholson made available free to the CWE each Sunday for one year, the space of one-and-a-half columns for articles promoting the Exchange. These appeared under the title "Exchange Notes" and were signed "XCHANGE."

Another significant strategy with long-term results was the CWE's active involvement in the 1884 World's Industrial and Cotton Centennial Exposition held in present day Audubon Park. The CWE assumed major responsibility for the Exposition's Woman's Department, requesting exhibits from women's organizations in every state as well as from women abroad. The report of this work constitutes one of the best systematic records of the names of consignors, their city of residence, and the work they entered for sale or for display.[16] The national and international attention gained from the CWE's Exposition work promoted both an increase in the number of consignors entering their goods at the Exchange and the sale of products. A less successful marketing strategy was the establishment in 1885 of a free-circulating library that was in part intended to bring patrons to the Exchange shop as they perused the available books.

---

[16] Reprinted in the Christian Woman's Exchange, Fourth Annual Report, April, 1885.

Newspaper ads, circulars, and often receptions also promoted the move of the Exchange salesrooms over the years. In 1922, the CWE sold their Lafayette Square property and moved the Exchange salesrooms to 522-524 Royal Street and, in 1937, across the arcade to 516 Royal Street. Although the CWE bought the property at 820 St. Louis Street in 1924, now called the Hermann-Grima House, they did not move the salesrooms to that location until 1946, when the rent on the Royal Street building became too expensive. First set up in the slave quarters of the House, the sales shop was moved to the carriage house to the left of the House in 1952.

The CWE, like several other Exchanges nationally, accepted on consignment "family heirlooms" that owners were "willing to sell in order to pay their debts during hard times." The commission on items such as "furniture, glass, china and silver," was always five percent higher than on items handmade by the consignors. However by the 1940s, the inventory of the CWE's Exchange shop consisted primarily of antique silver, crystal, and furniture and only secondarily of handmade articles and food products. In fact, their address was listed in the New Orleans City Directory under "Antiques."

Several factors may account for the visible change in products available for sale in the Exchange salesrooms. One reason might be its location on Royal Street clustered among blocks of other antique shops. Certainly the Great Depression and World War II forced many women to sell their family heirlooms while the purchase of handmade products, often more expensive than ready-made, was a luxury few could afford. In addition, ideas about women working outside the home were changing as employment opportunities and income potential were expanding. For these reasons, and likely countless others, the CWE, like many other Exchanges nationally, closed its doors in 1963. At that time, the CWE decided to refocus its mission on the restoration and maintenance of its historic home.

Overall, the efforts of the CWE to improve the economic security of women can be termed a huge success. In April 1913, Mrs. George Halbert, recording secretary, reported that during CWE's thirty-two year existence, the Exchange had paid nearly $500,000 (estimated as equivalent to $11.4 million in 2010) to women for work they had accomplished in the home.[17] However, no final tally is available. It would be nearly impossible to estimate how many consignors benefitted from selling their works at the Exchange, how many items were sold, and even how much money was paid to consignors who brought in their needlework or sewn work as opposed to those who brought in cakes, pastries, jellies or jams, or supplied products such as milk and eggs for the lunchroom. Numerous differences and voids occur in the CWE records concerning the reporting of disbursements to consignors. In some years, the number of consignors and the number of articles submitted are listed in the annual report; other years, not. In some records, the total amount paid to all consignors is provided, while in other years, the disbursements are broken down by Fancy Work, Table Supply (cakes, etc.), and Lunchroom. Early records are more thorough than later records, in large part because over time, the organization's financial strength (and therefore its own accounts) assumed greater importance than that of the consignors. Moreover, as the number of consignors and items in the sales shop declined, the CWE shifted their emphasis to the rental of rooms or redirected their attention to new projects such as managing a tearoom.

Perhaps somewhat ironically, the opportunities for working at home and entrepreneurship once afforded women by the Exchange movement are now provided by online websites such as Etsy and the upsurge in art markets in New Orleans as well as around the country. In 1997, the CWE, renamed the Woman's Exchange, reopened a shop for the sale of women's creative work in the carriage house of the Hermann-Grima House. Today, the Exchange Shop features the unique work of local women artists, jewelers, ceramicists, photographers, and authors with prices ranging from $10 to several hundred.

---

[17] CWE, Annual Report, 1913. Box 1, Folder 11; Officer and Williamson.

Needles of History: Embroidery of the Newcomb Pottery's Enterprise

Sally Main

> *The world of environment is subject for artistic*
> *interpretation. The examples of [Newcomb]*
> *needlecraft . . . illustrate this truth in some measure.*
> *Both are drawn from sources familiar in the daily*
> *lives of southern girls, and both of them are possibly*
> *used for the first time in decorative art.[1]*

The art of embroidery is often identified as "craft," a term placed low in the historical hierarchy of art, an artificial distinction that pivots on the word "functionality." Yet, in medieval societies, embroidery was considered equal to the "fine arts" of painting and sculpture, with embroiderers' guilds (whose membership was open to men and women) playing an important role in the cultural and economic health of their communities. As class status and gender roles changed in the fifteenth and sixteenth centuries, membership in the crafts guilds became exclusively male, and women were encouraged to take up embroidery as a leisure activity. Depending on social standing, needlework became either a pastime or domestic necessity. "Amateur" embroiderers' efforts became synonymous with bad workmanship and uninspired creativity. This impression was reinforced in the second half of the eighteenth century, when ready-made embroidery patterns put an end to the collaboration between head (imagination) and hand (skill). On the other hand, the leaders of the nineteenth-century British Arts and Crafts movement (1860-1910) attempted to close the gap between those who designed and those who executed by advocating "a good artistic training for artisans and a good practical training for artist-designers." They saw the obstacles faced by working or middle-class women as ones rooted in a lack of education and the limited means available for adequate training and materials. They thought of sewing as a skill

---

[1] Ellsworth Woodward, Director of Art Education, Newcomb College, "Needlework in Newcomb College," *Brush and Pencil* (June 1905), 314.

and an art that could lift women out of dependency on men, or, as imaginative but also functional.

An early institution for training women in secular embroidery was the Royal School of Art Needlework, founded in autumn of 1872 under the aegis of H. R. H. Helena, Princess Christian of Schleswig-Holstein (1846-1923), third daughter and fifth child of Queen Victoria and Prince Albert. She was encouraged to establish the School by William Morris and other advocates of the Arts and Crafts movement. Initially engaging approximately twenty women, by 1875 roughly one hundred to one hundred fifty women were employed; "their claims were poverty, gentle birth, and sufficient capacity to enable them to support themselves and be educated to teach other[s]."[2]

In New Orleans, Newcomb College's pottery enterprise (1895-1940) was established similarly on the principles of the British Arts and Crafts movement. The local impetus can be traced to the Woman's Department of the 1884-85 World's Industrial and Cotton Centennial Exposition, held in the city, and its president, Julia Ward Howe (1819-1910). Art demonstrations, carried on in the Woman's Building, were directed at encouraging women's "innate" artistic talents, which would, when applied, provide opportunities for financial self-reliance. After the exposition closed in June 1885, the Tulane Decorative Art League, an outgrowth of the classes offered at the fair by the University's faculty, provided instruction in "art pottery, woodcarving, fresco, and art needlework." The H. Sophie Newcomb Memorial College for Women of Tulane University grew from these efforts, opening its doors in 1887.

The Art School within the College was especially intended to prepare white female students with practical training, thus giving them financial independence and career opportunities other than teaching. Among the founding art faculty was Gertrude Roberts Smith. She, alongside William and Ellsworth Woodward, guided the development of what they called a "model industry" with clear design goals and standards.

Though Newcomb's pottery was the first craft to gain notice and receive prestigious awards, the second craft added to the art program was needlework. Introduced in 1902, the *Daily Picayune* wrote of

---

[2] Lady Marianna Margaret Cust Alford (writing as Lady M. Alford), *Needlework as Art* (London: Sampson Low, Marston, Searle and Rivington, 1886), 54.

it: "An interesting department recently opened is the textile works; this has been placed under the direction of Mrs. Gertrude Roberts Smith, and so far embroidery has been the principal work taken up. Prof. Woodward says that in this department the endeavor will be made to produce beautiful art needlework from the standpoint of design and color rather than from that of intricate needlework."[3] Smith was appointed to the College just before its opening session in October 1887 as a professor of drawing and painting, but her selection to teach the textile classes began a lifelong fascination with the medium.

Gertrude Roberts was born in Cambridge, Massachusetts, in 1869. From an early age she knew her vocation was teaching. Her desire to educate was so strong that she entered the Massachusetts Normal Art School at fourteen years old, training also at the Chase School of New York (now the Parsons New School for Design) and with a year of fine arts studies at the Colarossi Academy in Paris. At the age of sixteen she was recruited by Ellsworth Woodward to teach with him and his brother, William, in New Orleans. Immediately upon graduation in 1887, she joined the fledgling Newcomb College art faculty as a professor in drawing and painting; she was eighteen years old. Roberts married Frederick Smith in 1893 but was soon widowed. She remained at Newcomb for forty-seven years, instructing, inspiring, and encouraging many students who felt an affinity to their professor long after graduation. Throughout her career Smith exhibited her own work of watercolors and oil painting, establishing a link between the brush and the needle that is evident in all Newcomb textiles.

Ellsworth Woodward and Smith agreed that needlework was a chiefly feminine craft. To their minds, the basic skills were already in place because most Southern mothers taught their daughters to use needles and thread. Both instructors believed that only artistic training and design fundamentals were needed to develop women's skill into an art form. Reporting on the 1903 Founder's Day celebration at Tulane and Newcomb, the New Orleans *Daily Picayune* newspaper noted, "Among the recent additions to the Newcomb

---

[3] "Activity Among the Southern College. The Education Conference at Baton Rouge of Great Importance to Louisiana," *Daily Picayune*, March 15, 1902.

Library are: *Encyclopedia of Ceramics* by W. P. Jarvis; *Color (Modern Chromatics)* by O. N. Rood; *The Domain of Art* by W. M. Conway; *The Book of the Art of Cennino Cennini* by Graus C. Herringham; *Great Epochs in Art History* by J. M. Hoppin; *Embroidery, or the Craft of the Needle* by W. G. P. Townsend; and *Ornament in European Silks* by Allan Cole."[4]

Woodward spent the summer of 1903 visiting educational institutions and art centers in the North and East, observing their pedagogical ideas with the intent of applying the best concepts to his "model industry." On his return to New Orleans, the September 3, 1903 issue of the *Daily Picayune* newspaper featured an interview in which he addressed the events of his three-month vacation and the hopes he had for the Pottery enterprise. "My great ambition is to spread the name and fame of Sophie Newcomb's Art Department, with special eye to the extension of the pottery and the embroidery sections." [5]

In keeping with a tenet of the Pottery enterprise—the preference for regional materials—Smith added carding, spinning, and weaving of local cotton fibers to make the crash—a coarse, light, unevenly woven fabric on which the students would embroider. The process and purpose were explained in the March 3, 1903, issue of the *Daily Picayune* newspaper:

> *The art embroidery needlework under Mrs. Gertrude Roberts Smith also attracts much attention, as also the hand weaving and spinning. It is very beautiful to see the girls at work, the picture bringing back the representations seen of the women in households a century ago. The girls use the carding boards for the cotton and make it into thread, and so through the process, till cloth is produced from the hand looms. The industry is for the purpose of creating in the future designs for cotton factories and mills, and is in keeping with the industrial progress throughout this section.*[6]

---

[4] "From the Southern Colleges. The Full Programme for Founders' Day at Tulane," *Daily Picayune*, February 21, 1903: 11; "News From Southern Colleges. Newcomb Notes. Juniors Want to Present a Play – Progress in Pottery," *Daily Picayune*, March 7, 1903.

[5] Ibid.

[6] "News From Southern Colleges."

Thread used to illustrate the design was usually Persian silk that had been carefully selected and colored with Oriental dyes that didn't easily fade. Remaining evidence suggests that the weaving process used for embroidery eventually gave way to purchased linen and rough silk.[7] From a practical standpoint, art needlework had several advantages over the pottery: it required no expensive equipment, and was neither site- nor time-specific, which meant it could be carried out at the artist's discretion.

Designs for the textiles adhered to the same principles as the pottery, often depicting indigenous flora executed with Arts and Crafts aesthetics. In 1900, the Art School awarded two scholarships for deserving students, donated by an anonymous "friend," to attend Arthur Wesley Dow's summer school in Ipswich, Massachusetts. The first to travel there were Harriet Coulter Joor (1875-1965) and

Figure 3.11. Newcomb Artisan, Detail of Table Runner with Oak and Moss Design, ca.1915-20, silk thread in darning stitch on woven fabric, 12 x 17 inches, Newcomb Art Museum of Tulane University. Collection, 2003.5.1. Photograph by Owen Murphy.

---

[7] "Art Needlework in Newcomb College," *The Craftsman* 5, (December 1903), 265.

Amélie Roman (1873-1955). Dow's 1899 book, *Composition,* was seminal for the design fundamentals of the Pottery enterprise. In his exercise on "Arrangements in Opposition and Repetition – vertical lines cut by horizontal lines," Dow reduces a landscape to its essential lines then fits the components in a rectangular space. By shortening the viewer's depth of field, the treetops are not visible and the exercise is one of horizontals and verticals. One year after Joor returned from Ipswich, she executed a pine grove landscape on a three-handled cup or tyg in a design identical to the exercise illustrations in Dow's *Composition.* The treatment of the motif was innovative because instead of painting an outline, she incised and textured her composition into the clay before its bisque firing.

Figure 3.12. Marie Odelle Delavigne (1873-1963), Wall hanging with pine forest design, ca. 1902-05. Silk thread in linen in running and outline stitches on woven linen, 17 x 45 in. Newcomb Art Museum of Tulane University. Accession number D&MA 1973 210A. Photograph by Owen Murphy.

The graphic qualities of the new technique translated well into a wall hanging of similar design that was executed between 1902 and 1905. Attributed to Marie Delavigne, the silk threads on cotton crash address the same arrangements of verticals and horizontals as in the tyg; however, the motif is depicted in running and outline stitches. The stitches are not complicated, but they are used with skill and imagination. The wall hanging is covered in richly colored threads of orange, yellow, purple, green, and blue. In a sense, the textiles had an advantage over the pottery when it came to use of color. Newcomb's pottery adopted its "trademark" blue and green underglaze early in the enterprise's life; embroidery had no such restrictions. In fact, close inspection of the pine grove wall hanging reveals the juxtaposition of colors similar to that of Pointillist paintings by George Seurat. Writing on the use of color in Newcomb textiles, Woodward said, "In the subtle contrast of color, the deft choice of hues in infinite variety, lies half the power of the designer, and constitutes a resource for the needlewoman, which cannot be overestimated."[8]

A Newcomb textile began the same way a piece of pottery began—with a drawing. The design was laid down in pencil and a color palette was worked out in watercolor. Tonal variations are evident in the individual brushstrokes employed in drawing. A cut-out template was used to transfer the motif onto the linen by means of dressmaker's tracing paper. Various colored threads were placed parallel to one another, catching the warp or woof depending on the direction of the stitch, over and under so as to make the silk floss appear part of the woven fabric. Pieces judged suitable for sale had the initials "NTN" (Newcomb Textile and Needlework) sewn into the back.[9] Judging from extant examples, the mark was not used consistently.

As with the pottery designers, Newcomb's needleworkers also made recurrent use of indigenous flora. Gardening, especially the cultivation of flowers, was a pervasive influence on nineteenth-century American women. Popular women's magazines of the time encouraged their readers to establish flower gardens, not only for their aesthetic value but also for physical exercise. Men of science, religion, and literature praised the feminine mind that understood floriculture. Women decorated their homes with fresh-cut flowers and adorned their interiors with nature-inspired textiles—curtains, upholstered furniture, and quilts. Young women who attended college and followed a scientific track were encouraged to study botany. During the mid-nineteenth to the early-twentieth century, it became the preferred science for its conformity with contemporary views

[8] Woodward, "Needlework," *Brush and Pencil*: 315.

[9] M. G. Sheerer, "Newcomb Pottery Workers, An Appreciation," *New Orleans Times-Democrat*, May 19, 1907; Harriet Joor, "The Art Industries of Newcomb College," *International Studio*, 41 (July 1910), 10-12.

of acceptable, home-centered, feminine roles. Thus it followed that Newcomb's textiles became unique for the Gulf region's indigenous flora and the skill with which designs were implemented. Colors and shapes found in the students' home gardens presented infinite variety and inspired their art.

The work of Newcomb artist Harriet Joor again serves as an example. Besides her travels to Dow's summer school, she was among the first students in Newcomb's Normal Art program, decorating ceramics and crafting embroidery, but her academic major wasn't art, it was science. She received a Bachelor of Science degree in 1895, after which she enrolled as a Special Art student for the next four years. She was subsequently listed as a Graduate Art student in the 1900-1901 Tulane University catalogue and a Pottery Decorator from 1901-1906. Her keen eye for detail and knowledge of plant anatomy make her botanical drawings among the finest ever produced at Newcomb. Joor used her talents to explore diverse careers—South Dakota homesteader, author, art therapist, and ultimately teacher. Joor was greatly influenced by her father, Joseph Finley Joor. A native of Louisiana whose occupations included physician and botanist, his medical practice embraced New Orleans and Thibodaux, in the bayou area southwest of the city. He moved his family to southeast Texas where shortly after his arrival, he was appointed assistant commissioner for Texas to prepare a botanical exhibit for the 1884 World Industrial and Cotton Centennial in New Orleans. In 1886, he accepted a position at Tulane University's Natural History Museum, first as associate curator, and then curator and professor of botany in 1888.[10]

The distinguishing characteristic of Newcomb needleworkers' embroidery was the use of a darning stitch in an unconventional way, which gave a painterly quality to the design's texture. In most textiles of the period, stitches fully covered the woven base. With Newcomb's textiles, the weave of the cloth was allowed to show through, creating a texture to the contrasting smooth surface of the fabric foundation. The French knot stitch was used to illustrate a flower's stamen; an outline stitch would delineate the form for the satin stitch to fill in

[10] J. B. S. Norton, "Joseph F. Joor," *Botanical Gazette* 26 (4), 1898: 270-274.

the space between. The texture and harmony of color employed by Smith and her students on landscape wall hangings achieved an illusion of depth usually reserved for the best graphic works. Items sold from the Art School's Sales Room, or exhibited at expositions and arts and crafts clubs around the country, were created by "a student of ability having had four years' training in its courses in drawing, color, and design."[11] The products offered for purchase were table covers, table runners, lamp mats, wall hangings, decorative screens, and dress insets.

There are, of course, limitations to needle and thread, but the relationship between the worker and her art was immediate and intimate. Embroidery was a totally female product, not taught by men, not designed by men, not, as the pots were, shaped by them. Unlike pottery decorators, needleworkers had control of their pieces from inception to completion. The case for intimacy with items made by the needleworkers can be found in a 1903 article featured in the *Daily Picayune* newspaper reporting on activities in Southern colleges. The story contained the following: "The Embroidery Class, under Miss Huger's artistic supervision, is designing the most attractive sofa pillows. As another pleasant result of this new class, the young ladies appear frequently in waists that have been most beautifully embroidered by themselves."[12]

Emily Hamilton Huger (1881-1946) graduated from the Newcomb Art School in 1902 and began her teaching career at the Louisiana Southwest Industrial Institute, now the University of Louisiana, Lafayette, that same year. The course she was assigned dealt with clothing construction, called "Domestic Art," which had been added to the Domestic Science curriculum in 1902.

The Newcomb Art School received many awards for its industrial crafts over the years, but the first won by the embroidery workers came from samples sent to the 1904 Louisiana Purchase Exposition in St. Louis. A newspaper article in the October 30, 1904, issue of the *Daily Picayune* quoted Woodward as saying:

---

[11] "Art Needlework in Newcomb College," 282.

[12] "Southwestern Industrial" in "Tulane University Continues Founders' Day Celebration, All the Departments Acting as Hosts to Each Other," *Daily Picayune*, March 14, 1903.

Figure 3.13. Newcomb Artisan, Table runner with southern pine design, ca. 1905-10. Silk thread in running and outline stitches on woven linen, 23 x 52.5 in. Newcomb Art Museum of Tulane University. Accession number D&MA.1973.209A. Photograph by Owen Murphy.

The work in embroidery is steadily advancing in importance and in beauty of production. A number of new agencies have been established in the Northern centers. A very complimentary letter has recently been received from Mrs. Candace Wheeler, the Dean of American needlework.

Of the artistic crafts, which have been revived with so much advantage during recent years, few lend themselves to individual treatment so satisfactory as embroidery. In the hands of the skilled artist, its possibilities seem endless. Originality of design and charm of color unite with the interest of handwoven texture and the quality of permanence, and satisfy the requirement of art production.[13]

Wheeler (1827-1923) was in partnership at Associated Artists, New York, with Louis C. Tiffany (1848-1933), Lockwood de Forest (1850-1932), and Samuel Colman (1832-1920). She was considered by many to be the "mother" of interior design. She addressed the art classes at Newcomb in February 1908, taking as her topic the progress of interior decorating.

Newcomb's esteemed teacher Gertrude Roberts Smith, an inveterate traveller during her years at the Art School, began making regular visits to North Carolina in the late 1920s. Her heart went out to the mountain people living in and around Andrews, North Carolina. When she retired from the College in 1934, Smith moved to Asheville, North Carolina, hoping to revive the weaving tradition of the Appalachian mountain people. In her final days at Newcomb, she was interviewed by the *Times-Picayune* newspaper about her long association with the College and her future plans:

I don't know whether my plan will work or not. As yet it is only an idea of mine that I am going to try to put into reality. I have visited Andrews, North Carolina, many times, and have always wished I had some means to help those poor people up there.... I thought if I could go up there, and teach them to weave clothes for themselves from their wool, they would at least be able to keep good and warm.

---

[13] "Newcomb Art. Scores More Triumph at St. Louis Exposition," *Daily Picayune*, October 30, 1904.

It is a curious thing, the people still do a little spinning, but the art of weaving is almost totally dead. The old looms are all idle in the attics where they have lain for generations. I should like to have them taken out again, and put to work.... I want to teach the women to make practical articles for their own use, not necessarily to sell.[14]

She found money to purchase thirty looms, giving them to individuals for personal use in their homes. Always the teacher, she devised the patterns and designs for the woven rugs and fabric. The coarse material made "excellent sports costumes" and through the efforts of one of her former Newcomb students, Henrietta Bailey, Smith was introduced to a New York designer who in turn marketed the handiwork to colleagues. Former students interviewed in the June 10, 1934, issue of the *Item-Tribune* said, "We are only lending her to North Carolina for a little while. Louisiana needs her, and when she has realized that sweet, long-cherished dream of hers, she is coming back to us."[15]

Clearly Smith was the pivotal person around whom Newcomb's needleworkers had operated. Embroidery involved items of cultural aspiration, usually for home use, and instruction in creating them was intended to educate women into the prevailing feminine ideal. But the women at Newcomb did more than stitch expressions of femininity. They created artifacts that transcended their dependence and transformed them into artists who could support themselves, or provide income. Most important, their mastery of these arts was proof of success to the women themselves.

---

[14] Edith Loeber Ballard, "Veteran Art Teacher Leaves Newcomb to Teach Spinning," *Item-Tribune*, June 10, 1934.

[15] Unidentified clipping in the Newcomb Art School scrapbook, University Archives, Special Collections, Howard-Tilton Library, Tulane University.

DECORATIVE CLOTH CONNECTING A CITY
Susan Tucker

The queen of New Orleans Carnival, the Queen of Rex, in 1988 wore gold. Newspaper columnist Nell Nolan described the fitted "gown of fine French silk lamé" with a "godet-shaped skirt" as dazzling. She told of "hand-beaded lines cascading across the dress ... rhinestones and gold beads ... with a series of glistening tassels." One could read her reporting as a prose poem to the city itself, can imagine a cartouche on the map of the area decked with her description of "a Medici collar of gold lace" and a "royal raiment" complete with "sumptuous mantle, the tiara, and parure—the necklace and earrings."[1]

One hopes Nolan had lots of readers who could picture this gown. There are many other similar descriptions as well. Some two hundred women and men dress every year in this way to reign over some one hundred New Orleans social organizations called krewes. In addition, there are descriptions of costumes worn on floats, at balls, and on the streets. Carnival revolves around the cloth of these creations.

On the other hand, who understands the ancient vocabulary of the designers, seamstresses, and tailors of the city? Who really can picture a *godet-shaped skirt* or a *Medici collar*? Who thinks of a person's *parure*? Who knows this vocabulary of dress in terms of social class or details of artistry? Ask too: where does the cloth for these creations come from and what happens to such apparel? In reply, this essay is devoted to a few connecting biographical and historical accounts about people involved in this foundation of Carnival, those who also often continue work all year long, in the past and in the present, to build and maintain the textile infrastructure of the city: the owners, workers, and customers of fabric stores; the makers of slipcovers, baby clothes, and pillows, for some examples.[2] Their lives

---

[1] Nell Nolan, "The Monarchs of Mardi Gras," *Times-Picayune*, February 21, 1988.

[2] These other practices and the connections were suggested by Ilaine Hartman, designer, interview with Susan Tucker, October 17, 2011; Larry Mercier, tailor and designer, interview with Tucker, September 7, 2015; Nicole Gibson, seamstress and designer, interview with Tucker, January 21, 2014; Dottie Eaves Kostmayer and Lydia Eaves Trice, sewing teachers and seamstresses, interview with Tucker, January 8, 2014. Hartman is also a quilter; Mercier makes slipcovers; Gibson runs a shop called The Baby Boudoir; Kostmayer and Trice make pillows and purses to sell for charitable events. All interviews, conversations, emails hereafter are with Tucker.

suggest some of the ways we might consider decorative cloth as both functional and archival, that is, as used but also as saved.

I. Clothing and Costumes, Practicality and Design

Most cloth enters our consciousness today as covering for the body, and even in *haute couture*, starts as a practical matter. However, in New Orleans there exists a realm in which embellishment is more the rule than the exception. Here, there are plenty of bolts of taffeta, silk, satin, lace, and plenty of boxes of beads, sequins, and feathers. And, there are many people who work with these materials.

Carnival also fosters a conscious desire to remember. Photographs of families in costumes appear in almost every album in the city. Libraries, museums, and archives proudly focus upon their holdings about design and sewing. It is not surprising that the Louisiana State Museum (LSM) in New Orleans and the Louisiana State University Textile & Costume Museum in Baton Rouge are two of only some one hundred collections of costumes in the world.

Wayne Phillips, curator of that LSM Costume collection, suggested to me that to understand sewing for Carnival I begin my research with designer Ilaine Hartman (b. 1945). Hartman learned to sew in her grandmother's store, Gelman's. Russian-born Frieda Kaufmann Gelman (1901-1974) ran her fabric business from the 1930s to the 1970s as a key stop on Dryades Street, in what New Orleanians called the Jewish district, settled and dominated by immigrants from Eastern Europe and Russia.[3]

Hartman took over Gelman's on her grandmother's death, relocating it to St. Charles Avenue in 1978. By then, however, she felt the stiff competition that franchise stores like Hancock's brought. So, employing skills and connections she had had since childhood, she began to increase the amount of work she did for Carnival.[4]

Hartman saw this as a simple transition since a number of people from Carnival krewe design teams had often consulted her as they shopped in the fabric store. She also had the special experience herself of being queen of one of the children's balls of Carnival, and at eighteen, Queen of one of the oldest women's krewes, Iris. As a

---

[3] Wayne Phillips, Curator of Textiles and Costumes, interview, July 20, 2011. Hartman, interview.
[4] Hartman, interview.

Figure 3.14. Edith Stouse, Carnival designer, with unidentified knight of the Mistik Krewe of Comus, ca. 1928. Photograph by Moses Studio. Collection of Suzanne Whann, New Orleans, LA.

young adult, she had also worked as a buyer for Maison Blanche Department Store. On annual trips to New York City for the store, Hartman learned about the qualities of various fabrics. She would later recall all these circumstances when she ordered laces and silks from Europe and traveled to New York and Houston to shop for fabrics for costumes and ball gowns.[5]

II. Other Connections

In 1980, longtime designer and seamstress Claire Stouse called upon Hartman on Ash Wednesday, the day after Mardi Gras. Stouse handed Hartman a pair of pants, part of a costume for a Knight of Comus, another of the elite male krewes. "Sew this pair of pants," Stouse said.[6]

Claire Stouse was eighty years old then and had been sewing and designing since childhood. She and her three sisters (Edith, Eveline, and Yvonne) lived from the early 1890s to the early 1980s and had established themselves as critical to the elite Carnival krewes in the city. None of them married—thus showing something of how they wanted to be remembered for their work. They spoke French among themselves, an attribute that was symbolically important to the Francophiles in the city but also practical since they often contracted with Acadian women in rural Louisiana for some of the sewing on their creations of hundreds of costumes. They were devoted professionals at a time when most women were not, and their profession allowed them some income, prestige, and travel. They sewed all year for some four or five krewes. In 1928, for example, the krewe of Rex paid them $6,850 for costumes to be allocated to expenses and income for the four sisters. This amount in 2015 would be close to $95,000. They also knew Carnival from the inside out: the color and sizes of tights needed; the mechanics of frames to construct mantles; the sizes of the trims of fur and gilded rope; the textures of silver and white wigs; the formalities of symbols in the costumes of royalty, including the hierarchy of the

---

[5] Hartman, interview; Susan Langenhennig, "Designing Carnival's Queen Gowns Takes a Couturier's Eye and an Aptitude for Engineering," *Times-Picayune*, February 12, 2012; Christina Masciere, "Crowning Achievements: Carnival's Royal Costumer," *New Orleans Magazine*, January 1, 1997.

[6] Hartman, interview.

captains, pages, and other specially chosen role players. The sisters also understood and indeed lived within the domain of social connections. They were daughters of a Rex member. And they had another more important lineage. Their aunt, Anna Forstall, had been a designer for Rex.[7]

By 1921, Forstall had taught them all she knew and handed over her work to them. Each of the sisters developed her own specialty. One drew; one made patterns; one excelled at details of fabric, mantles, and collars; one managed the accounts. Claire was the only one who did not work full time in the Carnival work. Instead, she also worked as a bookkeeper for Pan American Life Insurance Company and other businesses.[8]

In 1980, Claire approved Ilaine Hartman's efforts with the Comus pants. "Willy-nilly I had some 12,000 square feet of fitting rooms, sewing rooms, and storage," Hartman recalled. She took over, in other words, all the work of the four sisters.[9] Ilaine Hartman Designs operated from 1980 to 2015.[10]

III. Inside, Outside, and Moving Towards the Mainstream

Many other experts have dominated the informal and formal apprenticeship system that exists among New Orleans designers. Male designers are part of this system too, and perhaps better known. Journalists often enough discuss men such as Larry Youngblood, San Nicholas, Anthony Colombo, and Carter Church. No one has compared the number of men to the number of women in Carnival designing, but an overview of most writing on their work suggests that women predominated in the past since such seasonal work was more amenable to homemakers.[11]

---

[7] Joanna Tabony, "The Stouse Girls: New Orleans Ladies," Master's thesis, University of New Orleans, 2011, 4; Dollar-value calculations are based on the MeasuringWorth.Com Consumer Price Index.

[8] Tabony, 9-12; Hartman, interview; Suzanne Whann, cousin to the Stouse Sisters, email, March 17, 2016.

[9] Ibid.

[10] Today, her work, as well as the legacies of her grandmother, Forstall, the Stouse Sisters, and others, lives on in a new place, the Royal Design Shop, established in 2015 by Ashley Seehorn and Katie Johnson. Ashley Seehorn, conversation, July 23, 2015.

[11] For information in general on designers, see Tucker, "Coralie Guarino Davis (1926–2004): Claiming Status and Constructing Legacies," in Louisiana Women, vol. 2, ed. Shannon Frystak and Mary Kaiser Farmer (Athens: University of Georgia Press, 2016); Lynn Jensen, "Life is Sew-Sew for Rex Costumer," Times-Picayune, February 12, 1996; Mark Lorando, "Carnival in October," Times-Picayune, October 25, 2008; Wayne Phillips, "Behind the Scenes," City Life, February 2004; Errol Laborde, "Sew Me Something, Mister: Rex at 125: Some Theories of Evolution," New Orleans Magazine 31, no. 4 (1997);

In general, designers are relatively unknown, said Curator Phillips of the Louisiana State Museum. Most designers do not mind this anonymity, he said, since, "The theme of the balls, the design of the ball gowns and floats, all this is secret, and so they don't want people to know them and then ask [about their designs]." Memories about the life of designer Durelli Watts (1916-2004) reveal a special variation on this secrecy for the elite, primarily African American, Zulu Social Aid and Pleasure Club. "Durelli created the gowns from scratch," said one Zulu krewe member after Durelli's death. "The theme was a closely guarded secret and she was only one of three people to know it....She designed each dress differently and no one, not even the girls or their parents, could see" her creations before the ball.[12]

Sewing itself can be a meditative act, attached always to periods of silence, as well as connections to others. The most crucial beginning for all the designers, male and female, is usually learning to sew from their mothers, grandmothers, and other women.[13] Yet sewing is a skill not often taught today. Indeed, over the last century and earlier in some places, ready-made clothes replaced the need for most people to learn to sew. Still immigrants' sewing skills and indeed all work with fabric have, for centuries and in many cultures, enabled important entry points into new homes and new lives. New Orleans is no different in these circumstances.

Vietnamese American Nguyet Vu (b. 1956) is one contemporary designer and seamstress in New Orleans who emphasized both the portability of her skills and the status it has given her. Vu was born in Laos in 1956 and lived ten years as a refugee in Thailand. It was there that her mother encouraged her to study sewing and tailoring at a vocational school. She became involved in one of the most prestigious of all tailoring cultures in the world, that of the Asian shop attached to a hairdresser. As she noted, "Loyal clients come in

Brock N. Meeks, "Carter Church: The Mardi Gras Man, in *Rising from the Ruin*, MSNBC online, December 26, 2005. For flexibility suggested, see lives as described in obituaries of designers and seamstresses for Carnival, for example, "Grace Wood Blanchard, Designer and Draftsperson for Ball Gowns and Crescent City Connection," *Times-Picayune*, July 10, 2011; "Amy Marie Zeringue Roux," *Times-Picayune*, July 14, 2011.

[12] Phillips, interview; Karen Sommer Shalett, "Tribute to a Couturier," *Times-Picayune*, January 21, 2005.

[13] Hartman, Mercier, and other designers mentioned this connection; for influence on Marigold Hardesty, see John Pope, "Carnival Sparkles with Her Couture Creations - Tailor has Costumed Krewes for 30 Years," *Times-Picayune*, January 21, 2008.

for beauty needs…brought their fabrics and photos of dresses, suits, and other outfits they would like made."[14]

Vu arrived in New Orleans in the early 1970s and began work sewing with an earlier immigrant, a Mr. Gonzales who had been in the city for some forty years. He came from Honduras. "He had the shop from his brother, who first came to this country and then after his tailor shop became successful, he could bring his brother." Vu remembered many immigrant tailors and seamstresses with shops on Rampart and Common Streets.[15]

Mr. Gonzales introduced her to what became one of Vu's favorite places in "all America: Krauss Department Store. Beautiful," she said. "Everything better there. Fabrics you could not find anywhere else."[16] Leon Fellman and his nephews, the four Krauss brothers, founded the department store much earlier, in 1903. They located their store right on the edge of Storyville, the district of legalized prostitution (1897-1917). In the apocryphal lore of the city, Krauss catered to the ladies of the night. The store set other more verifiable trends: In 1925 it was the first department store to provide air-conditioning. It had the first escalators (wooden mechanical stairs). It had the city's last functioning pneumatic system for moving information between its six floors.[17]

Until 1968, the fabric department was located on the first floor, but management noted that people came so often for material that they would certainly take the stairs or elevators, if they had to, to the third floor. That way people would see other possible purchases. On the third floor, this space occupied 25,000 square feet. The fabric itself was given 14,000 square feet. Clerks placed eight-foot square cutting tables with mechanical measuring devices around the floor in different spots. According to the last manager of the store, Hugo Kahn, Krauss staff and managers always considered customers who sewed as special, as "skilled and smart…as experts."[18]

---

[14] Nguyet Vu, interview, January 17, 2014.
[15] Ibid.
[16] Ibid.
[17] Carolyn Kolb, "Krauss: Last of the Classic Department Stores," *New Orleans Magazine,* December 2010; "1997: New Orleans Icon Krauss Department Store Closes," *Times-Picayune,* January 9, 2012; "Historical Note," Finding aid, Krauss Department Store Collection, Earl K. Long Library, University of New Orleans.
[18] Hugo Kahn, Manager for Krauss, 1967-1997, interview, February 7, 2014.

New Orleans has been called often enough one of the most class-divided of American cities, and Carnival's part in this status is generally acknowledged by locals. Sewing, it follows, might reinforce social, economic, race, and religious divisions. Yet, Krauss defied these separations within the city, at least in some daily interactions around fabric, conversations between people of all classes, all races, ethnic groups, religions, and as noted in this volume, sexual orientations. Kahn noted about Krauss: "Old, young, black, white: great mix, and our staff was equally divided there. People felt good about the store. We were New Orleans."[19]

Can one associate these feelings and interactions with other steps in creating a more democratic society? Perhaps: Kahn remembered seeing architectural plans dating from before the 1960s that showed fitting rooms and a lunch counter for African Americans, features uniformly denied in other stores.[20]

There also were other ways that sewing revealed itself as a skill that commanded some deviation from the customs of strict segregation. In the late 1970s and early 1980s, when I was trying to understand what domestic workers and their employers could reveal about divisions among American women, I found that seamstresses were given special status among African American women working in white households. White women deigned to allow these seamstresses to enter by the front door when all other African American workers had to use the back door.[21]

Of course, these were miniscule steps toward equality. In addition, these and other African American seamstresses had more cause to learn to perfect their craft than did white women. Another statement heard often enough in oral history research was that many African American women dressed more stylishly than did their white counterparts. In the Jim Crow era, African American women had to sew to have access to better clothing, had to learn alter and "to fit" their clothes. They were not allowed in fitting rooms (what we

---

[19] Kahn, interview; Kim Lacy Rogers, *Righteous Lives: Narratives of the New Orleans Civil Rights Movement* (New York: New York University Press, 1993); Robin Roberts, "New Orleans Mardi Gras and Gender in Three Krewes: Rex, The Truck Parades, and Muses," *Western Folklore* vol. 65, no. 3 (Summer 2006), 303-328; Malcolm Gladwell, "Starting Over," *New Yorker*, August 24, 2015.

[20] Kahn, interview; Kahn, telephone conversation, September 6, 2015.

[21] Tucker, *Telling Memories Among Southern Women: Domestic Workers and Their Employers in the Segregated South* (Baton Rouge: LSU Press, 1988), 79-80.

usually call today "dressing rooms" since we don't so often "fit" our clothes) in department stores. The very term "fitting room" suggests also what this segregation meant: African Americans could not know if the clothes they wished to purchase fit since they were not allowed to try them on. They also could not return clothes that did not fit and thus had to learn to alter clothing.[22]

Born after the end of legalized segregation, an African American seamstress named Nicole Gibson (b. 1974) follows other traditions connected to Louisiana women who specialized in baby clothes, and discussed elsewhere in this volume. Gibson, a mother of four children, is the owner of a St. Roch's establishment called the Baby Boudoir. After the flooding of 2005, she followed her dream to find

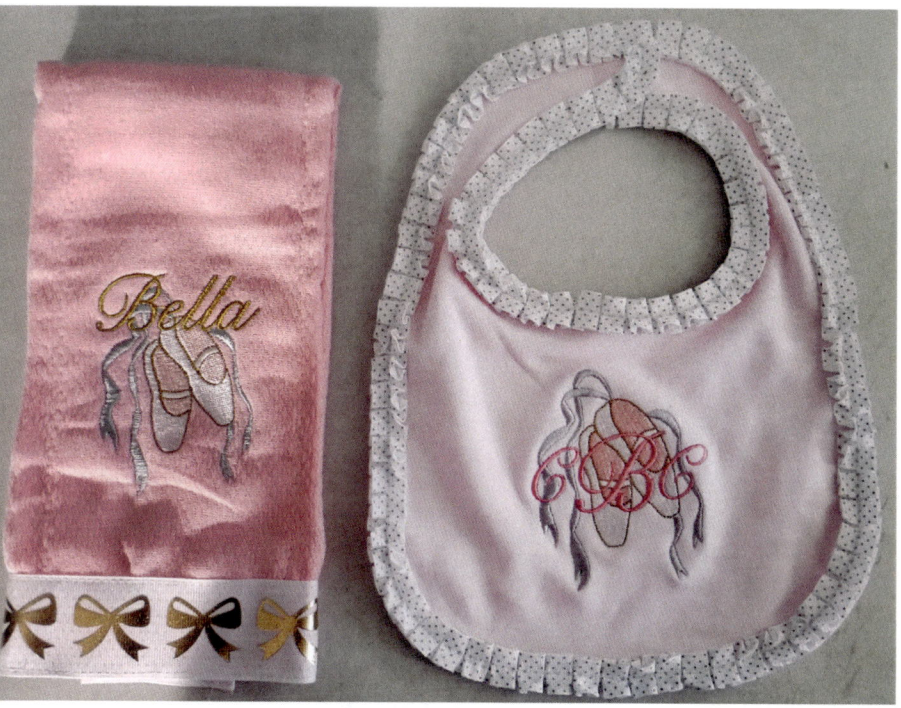

Figure 3.15. Baby cloth and bib. Created by Nicole Gibson, 2016. Photograph by Nicole Gibson.

[22] Herreast Harrison, telephone conversation, September 15, 2015; Wendy Ann Gaudin, "Autocrats and All Saints: Migration, Memory, and Modern Creole Identities," PhD diss., New York University, 2005. See also Civil Rights Movement Veterans, Timeline: "Sit-Ins Background & Context," http://www.crmvet.org/tim/timhis60. htm#1960nosmb. Accessed September 6, 2015.

more time to sew at home. She remembered Krauss's sale of bib cloths and the many different women who came there to buy them. Today she specializes in these cloths, adding embroidered initials, first names, or designs to them. She also specializes in quilts for newborns and ball gowns for young women. Gibson picks up clients from all sorts of backgrounds since Jo Ann's Fabrics in the suburbs suggests her to others.[23] Sewing then again creates connections that extend across racial, geographic, and class lines.

Vu's and Gibson's connections to Krauss Department Store circle back to Gelman's. Like Frieda Gelman's beginning in Russia as a part of a Jewish family, Krauss's founder came as a Jewish immigrant. Leon Fellman came from the Germersheim district of present-day Germany. Born in 1846, he arrived in New Orleans in 1865 and twenty-one years later married into the Godchaux family. New wife Blanche Godchaux was a lucky match for him. Twenty years his junior, she had important connections to the mercantile life of the city. Her father, Leon Godchaux, had come to New Orleans from Alsace and began as a peddler of needles, thread, and other household goods. Soon enough he had the preeminent department store on Canal Street, as well as a controlling interest in a sugar plantation and various other businesses. Another daughter, Leonie, married yet another immigrant, Augustus Mayer, who founded yet another department store, Gus Mayer's. Many other connections of Jewish families and their commerce in fabric can also be found, as noted elsewhere in this volume.[24]

People today still tell about Godchaux's Department Store (1840-1986) and its particular way of making handsewing part of its special appeal. There one could find not only expert seamstresses on staff but also a specialty shop that sold baby clothes created by rural Acadian and urban Creole women, a means for them to work from home, noted in this volume in several essays. Ida Kohlmeyer, famed New Orleans artist, found her first job in Godchaux's department of handmade baby clothes, located in the niche of an old elevator shaft.[25]

---

[23] Gibson, interview.

[24] 1910 United States Federal Census, Ancestry.com, Online publication - Provo, UT, Ancestry.com Operations Inc., 2006; original data - Thirteenth Census of the United States, 1910 (NARA microfilm publication T624, 1,178 rolls); Kahn, interview; Catherine Wolf, conversation with Susan Tucker, July 10, 2008. The families also had important connections with "junior" (smaller) department stores in rural Louisiana.

[25] "Ida Rittenberg Kohlmeyer, 1912-1997: Oral History interview, from 1986 by Adele Salzer," in Newcomb College: Higher Education for Women in New Orleans, 1986-2006, ed. Susan Tucker and Beth Willinger (Baton Rouge: LSU Press, 2012), 365.

Figure 3.16. Canal Street, showing Lazard's Clothing. Detroit Publishing Company, between 1900 and 1920. Courtesy of the Library of Congress, American Memory.

The Lazard's Clothing sign here shows another connection of cloth across the families who are mentioned in this anthology. Besides being the daughter of Mark Isaacs who helped found Maison Blanche, Flora Isaacs Lazard (who ran the Louise Shop in the French Quarter and who is mentioned in the essay by Rabalais-Vinci) also married into the family that ran Lazard's.

IV. Remembering

Remembering generally requires jogs of memory, often the connection of an emotion to the picture (literal or imagined) of an object. People on the street often greet Hugo Kahn, the last manager of Krauss, with enthusiasm. He has a downtown office and he can offer them a Krauss shopping bag. "They react as if they have won the lottery." This is particularly so "for the women who bought fabric there," he said.[26]

Cloth, to him, shows other connections to the remembered or forgotten past. When he was a young teenager, he and his family escaped Nazi Germany in 1940. Only in the early twenty-first century did he see something his mother had brought with them: a tablecloth she had made. It was light, like most fabric. It could be packed even in a small package and carried in haste.[27]

What does keeping fabric mean and require? Fabric can impart a story, but the story may not ever be fully told. Keeping the physical object entails careful housing: darkness, proper and stable temperatures, isolation from other fabrics, and many more particulars dependent on the type of fabric one has.[28]

Both the Louisiana State Museum Costume and Textiles Division and the Louisiana State University Textile and Costume Museum hold quilts and other bedding, dinner and furniture coverings, Acadiana textiles, uniforms, ceremonial artifacts from religious services, flags, embroidery, and much more. Founded in 1906, it was not until the 1920s that the State Museum began to think, however, of the collection of Carnival costumes and ball gowns as something truly unique and worthy of care. It was not until the 1970s that the collection began to grow quickly. What took so long? The simple answer is that those pieces familiar to the very life of a place are not always what are desired first in collecting. A more complicated answer is that Carnival sewing and designing were long both revered and tucked away, central and secret.[29]

---

[26] Kahn, interview.

[27] Ibid.

[28] "Textiles," Sustaining Places: Resources for Small Museums and Historic Sites, *http://sustainingplaces.com/read/ collections/collections-care/textiles*. Accessed September 13, 2015.

[29] Phillips, interview.

But the 1970s at the Museum, as elsewhere, proved a watershed decade for decorative cloth largely because of rising interests in women's history. Both the State Museum and the LSU collections expanded especially from the 1980s on, building on what they were lucky to have earlier decided: textiles are parts of public, commercial, private, and artistic endeavors.[30]

At the State Museum, one of the most recent acquisitions tells the intimate rewards of designing and sewing. Philip and Lucia Liuzza used their creativity in the floats, costumes, tableaux, and other pieces needed for some seven Carnival krewes from 1950 to 1980. Lucia Liuzza, in turn, also acted as archivist, documenting their work in scrapbooks. She sketched and wrote about costumes and the people who wore them. She, like so many others, loved her work and found it a calling that required imagination, tact, and a sort of otherworldly presence. As she asked in the last of her entries: "Who can say where the real & unreal begin & end?" Often offered jobs in Hollywood, the Liuzzas would not leave New Orleans.[31]

Figure 3.17. Page from a scrapbook entitled *TREASURED MEMORIES of Lucia & Philip Liuzza, Our Lives & Work in Mardi Gras 1950-1980.* Courtesy of the collections of the Louisiana State Museum.

---

[30] Phillips, interview; Pamela Rabalais -Vinci, email, September 4, 2015.

[31] Phillips, "Handwritten Memories," September 28, 2012. Paper in possession of author.

The decorative cloth of Carnival held them in the city, as it has held and continues to hold so many others. Eventually, too, many Louisianans learn to recognize that Medici collar and many other flourishes of fabric as they make themselves a fitting costume for the streets, floats, or ballrooms of Carnival.

Figure 3.18. Image of Medici collar from the scrapbook entitled *TREASURED MEMORIES of Lucia & Philip Liuzza, Our Lives & Work in Mardi Gras 1950-1980.* Courtesy of the collections of the Louisiana State Museum.

SARTORIAL SUNDAYS: SOCIAL AID AND PLEASURE CLUBS CRAFT IMPECCABLE STYLE FOR THE STREETS

Rachel Carrico, from interviews with Edward Buckner
and Sue Louis Press

Nearly every Sunday afternoon, huge crowds of people flood the streets of New Orleans to dance in participatory, neighborhood-based processions known as "second lines." The form of a second line parade is simple. The hosting organization and brass band form the first line or main line, and the trumpet's blare invites all within earshot to form a second line behind the band, giving the event its name. Second lines are thrown in New Orleans for all sorts of occasions: weddings, conventions, holidays, festivals, family parties, and (notably) funerals, but when New Orleanians talk about "*the* second line," they are most likely referring to the parades that are hosted each Sunday by one or more social aid and pleasure clubs. These African American mutual aid organizations grew out of nineteenth-century benevolent societies, which hosted processions led by brass bands, including funerals for their members, starting in the early 1800s.[1] Today, social aid and pleasure clubs do not wait for a funeral before they hit the streets, but plan second lines to celebrate each club's anniversary in its home neighborhood; and the affair is anything but simple. It is a spectacular performance that processes through public streets with live and recorded music, dancing, elaborate regalia, truck-pulled floats, food and drink, theatrical ceremony, spoken, written, and visual rhetoric.

Each Sunday's second line begins at 1:00 p.m. sharp, when club members "come out the door" of a house, barroom, or other building significant to its members.[2] As the brass band strikes up, the "main liners" burst into the street, showing off their best second line dance

---

[1] On the history of New Orleans brass bands, see Henry Kmen, *Music in New Orleans, the Formative Years: 1791-1841* (Baton Rouge: Louisiana State University Press, 1966); and Matt Sakakeeny, *Roll With It: Brass Bands in the Streets of New Orleans* (Durham, NC: Duke University Press, 2013). For more on the history of African American mutual aid societies in the nineteenth and early twentieth centuries, see Jacqui Malone, *Steppin' On the Blues: The Visible Rhythms of African American Dance* (Urbana, IL: University of Illinois Press, 1996), 167-186.

[2] During the winter months, the parades kick off at noon so that they can end before sunset.

Figure 3.19. *Ole & Nu Style Fellas.* Photograph by Judy Cooper, April 24, 2014.

moves—dropping low, jumping high, pausing dramatically, spinning, and working their feet so fast that they hover *just* above the pavement. As club members come out the door, they reveal a guarded secret: their colors. Every year, each club chooses a brand new color scheme, and everything they wear and carry, inside out from head to toe, is made in these colors: matching suits, accessorized with coordinated hats, socks, gloves, and shoes. A sash, called a "streamer" or "yoke," drapes across the members' torsos. They wave feathered fans above their heads and carry decorated umbrellas, canes, and/or buckets. While some clubs emphasize dancing and some, clothing, each club performs neighborhood and club pride both with their dance steps and sartorial style. In fact, clubs' clothing choices must be fashionable *and* functional, as club members execute intricate footwork, high-knee stepping, even aerial leaps and drops to the ground. Decked out in a riot of color and texture, the club members lead the brass band and a gathering crowd, which can number in the thousands, in a four-hour, processional dance party through New Orleans's historically black neighborhoods.

Functional yet fashionable, clothing and hand-held decorations are a major element of second lines' spirit of friendly competition, a one-upsmanship that keeps each club striving to come out bigger, better, and "cleaner" than the year before. Color schemes are kept top secret until the members come out the door on parade day when the crowd dispenses their approval and, not infrequently, their disapproval. The two clubs featured in this essay parade in the latter part of the season, which runs from September to June, so they have the added benefit of scoping other clubs' sartorial choices throughout the year before choosing their own themes, decorations, and color schemes.

Social aid and pleasure clubs are not the only street parading groups in New Orleans who engage in cloth-and-feather performances; so do Mardi Gras Indians, albeit in very distinct ways. Both traditions are unique to New Orleans but can be viewed in a historical context of the African Diaspora. In her study of black style and fashion, Monica L. Miller observes that black people "use clothing and dress to define their identity in different and changing political and cultural contexts." For people of the African Diaspora, who have experienced "an attempted erasure or reordering of their identities in the slave trade," *stylin' out* has long carried the political possibility of "converting absence into presence through self-display."[3] According to Miller, when black people indulge in finery, they can engage with two possible histories. They might make homages to "not uncomplicated African traditions of displaying status," and/or can challenge, through signifying, those who hold the same status in America.[4] Today, social aid and pleasure clubs transform the trappings of mainstream success, such as business suits, patent leather shoes, and fedoras, into something signified by using eye-catching color combinations, piles of bows, and silky plumes. Seen through the lens of signifying, social aid and pleasure clubs' sartorial performances are more than a show of frivolity, but part of a long history of black challenges to dominant aesthetics.

Beyond the political dimensions of dress, there are spiritual dimensions too. Second lines occur every week on Sunday, and many New Orleanians attribute this tradition to the fact that, during slavery, free(d) and enslaved people of color were permitted to gather at Congo Square to drum, dance, and sell goods. While many parts of the rural, mostly Protestant United States remained quiet on Sundays, the mostly French-speaking, mostly Catholic, black majority port city of New Orleans was rocking.[5] Sunday gatherings at Congo Square provided an occasion for black New Orleanians, enslaved and free alike, to don their best attire. Stylin' out on Sundays was not unique to antebellum New Orleans, but common throughout the African Diaspora. Miller concludes, "The spiritual has always had a sartorial dimension for black people in America."[6] Sunday is still the day that African Americans in New Orleans "rock the city" and style out, at church in the morning, at second lines in the afternoon, and, during Carnival season, at Mardi Gras Indian practices in the evening.[7]

---

[3] Monica L. Miller, *Slaves to Fashion: Black Dandyism and the Styling of Black Diasporic Identity* (Durham, NC: Duke University Press, 2009), 1, 10.

[4] Miller, 16, 90.

[5] Ned Sublette, *The World That Made New Orleans: From Spanish Silver to Congo Square* (Chicago, IL: Lawrence Hill Books, 2008), 3.

[6] Miller, 3, 91.

[7] Sublette, 3.

Figure 3.20. *Ed Buckner of the Original Big 7 Social Aid and Pleasure Club.*
Photograph by Judy Cooper, April 21, 2014.

Making Something Out of Nothing: The Original Big 7 and the Ole N Nu Style Fellas

These days, it is customary for social aid and pleasure clubs to outsource the construction of their streamers or yokes, hand-held fans, umbrellas, canes and buckets. Several artisans in New Orleans, and some far away, specialize in crafting these custom items. However, at least two clubs still handcraft every item that they carry into the street: the Original Big 7 Social Aid and Pleasure Club, based in the Seventh Ward, and the Ole N Nu Style Fellas Social Aid and Pleasure Club, from Tremé.

The Original Big 7 was founded in 1995 in the St. Bernard Housing Project and held their first second line parade in 1996. Club memberships are always fluctuating, however, in 2013-2014, the Big 7 boasted a healthy roster of 16 members, including four children. Edward Buckner has been the club's president since around the year 2000, but even before that, he was designing the club's outfits and decorations each year. As part of the Big 7's charitable work, Buckner also directs the Red Flame Hunters Youth Mardi Gras Indian Tribe, a group of boys and girls ages four to sixteen who sew suits to wear on Mardi Gras day.

Sue Louis Press founded the Ole N Nu Style Fellas in 1997, and the club's members have always been recruited from her family. Sue is the only female member of this club, but she is the figurative glue that holds it together. Her son, Tyrone Miller, oversees the literal glue, meticulously designing, constructing, and decorating every fan and cane. As Ms. Press's other son, Askia, describes it, Tyrone starts "from scratch, from blueprint. [...] From our yokes that go around our neck to the shoes, is done by his hands. [...] Other clubs, they may get other people, they may pay people to do their decorations, but with us, it's all done by him and members of the club. We all do it."[8] Buckner, his family, and his fellow Big 7 members do the same.

During the summer of 2013, I conducted separate interviews with Buckner and Press. I have organized the transcripts of our conversations around several overlapping themes that thread

---

[8] Askia Bennett, audio interview with DJ "Action" Jackson, WWOZ New Orleans 90.7 FM, April 6, 2014, http://www.wwoz.org/events/230549, accessed April 14, 2014.

the interviews together: details of the creation process, the inter-generational aspects of the work, and the importance of making something out of nothing.

Why Make Your Own Decorations?

SUE LOUIS PRESS: [The first year we paraded,] the guy made the fans that fell all apart with the plumes when we walked out the door. We had five plumes and then when we got to the corner we had three plumes on it. That was horrible, and the next time it was even worse. So it was like, no no no no no. We got it, we been beating and hammering and hot gluing and stitching and sewing ever since. […] Sewing is a beautiful thing. Art is beautiful. It's creative and that's what I think my whole love is, creativity and making decorations. Most clubs don't do it, and I don't know too many clubs that actually do their own decorations.

Figure 3.21. *Original Big 7, posing before beginning.*
Photograph by Judy Cooper, May 10, 2015.

...

EDWARD BUCKNER: The reason why I learned to do the work with the Original Big 7 is, you know, it's 2013 right now. In 2013, we're still paying three hundred dollars for a streamer. You're paying another fifty dollars for a fan. So you look at that coming out of your pocket as a club expense. If I can build it for you, that three hundred and fifty dollars turns to a hundred and fifty, so you save money, and all you got to do is spend your time helping me construct it all.

RC: When do you start designing? When does the process of envisioning start?

EB: Oh, immediately after the parade is over. Actually, during the parade. Before I was president, the old president of the club used to have to always tell me halfway through the parade, "Ed, stop thinking about what you're going to be doing next year. Enjoy the rest of the parade!" And he was always telling everybody, "This guy is going to be the next president. I can tell you, Ed is going to run this thing." You know because at the midway part of the parade, I'm trying to get on the float to see the crowds front and back, I'm trying to get to areas where I can see how it's moving, how it's looking so next year I can try to create in another way maybe to take in whatever I didn't see look right, I can fix it.

...

SLP: With us, it's up to the five minutes till we parade. When it comes to us, it's five minutes.

RC: You were telling me a story, before we turned the recorder on, there was a reporter in with you one year, and what was he saying?

SLP: He said, "It's 12:53 and they're putting the last bow on!" And we parade for 1:00. [...]

And you know, everybody have to work, we don't sleep. My son and I, his fiancé, and my brother, it's mainly four of us, that every day leading up to the parade, at least four weeks, we'll be up till two, three o'clock in the morning and still go to work, and come back that night leading up until that day. That weekend, that Thursday, that Friday, that Saturday—you do not sleep. You may get an hour, or whatever, but Saturday before the parade, I don't care who in here,

76

we have almost a whole family, because we teach them how to bust bows. [...] But you know, you got to get it done, you know, that's it. You know, you got to get it done. "Why y'all wait?"—my family, my mom—"Why y'all always wait till the last minute?" It doesn't be that. Because my son don't want nothing to get mashed up, you know, he wants it to be right, you know, he wants, it's got to be *right*.

...

EB: Culturally, when you're doing a second line or something, Mardi Gras Indians or stuff like that, it's about the creation of the art and the artists. The artists are having a vision that will end up on paper, that will transform from paper to wood and materials and fans and plumes and quail feathers and then that work itself becomes the beauty piece, but from that vision. It all starts on just that little piece of paper though.

Making Yokes and Fans

SLP: The yoke is cut out of a piece of backing material, on that part, you put a whole other piece of material on it, to give it a smoothness. Then you're going to put strips of material on top of that, and strips of trim. Sometimes you may have stones [large plastic jewels] and then sometimes you may not, because the time run out on us. Each one of them, they going to have a stone. Each one of these things have stones all around it, that you got to place it, you cannot have the glue or whatever you're working with, the hot glue showing or dripping or anything. [...] It's tedious so you have to take your time and do each one with a little dab. A little impression and [make] sure it doesn't fall off. This particular club, you don't see bows in the street, you're not going to see plumes dropped in the street. Nothing leaves out of here unless it's inspected.
RC: And how would you describe what a yoke is?
SLP: A yoke is ... it's a piece of material, it's your first decoration that lays upon your clothes, it's like a streamer. Most people call them streamers, we call them yokes because we don't have it laid across our shoulder, we have on each, pinned up on each shoulder. It doesn't go across our body, so it's like a yoke of a suit or something,

Figure 3.22. *Sue Press parades with Ole & Nu Style Fellas.*
Photograph by Judy Cooper, April 24, 2015.

it's the yoke part of it, and that's why we call it a yoke. On that, you also have to put your birds on it.[9] [...] Your leaves, your little flowers, your corsage—your carnations. You hook all that onto your bird. Then you take it, twist it up and sit it on your buckle on your felt. Then you put your bows around it. The bows are made actually with a bow machine. You actually bow them with a bow machine and we actually bust them ourselves, bring them out to a beautiful bow.

Everybody says I have, like, beehives, I go so high. I was taught you put four on, but I use maybe like eight to ten on each side, for each shoulder that go underneath each bird. We also have the little tassels that come down from the yoke. On the tassels I usually do three wide strips of a ribbon, and on each ribbon I put two ribbons on each side. So that gives you two, four, six ... that's approximately six of them hanging down off your shoulder.

RC: (*Pointing to a picture*) And this is the circle part that hangs at the waist?

SLP: At the waist part, it hangs at your waist. And you have to measure each man, because you don't want them hanging too far because some people show them, some don't. So everything is a different height, everything have to be measured. Because you have short guys, big guys. [...] Yeah, and that's basically the yoke.

...

RC: Ed, can you tell me about the fans?

EB: Well, the fans start out ... making the fans is ... well, you got to imagine Vegas showgirls if you want to come close to the imaginatory space of seeing a fan. You buy the plumes [ostrich feathers], you send off and you purchase plumes and you get the plumes dyed to whatever spec [specific color] that you want them. And then what you do [is] you draw your design on a piece of paper. Because everything, like I said, everything starts in your head and goes on a piece of paper. Once you draw your design on a paper, then you have to transfer the design that you drew on paper to a thin plyboard. Then once you draw the design on a plyboard, then you have to get your jigsaw and cut that out off the plyboard. So, like, with my club,

---

[9] Customarily, artificial doves are affixed to one or both shoulders of the suits. Many believe that this references the custom of releasing doves at funerals.

I may be cutting out twenty pieces off the plyboard to create the fans. So once you cut the pieces out, then you take a material, you glue the board, and you do a material over-layer to cover the wood. Then you create whatever writings you going to do and whatever other design that you may have had. You take your gimp and you wrap the ends because when you cut the material and you glue the material down, there's still ends that's raggely around the sides of the wood. So you take your gimp and you cover that end—

RC: What is a gimp?

EB: Gimp is another type of material, a ribbon that they sell at the cloth store, at the fabric store.

RC: Okay.

EB: But you buy the gimp and once you add gimp to it, it cleans up all the raggely edges you have, then you go back to the bows. We spoke about earlier the bows. The bows play an important part, help build the piece to this big nice fluffy beautiful design of a piece. And once you've have all your printing and your work done on the wood, then you go back with your gimp and your bows and you put your bows there. But before you put your bows on there, you need to staple down the ostrich plumes that you get. They're so pretty and fluffy. Once you staple all of them down, and what I do, I do a process to make sure that none of that stuff comes apart. I do a glue edge to make sure that everything that's tacked down with thread and still has that little bead of glue around the edges to make sure that it continues to be tacked down. Basically you have some beautiful fans that you just created with nothing but some print work, some wood and a very great idea you might have had of cutting your wood design.

Messes, Accidents, and Injuries

EB: The process is not hard to do, it's just a tedious process because if you don't have a big enough house, a big enough work space, you're basically working on top of yourself. Like myself, I have enough room to work with, so what I do, I have a work space out in front of my house which used to be my son's bedroom before he went to college. So I'm in his old room and also I have a studio apartment in the back of my house I also use as a workspace. So I have those two spaces to really create and lay stuff out, because you know you can lay the work out and easily assemble that to be able to cut the work and everything. The only thing that my wife hates so much about all of my creating and sewing and beading and everything is the mess that I make in our house from feathers and stuff like that. There's just too much feathers running around, and you don't never get rid of the stuff, believe me. You can go in a corner and find some feather somewhere from three years ago and we can vacuum every day over and over with the shop-vac and they're still here! You know they're here, either in your truck, your glove compartment. You know, somewhere you'll find [something from] two years ago. It's everywhere! And beads, every crack of your house. You can go back with that vac over and over all year and all year long you going to still be sucking up beads from somewhere.

...

RC: And this is your workshop right here, huh?
SLP: In my house.
RC: Right where we're sitting.
SLP: Yeah, right, we have to move this here, put cardboard on the floors, move all that—
RC: It just transforms.
SLP: Oh my god, it's like, it's like—it be so much! Everywhere! Just like, tables all over. Ribbon, everything. And it takes me about six months to actually make it look decent. I'm still not finished. It takes that long to actually make it.

...

EB: Early on I ruined a lot of pieces.
RC: Did you cover it up with a bow or did you start over?
EB: Well, I learned too early on if I ruined the damned thing, just take it and put it in a washing machine and wash the material and all the stuff is going to come back out. But early on, I thought I had to throw everything away. So one evening, it was a green and blue Mardi Gras Indian suit, and we had everything going and I had this one piece of material left because the Indian wanted a fan like the social aid and pleasure clubs, but he wanted it to come on the end of a stalk he was going to have as a staff. And so I had put the material on there too early, and that was the last piece of the green,

so that's when I learned that: put it in the washing machine, wash it, dry it, get it out, after the drying, and you can put it right back on there. Oh, I saved myself that time, I really did. […] So it teaches you, you learn, and that's the process, that's the whole thing. The beauty of the art that you think of and create. The beauty of the art is that sometimes you ruin a piece.

…

SLP: You will get burnt up. One time I stuck that [*makes a gesture like a glue gun*] right on my finger! I stuck my finger in my mouth, had a big old blister on it, skin off my leg! One guy [was] putting on the yokes, and did something, went to flip it over and his whole hand burnt up, blistered up the day before the parade—okay? Blistered hand! So you have to be careful, you know, you'll get burnt up. So that's why you have to just take your time, you know, do it right.

Needles, Thread, and Hot Glue Guns

RC: So most of the decorations are made, you said, with glue, with the bow machine. Does any of it happen with needle and thread sewing?

SLP: Yes, some of it have to be sewed with a needle and thread. Some things that you do, it all depends on what fabric you using, what type of trimming you're going to use, to make sure that it's laying and it won't buckle loose or anything like that. You may stitch up the edges of, you know, or you may take the yoke, take the back of the yoke use some heavy material with your first material you put on it, just to give you a little weight, because you don't want nothing flying, or anything like that. So they'll stitch up the edges of your yoke with the material backing, and everything else is most likely glued on. We glue everything. Some people take a needle and thread to make they ruffle, and take needle and thread and put a piece of thread through a piece of material and just make a ruffle with it like that. I mean we have done that in the past also.

RC: And you were telling me earlier, too, that your sister sews and sews your tops for each parade, right?

SLP: Yes. I'm the only lady, and you can say this about everyone come out there wants to see the top that I'm going to have on this year. Every year, it's a big—I don't know how it get like that—but it's this big, amazing thing about the tops that I wear. And my sister actually sits and hand sews the tops that she makes. Most of them are like corsets, and she decorates the whole thing like that. Takes the pads, you know, bra pads and decorate on top of that, whatever design. I don't really give her designs, I just give her colors, maybe pick out and say "I want feathers this year, I want...." (*rustling*) Here we go, one minute, this is this year. (*Pulls out a photograph.*)

RC: Oh yeah, I came to your parade this year and I remember seeing this, mm-hmm. Oh yeah, that is beautiful. So this is kind of like a bustier top—

SLP: Yeah, most of them are.

RC: —with purple and green, umm, what kind of feathers are those?

SLP: Peacocks.

RC: Peacock feathers. Mm, so, and your yoke comes around your waist.

SLP: My yoke always around my waist....

RC: Well, and you wouldn't want to cover up that pretty top.

SLP: That's right, so my son come up with that, and then had a club, last year, year before that, ask him, can they do that. A lady club came, would it be all right if they would put, you know, make their things around their waist. And my son, he's humble, it didn't bother him.

RC: Not many people do that. That's kind of like a signature style.

SLP: Mm-hmm. And she actually makes that with her hands. Sew the feathers on, sew the birds on and everything she have to do, she sews it on.

Older Generations

EB: I've been sewing ... the past ten years I've been sewing. This is something that just was handed down to me from another Indian that needed help on his suit and I was helping on her, well it was her suit. And I helped her, Miss Jones, on her suit because she was a queen, a Mardi Gras Indian queen. And I used to help her sewing, take a ride with her, go collect beads and pearls and stuff like that here.

RC: Mm-hmm. So you got started sewing within the Mardi Gras Indian tradition?

EB: Yeah.

RC: And have you ever masked as Indian yourself?

EB: No, I've never masked as an Indian, it's too much to put on. For me. It's too hot. But I love, I love making the Indian suits, I'll be honest with you. It's almost something that I look forward to every year, see what my mind can recreate. […] Second line, I've been second lining since before I knew it. My daddy was bringing me to parades, hanging out at the second lines, so all of the stuff that came to me just so easy from family members and stuff. Being involved in it, hopefully I can nurture them through some of this, and hopefully they can understand the great quality some of the very unique culture that only happens here in New Orleans.

...

RC: And you were telling me earlier too that your mother did a lot of sewing, right?

SLP: Ooh, my mom sewed for years, um, clubs like the Jolly Bunch, the Lady Jolly Bunch, she sewed for them. She sewed for a lot of clubs, um, the Baby Dolls.[10] The original Baby Dolls when they first came out, with the fishnet stockings and the little fake money in they stockings and the little bustiers on and the little bloomers on, the little pants. My mom sewed for a lot of clubs. […] She made my crown when I was the queen. And she actually beaded it with her hands, with the beads and the diamonds on it. When I was the queen, that was years ago, but I was a queen for the Money Wasters Club, and she actually made the gown, she made the maids, I had like eight maids, she made all the gowns and everything like that.[11]

RC: Wow. And what year was that?

SLP: Oh my god, that was in …'95? Something like that? It's been a minute ago.

RC: And what years was, about what years was your mom doing

---

[10] The Jolly Bunch was a second line group that paraded in the Tremé from 1941 until the early 2000s. The Baby Dolls are a female masking tradition in New Orleans that dates back to the early nineteenth century. For more on the Baby Dolls, see Kim Marie Vaz, The "Baby Dolls": Breaking the Race and Gender Barriers of the New Orleans Mardi Gras Tradition (Baton Rouge: Louisiana State University Press, 2013).

[11] Social aid and pleasure clubs often honor their chief supporters and other significant people by bestowing on them the title of King or Queen, or making them a member of the royal court during their second line parades. The court usually rides on truck-pulled floats in front of the marching members, sporting elaborate gowns, suits, and headdresses that tower several feet above their heads.

most of her sewing, like for the Jolly Bunch and the Baby Dolls, when would that have been?

SLP: That had to be up in, it had to be in, um, in the sixties and the seventies. She did a lot of sewing in the sixties and the seventies.

RC: And was she a member of those clubs or did they hire her to sew their stuff?

SLP: I don't even know if my mom got paid, she probably did get paid a little something. Most of them was friends. She paraded with the Jolly Bunch, the Lady Jolly Bunch, she paraded with that club. And um, she would do a lot of sewing and she would do a lot for Mardi Gras. She did a lot for, like, guys that was homosexual, you know how they come out on Mardi Gras with their beautiful outfits? She do a lot for Sugar Doozie, everybody know Sugar Doozie from the neighborhood, she sew for Sugar Doozie, she sewed for Precious. These was gay guys that she would [sew for], they were wearing gowns and all that stuff. But if somebody was going to the Zulu ball, she would do their gowns. She did a lot of sewing. She's still got the sewing machine.

RC: And worked with newspaper patterns, you said?

SLP: Oh yes indeed. We couldn't afford, she didn't have patterns. Newspaper. She'd measure, "Come here girl." She'd put that little piece of paper, cut that drawing and that was your outfit. When I had my prom, she made my gown and there was no pattern.

Younger Generations

SLP: I love what I do so much because I love the children, I love to sit down and talk to them, I love to listen to them, you know, and they be going on, and they have a little conflict between themselves and how easy it is to resolve, you know? "Come on, we all, you know, we all the same, we all, we here to work together, we supposed to be uniting with each other, we not supposed to try to out-dance each other. We not supposed to say who going to get more approval, it's not about that." [...] And what I like so much is like, the children listen, they actually listen. They look out for the younger ones, they get together. You know, the older ones take and get the younger ones before the parade, give them something to do, get them chicken. The older ones showing the younger ones what moves to make and all like that. When you get ten children together and you see them getting along like that, it fills your heart, it just be like, "We got that." A lot of people say, Nu Style Fellas ... that's what I thought about, it's like, you get the older guys intertwined with the younger guys and make a difference. You know, show them that things can be different, you can do this and enjoy yourself, you can learn about this. And have it be fun for them. "Oh, children don't listen, he can't mess with...." It's not true, I did it. I've been doing it—I been doing it before that, but I been doing it for fifteen years. If you see them little young boys come here, so enthused about wanting to help out, so enthused about their day, so elated, like, wow, you know, and you can do it. They just want to be around something that's positive. But if you sit around with this and that and all that, you going to lose them, you going to get negativity from them, you know. [...] Seeing that they love to be around me and they want to be a part of it, even if they're just handing you something, you know, putting the glue stick, when the glue stick running low in the gun, they pushing it in, they just amazed to be around it to do something, you know, "Cut this, cut the cardboard here," just, they want to be a part of it.

...

EB: I've learned to do a little bit of the work at a time and call my great daughter Samantha. Oh she's fantastic and much faster than her daddy, and she's learning, you know. She comes in and does all the bow stuff and makes the beautiful stuff that happens that frames all of the work. Samantha will come in and put in all the sequins on the string or she either do the gimp. She has the hang, and she'll be like, "Daddy, I got it, I got it for you." And I'm so happy though because she picked up a traditional art that not a whole bunch of young people know how to do, first off, but then not a whole bunch of people who's involved in the culture. You look at a hundred percent of the people in the culture, you may have twenty-five percent that actually know how to create. The rest of the people are just basically there trying to pay their money to parade but don't have anything to do with the building and construction side of making all the things.
RC: I wanted to hear more about the Red Flame Hunters and the

Figure 3.23. *Tyrone Miller of Ole & Nu Style Fellas.*
Photograph by Judy Cooper, April 24, 2015.

beading work you do with the youth here, because that's a whole other aspect of sewing you do around the year.

EB: Well. I kept trying to search for ways. I had young guys. I was working with another organization that did cultural work in New Orleans, but they work with children. We had a group of boys, maybe about six or seven boys, that just was running in people's back yards, causing havoc in the neighborhood, and I got to know the boys, got to know them real good, and I kept trying to work with them, and trying to figure out what could I do to help…. The minute I said, "I'm going to try the Mardi Gras Indian thing," it hit me that I might have finally fell upon the right thing, because I know the concentration it takes to bead and sequins and sew a piece and pearl it and all the other stuff. And it takes a little concentration, because now you're trying to sew on top of something that's been drawn for you, so you're trying to sew on each line. So to try to keep the lines and the curves and all of the stuff that happens with the drawing correct, it takes a little more concentration because it means you're going to be needling into the canvas or upholstery board or whatever you're using to sew on.

So when I found that, I got the guys and they all joined the Indians, and everybody sewed. But all of a sudden, I started getting a response from the neighbors . . . saying, "I don't know what you did Mr. Ed, but those boys ain't been through my yard, ain't been messing with this here and that there, I ain't seen the boys running and trying to catch chickens or all of this stuff here." So I realized, "Yeah, they are always with me, and they're sewing." […] My thing is, with so much killing that's going on in the streets of New Orleans, that we're one of the highest murder rates in the country, with so much killing, I can't turn not one child away. So I will have to figure out more creative ways of getting funding to help me with those suits. But I'm not going to turn them away, I'm going to keep them here with me till we're all eating dinner, or we're all playing drums together or something. But I won't lose them to the street, won't lose them back to the streets. […] I'm always hoping more clubs have more children in on the building and designing on what happens for that one day every year. Because, if we don't get a lot of these children knowing how to build and construct this stuff, we can have clubs forever, but then we'll be outsourcing to manufacturers maybe by that time. I found a company in New York, that everything we do by hand, they do by a computer and a machine. So they can create the piece even better and quicker. My thing is, since it's been a handcraft and how you do this art and the artistic technique of beading by hand, I don't think I ever want to see it get to the point where we're actually outsourcing the contractor work through a company that would machine build the work.

RC: Does that company do the beading work with the Indian suits?

EB: They do the beading work with the Indian suits and also make the streamers and everything. They do a lot of the New Orleans work right there in they shop there. And the guy told me when I met him, he said, "Ed you should send me a picture, I can create anything." And I sent him a picture one time because I really wanted to see. And he created a piece better than I could sew it. But the difference was that he didn't labor with the time and love that I put into it. You know it was strictly business for him. It was a labor of love for me to be ready for this certain time, so I can greet and meet with all the social aid and pleasure clubs, all of the Mardi Gras Indians who greet and meet with my children. It just was a labor of love. I don't think I'd ever be happy, it would just mean I'd be bored to death in my house, I'd have nothing to do for a bunch of months out of the year.

RC: It sounds like you're saying there'd be a lot that would be lost if the focus was strictly on—I mean it's important how people look when they come out the door, but it's how you get there that's important.

EB: It's very important how you get there, how you create it. And I'll say this: people ask the question, "Who was the designer? Who was the creator? Who was the person in charge of wardrobe?" And stuff like that there. People ask those question. And I like to say, "It was Mary over here. Or George over there. Or Sam over here." To be able to point out the people that actually did the hand work. Because you think about it, once things start being factory built, the piece loses its value, everything loses its value at that point. You would have to then actually unroll the Indian to go under everything and start pulling material and everything to find out if it was hand-stitched. You would have to unroll the guy at that point. Hopefully we never get to that point. I think more Indians might have met the guy in

New York and I think more Indians took the avenue, whereas I took that we better just keep on sewing. [...] I don't think the people of the culture will smile upon us at that point. They'll be very upset that like, "You've got the nerve to wear that on the street here in New Orleans? Somebody else made it? You didn't sew none of it?" Because the thing is if it's the Mardi Gras Indians, if you don't sew it, you shouldn't wear it. You shouldn't wear it. And I'm sticking closely to tradition. My Indians will sew all the time. All the time.

Making Something Out of Nothing

SLP: It was amazing to me when I was coming up, to take a hanger, a raw hanger, an iron hanger, and open it up, and make a shape, you know, shape that hanger, and stick these bows so you didn't see no hanger, you didn't see the iron, and stick the bows all around and you'd be like, ah, you know, this is newspaper, hangers. That's why I think I love what we do, it's so much about our culture.

...

EB: I did a bucket. Took an actual bucket, and did a Mardi Gras bucket, second line bucket, and that was material and overlay again and stuff like that. That was more cutting out material, covering the whole thing and then coming back with another type of material [you] might have, cutting the holes and circles and overlay with it and then I might take another piece of material, cut some more circles to add to those circles. [...] When you put it all together with some bows again, and everything, and once you put it all together you got a hell of a piece sometimes.

RC: And what is a bucket?

EB: A bucket is actually like a regular house mopping bucket, a big five-gallon paint bucket, just those type of buckets. And they used to call them baskets and stuff like that there. Like, they had the Bucket Men Social Aid and Pleasure Club who really had buckets every year. It's actually a bucket that's been decorated. New Orleans has this special piece of culture that you can take most anything and bring it out.

...

SLP: I love the order of it all, that you can take, it's so amazing that you can take a piece of cardboard, flat cardboard and come up with a whole cane, you know all these shapes, it's just amazing to me […] You know, given that dimension, that 3D look you know, that come out. It's amazing to me that I sit there and, you know, you're like, "Wow, this is something, that it's just amazing to me." I be so amazed at my work. You know you look back at all that work, all that ripping and running and you're worn out tired and you sit back, look at it and you're like, I did that. You know. You don't get no credit, but it just makes you feel good, the children feel good, you know, the children, I know they just, "Thank you, Miss Sue, thank you Miss Sue."

Coming Out the Door

SLP: What makes a club feel good? When you walk out that door and you see the people that come to see what y'all going to do this year and that's magic. Most of the time we get a nice crowd, a real good crowd, in the beginning, and we talk about, when we come out that door once we change, they be like (*whispers*), "Wow, where these people come from?" They be like amazed like, "Oh my god. Where do they come from?"

…

EB: When you come out that door if they're chattering and hollering and people loud saying, "Oh them boys is beautiful!" And the word is, "They're so pretty on Sunday." You know. And "Them boys are so beautiful, when you see them they're pretty this Sunday." "Oh lord, they're pretty like Sunday."

IV. Inscribing Sewing through Poems

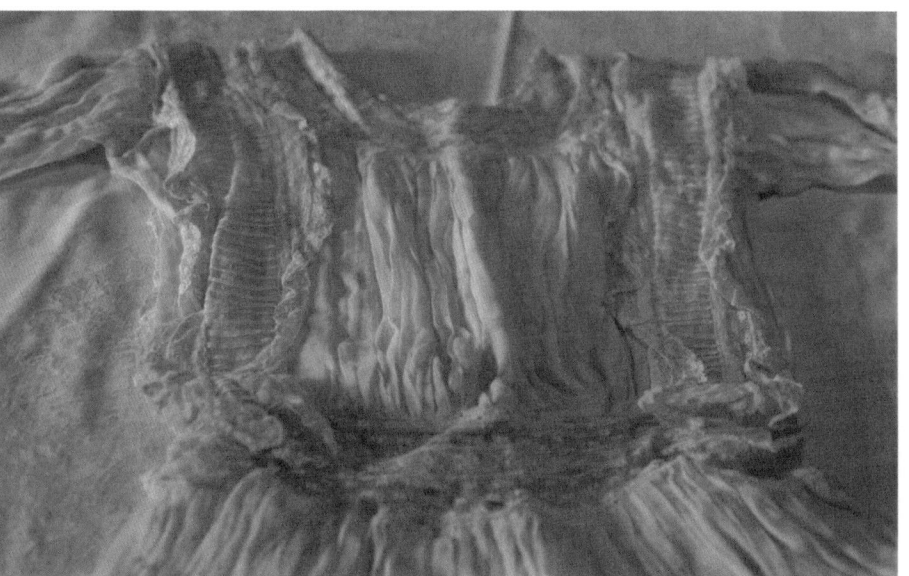

Figure 4.1. Detail of dress for crowning ceremony, to be worn by Agnes Mary Bethancourt in 1913. From the collection of Augusta Elmwood. Photograph by Yuka Petz.

THE SEWING ROOM

Malaika Favorite

A spider is a master weaver
    weaving window curtains to hang
        between trees. Pearly lace tatting
            that reflect gems of dew,

            glowing prisms of pure light.
        She crochets round doilies
    On top floral arrangements
in her living room

there to ensnare crumbs
    that fly by and get entangled
        in her tapestry laid out
            on her children's table.

        Her mantle is covered in
      Alençon lace with a delicate
    mesh background. She dazzles
butterflies with her curved lines

and drawn work; uses their wings
    as punch-work designs
        for her pillow shams.
           Leaves dangle on the fringes

            of her bobbin-lace curtains
      that dance in wind,
    revealing paintings on view
in her open window.

THE BOBBIN REELS

Lee Meitzen Grue

my head given over to thread
whirling
      off a spool

skin tight
strung out gut thin
trying to sew up
holes

sound as a roach

eating
glue off books
in a house
full of glass monkeys

not able to mend anything.

NEEDLEPOINT

Wendy Klein

She's watching the new Sunday series.
She doesn't know what it's called,
and she'll probably forget to watch it next week,
unless I remind her—if I'm here to remind her,

if I can bear to be here to remind her. Anyway,
she's not really watching it properly; she's doing
her needlepoint—not like those printed pictures,
the ones that tell you every colour to use.

She just keeps a roll of canvas behind the sofa
along with a patchwork bag of yarn;
cuts off a length, grabs a handful of colours,
frowns them into submission, starts.

In the cathode flicker of the screen, tapestries
emerge of owls and flowers, land and
seascapes; she hands me a piece
of her canvas, watches as I smooth

its roughness, inhale its new-cloth smell, smiles
encouragement, offers me wool, balls
of all sizes, neatly wound, night
after night in front of her TV.

I take some black yarn, moisten it with my tongue,
jam it into the thick tapestry needle,
while on the screen, Fred Astaire
begins to dance on the ceiling.

Seamstress

Lenny Emmanuel

Her hands were extraordinary—neat, clean,
very precise with every stitch, not in the least
was she concerned about the world, so keen

and yet without a sense of the mythic beast,
of rivaling God's creations, nothing like that,
as some believe we shame His masterpiece.

Simply kind, bringing me near where she sat,
she turned scraps of cloth to mythical designs,
my mother, my mentor, and I a spoiled brat.

But somehow the magic patterns of her mind
became the notes and measures of my riff,
savoring the bitter lemons and viscid rinds.

The threads and needles of her joyous strife
are the magic in the ragged scraps of my life.

GRANDMOTHER

Jessica Mitchell

You're gone now.

You've left your crocheted afghans,
the flowers you grew from yarn
and strung together for me.

Your showy blossoms mock me now,
shamelessly red when they ought to be black.
Unfathomable, the survival of these bright
blooms in the absence of their creator.

I wrap myself in the rough yarn,
this polyblend garden of yours.

I wrap myself in you.

I try to hook your essence
and pull you into me.

PERSISTENCE

Malcolm Willison

Her thimble

    still neatly burnished

waits in lamplight

    ready for its smooth fit

to crooked finger tips,

    start of needle rocking

    down one more grandchild's seam.

Figure 4.2. WPA Sewing Room, Faubourg Marigny, New Orleans, 1939.
Number 69-NS-22M-01, National Archives at College Park, College Park, MD.

During the Depression, unemployed women could come to one of some four
hundred sewing rooms around the country. There they could use sewing
machines and be paid to make uniforms, other clothing, and toys to be sold,
or make clothes for their families. Marie Odelle Delavigne, one of the Newcomb
embroiders whose work is explored in Section III's essay by Sally Main, found
work as a supervisor of such a room. Extant photos of the WPA Sewing Rooms,
such as this one, indicate that there was some segregation, though also some
integration, by race in the rooms.

The Dressmakers

mary mac jones

sunday was our day of WarpShit.
they sewed me in smocked dresses.

ribboned and bowed my head before Him.
all week long i sat still amidst patterns.

listened to a Sunbeam metronome.
shining tooth biting the thread with a hunger.

silver foot lining smiles in elephant faces,
seeds in watermelon real godlike.

depressed because i knew my chicken
rebekah was doomed to hell.

i could not, for the life of me
or a juicy nightcrawler,

get her to ask jesus into her heart.
He died for our sins.

peck and shudder.

I Hate to Iron & I Hate to Sew

Roselyn Lionhart

I HATE TO IRON, I HATE TO SEW. IT'S ALL MISS MILLER'S FAULT!
    FOR SHE WAS OUR OLD HOME EC TEACHER, LORD HELP THOSE
        SHE TAUGHT!
SHE MADE OUR HIGH SCHOOL LUNCHEON AND NOBODY CARED TO EAT,
    WE'D SLIP OUTSIDE AT LUNCH TIME AND EAT JUNK FOOD DOWN
        THE STREET!
MY MOTHER TAUGHT ME HOW TO SEW, GRANDMOTHER HOW TO BAKE.
    I DID NOT WANT TO TAKE HOME EC. THAT WAS MY
        FIRST MISTAKE!
I SAID I WANTED SHOP CLASS, ALL THE GIRLS SEEMED TO AGREE!
    A BIRDIE TOLD MISS MILLER AND OF COURSE SHE HATED ME!
I WATCHED THE BOYS GO OUT THE DOOR, ALL MARCHING ROW ON ROW,
    & THEN I DRAGGED MYSELF UP STAIRS, SO SAD I HAD TO GO!

MISS MILLER TOLD US SEVERAL TIMES, WE HAD TO SHRINK OUR CLOTH,
    & SO I TOOK THE STUFF I BOUGHT & PUT IT IN SUD'S FROTH.
MY MOTHER POINTED OUT THE FACT THE CLOTH WAS ALL PRESHRUNK!
    SO I EXPLAINED MISS MILLER 'SAID!' ALTHOUGH I THOUGHT
        IT STUNK!
THE WASHER FINISHED SPINNING, IT WAS VERY CLOSE TO TEN,
    BUT I STILL HAD TO IRON IT DRY & THEN MY TRIAL BEGAN!
I TOOK IT QUICKLY OUT THE WASH, I FOLDED IT SO NEAT,
    I PLACED IT GENTLY ON THE FLOOR, UPON A NICE CLEAN SHEET.
MY MOTHER TAUGHT ME HOW TO IRON I IRONED MY DAD'S WORK
        CLOTHES.
THIS FLAT CLOTH WAS MUCH EASIER, NO SLEEVES, NO COLLAR
        WOES.
BUT THEN I MADE MY NEXT MISTAKE, I LAID MY CLOTH OUT FLAT!
    I PUT IT NEATLY IN ITS BAG & SMILED & SAID THAT'S THAT!
I HEARD THE BIG CLOCK SOUNDING AS I WENT UPSTAIRS TO BED.
    I COUNTED UP TO NUMBER THREE AS I LAY DOWN MY HEAD.

NEXT MORNING AS I ENTERED CLASS MISS MILLER GRABBED MY BAG!
    SHE PULLED MY CLOTH & SHOOK IT OUT & SHE BEGAN TO NAG
I TOLD YOU ONCE I TOLD YOU TWICE, YOUR DENIM YOU MUST SHRINK
    & THEN SHE BALLED MY DENIM UP & THREW IT IN THE SINK!

I DID NOT STAY TO HEAR HER YELL, I COULD NOT STAND TO LISTEN
I RAN OUTSIDE & DOWN THE STAIRS AS TEARS BEGAN TO GLISTEN
I RAN TO GET MY MOTHER I RAN FIVE BLOCKS OR MORE!
I RAN TO WHERE MY MOTHER WORKED AT THE THREE SISTER'S
STORE!
I RAN INTO MY MOTHER'S ARMS, I SOBBED MY TALE OF WOE!
SHE TOOK ME TO HER WORK ROOM, TOLD HER BOSS SHE HAD TO GO
WE MARCHED BACK TO THE SCHOOL & TO THE PRINCIPAL WE WENT
MY MOTHER WAS SO ANGRY SHE COULD COW THE PRESIDENT
SO UP THE STAIRS MY MOTHER MARCHED, THE PRINCIPAL IN TOW
THEN MOTHER QUITE POLITELY IN A VOICE THAT WAS NOT LOW
INFORMED MISS MILLER SHE HAD ERRED, "APOLOGISE!" SHE SAID.
MISS MILLER LOOKED LIKE SHE WAS SICK, SHE STOOD THERE
TURNING RED
& THEN SHE SAID "I'M OH SO SAD, I DID NOT KNOW!" SHE PLED.
I KNEW THAT SHE WAS MAD! IF LOOKS COULD KILL THEN I'D BE
DEAD,
SHE MADE A NICE APOLOGY, & MOTHER LEFT THE ROOM.
MISS MILLER WAS SO MAD SHE SHOOK, SHE LOOKED AS THOUGH
SHE'D SWOON
SHE TOLD ME NOT ANOTHER THING, I GAVE A QUIET SIGH,
I STILL MUST TAKE MATERIAL & IRON 'TIL IT WAS DRY

I THINK APOLOGIES ARE NICE, I'M GLAD SHE HAD TO SAY,
"I'M VERY SORRY ROSELYN." ALMOST MADE MY DAY,
BUT I WOULD BE MUCH HAPPIER IF SHE HAD HAD TO IRON
THREE YARDS OF WRINKLED DENIM, THEN, I'D FEEL THAT I HAD
WON!
I HAD TO MAKE THAT STUPID SKIRT. NOW DO YOU UNDERSTAND?
SHE TOOK A TASK I'D LOVED TO DO & CHANGED IT OUT OF HAND!
I'VE HEARD IT SAID BY TEACHING FRIENDS "BY STUDENTS WE'VE
BEEN TAUGHT!"
BUT I HATE TO IRON AND I HATE TO SEW & IT'S ALL MISS MILLERS
FAULT!

QUILT REPAIR
Melody Davis

I sew over the seams
of my grandmother's quilt
restitching stitches years
have loosened.
So long it kept our marriage bed,
no wonder it's falling apart.
Was it passion or lack of care?
Now squares gape
like doorless houses, all the sides
need battening down,
the backing tattles like town gossips.
How long did I let this go?
Forever the single word QUILT
held its line on my To-Do list
that shrank and swelled, vertiginous
as love. Now, I'm crossing
items off, here complete,
there unnecessary.

On the machine I trace
my grandmother's lead, and a strange
peace comes to me, I who've always
declined to sew, abjuring the tedious,
the stitch by stitch, allowing shirts to
dangle buttonless, holes to widen,
tears to mouth pink flesh.
I wore my *deshabille* like a career.
But my grandmother's hands, near the time
of my birth, placed red and green together
with no thought of Albers or Hoffman
and there they blinked, come on
now stop, like all those crossed
messages down the years.

Did I ever think of this as I smoothed
the quilt after you left for work?

Sometimes no doesn't mean no,
you said, without apology.
I keep on tracing seams,
securing blocks, building towns
with my fingers, as boys built walls
no girl in class could touch. Does yes
also unravel to its opposite? Is no
a border for folding back? I place
and save, like children's play—
everything real is constructed,
joined by contradiction.
Only the corners are true.

All day long my grandmother's with me,
my stitches white on her white.
I try to trace them perfectly,
like bodies at noon, without
shadow, but I shift a little here
and there, so that the seams,
hers and mine, are sometimes in union,
sometimes side by side, like music,
that little drunk physics.

My son cries and I leave the machine,
between comfort, milk, and dinner I return,
then at night in the sweetness of his
breath descending on the house,
children tucked in their beds
like spools of thread, I return
to the single lamp, the centered eye,
the needle gunning fit, lines pulled

through stretched fingers for hours,
the darkness bunching about me.

It is our anniversary
and I've a mad idea to leave the threads
untrimmed, dangling loose like lines
from the mouths of fish that broke free,
ugly tattles. What a great statement
I think, the fray left showing, flagging
repair gone public, scars and squares
blown out to sky, loose ends in wild
babble about some sort of right...
but I am my grandmother's daughter,
and I know I will clip them,
tidy them up, finish the job,
cross it off the list.

Figure 4.3. *Sewing a quilt. Gees Bend, Alabama.* Photograph by Arthur
Rothstein for the U.S. Farm Security Administration. Courtesy of the
Library of Congress, American Memory.

PICTURE OF THREAD AND SUGAR CHILDREN

Megan Burns
after Vik Muniz photographs

the shuttle blinking open and close
on the loom, it is never going backward
laying hues and tints that cannot be undone

it's being carefully marked by a kiss
the wink of an eye from the future
a small step in landing upright

it's a sea holding up the island
while the city hooks and sways
dawn in January, forgotten and crisp

the pages as nimble and bare as a first
a history book before it's written
and then that like our own past

turns over, remembering to do this
back on the streetcar before the New Year
where the statues are half-moved

a narrow walk from Julia to Lee Circle
a picture of a picture of sugar and smiles
it's the threadwork holding together the castle

Figure 4.4. Crazy quilt made from men's silk and cotton ties, ca. 1880. Made from silk and cotton ties. Unknown creators, passed down in the family of Susie Owen Quigley (1862–1944). Photograph by Jane Tucker.

THE NECKTIE QUILT

Wendy Klein

After his death she set about thirty years of his neckties,
the gifts of grateful clients whose grubby affairs
he'd settled in and out of court, while she'd looked on,

applauding his victories, folding away ties. Now she selected
only the silk ones, unpicked them with meticulous care,
pressed them under a damp cloth until every crease

was smoothed, arranged them on the dining room table:
the bold paisleys, their backs curled against regimental stripes,
the gaudy florals that had made him smile, but were never worn,

cheeky polka dots, a couple of sombre knits she suspected
were synthetic. Day after day, the old Singer hummed
and whirred as she tacked the strips together,

and when the backing was attached, the borders feather-stitched
by hand, she found a place for every scrap left over: trim
for a dresser scarf, appliqué for scatter cushions,

a white curtain tied back with a sash of hand-painted peacocks,
an old dressing gown with a new belt, flaunting wild geometrics.
Swathes of unexpected colour cropped up in unexpected places,

the fallen-fruit silks of mulberry, gold and plum, a splash
of scarlet in an inner sleeve, reminding her of the flash
of a certain petticoat—a woman she saw once,

slipping out of his office. When it was finished,
she shook it out, flung it across
her single bed, covered it with her body.

Reflection

Jan Villarrubia

She needed to clean the window. For weeks she studied the faint outline of dust on the glass outside her sewing room. A pale woman's powder, translucent, almost. Her eyes would drift from needle and fabric in her lap to trace faint brush strokes, pitch of wings, imprint of each feather. The design, precise as pattern for bird.

She was not there when the bird hit, but had memorized the slant of flight, not head on, but soaring into trees at an angle. Nor had she heard the telltale plunk the instant of flight's celebration, the instant of release.

Today, in the rain, she will take rag in hand, smear off the notion of escape, wind the bobbin, thread the sewing machine, start the hand wheel, place her feet on the treadle (right slightly higher than the left) and sew.

Figure 4.5. Original photograph by Lee, Photographer, N.W. Cor. 5th and Penn Sts., Reading, PA. Photo of original, framed portrait by Jan Gilbert.

Jan Villarrubia's poem "Reflection" was inspired by this portrait. This is one in the author's collection of approximately seventy-five photographs of elderly women found in antique stores and flea markets in New Orleans, various cities in Oregon, and in Paris. The women are all unknown to Villarrubia, even though a small fraction of photographs have names handwritten on the backs. One entire wall in her home is covered with such photos, and many of these portraits have inspired her to write poems, prose poems, and monologues. Villarrubia's book entitled *The Wall of Forgotten Old Ladies*, including her written pieces with corresponding portraits, is forthcoming.

A Stitch-in-Time

clare e. potter

There was the gathering   of pieces:

                this chin

             an arm

          my slab of gut

that still held
all that stuff;

un
    rav
        elled I was.

Soon after, we scattered
her, and when I needed it: my grandmother spoke
                    through her cottons,
                    needles, loose buttons,

and one of her silks
—which I found
the day after I'd spilt it all out
in court–
called 'Forget me not,'

and I knew
my grandmother
sung
beyond the grave
in blue,
and it shimmered
and it stitched
me whole.

INVISIBLE MENDING

Wendy Klein

On Sundays we could go
to the refugee's—
the only shop open.

Down the alley, past the smell
of boiled cabbage, past
the rubbish bins; it looks closed,

always. Vintage spider webs are there
thick with dust
behind a streaked window,

and under a naked bulb,
the midday light
of the refugee, she works.

Her cat, a calico
has found
the only patch of sun—dozes

on a ragged cushion. The bell
pings when we open
the door. There is the smell

of hot iron and scorched cloth
from the corner
where her ironing board crouches,

its cover daubed with stains
Her iron
spews out steam. The refugee

is always there, at her place
in silhouette,
bent over her stitching.

She is busy; her hands, clever fingers,
that can mend
anything, twist and turn.

Two streets away, the waves dance.
The beach is white.

Miss Brontë's Comb

Martha McFerren

She's up at seven, as always,
dressing in painful silence.
As she lifts it, her old bone comb—
yellowed, four teeth missing—
slides from her fingers, lands in
the hot grate. It can't be reached.

She's too weak, too not-there
to pummel the morning's dough
and peel an eternity of potatoes.
She's peeled herself away.
Now her sisters do all the cooking.

She won't eat, though they beg her.
She can't speak, her only strength
the force of her scantiness.
She sits sewing an hour
but can't and won't sew flesh
back to her narrow skeleton.

Now her father's lifting her
onto the sofa. She's burning,
flames never meant for
this frugal parsonage hearth.
She seizes her fever. Dies.

Five people own burnt combs.
Each says his was Miss Brontë's.

STORM

Malcolm Willison

As the sun slowly filled our fields
my mother, just up
came into the little kitchen.
She, who sometimes told her dreams
about passing Janus-faced strangers
in the street, with their accusing
extra eyes, said perplexed
"I had a curious dream last night."

My father and I, an adolescent,
looked at her, "Oh?
How did it go?"

"Well," she reported, "we were all
here in our house, and I went
into the living room. I noticed
the low white plaster ceiling
reflected the light the way it does
only when it comes
through the windows from the horizon
if there's a huge thunderstorm
covering most of the sky.

"At the back of the room
my mother, here from the City
was sitting with her old friend Emma
who lived with her
in those low chairs; they had a cloth
stretched across their laps, and
they were sewing.

"I asked what
they were working on."
My grandmother had replied
(in her brief way)
"A shroud."

Standing by the stove, my father
and I agreed: "It has to be
a death dream."

My mother seemed
surprised, but not startled.
"Yes, I guess it is."

We were still having breakfast
when the phone rang
off the living room.
My mother went to answer it.
When she came back, she said,
"Emma died last night."

115

Figure 4.6. *Madonna of the Book*. Malaika Favorite, 1997. Mixed Media on frame and canvas with found objects, 24 x 18 in. From Favorite's series: "The Garment as Muse." Courtesy of the artist and poet.

I CAN SEE YOU

Moose Jackson

i can see you
sewing fingers on a white glove
sitting on a white couch
white light poking
through your red mop of dreads

i am happy to record these moments
that float gently groundward
red and yellow and spring green
for all the lives cut short
someone will stand in the grey wind
and shout out their names
our quiet moments of peace
are adrift in a river of heartbreak

we keep flowing into one another
like neighboring tidal pools
one day soon
early in the morning
we shall join forces
flood these provincial dams
and run down to the mississippi

Pulling Pieces

Jessica Mitchell

My great-grandmother pulls quilt pieces from the top of a closet.
 They cascade over her
bits of fabric cut from seventies polyester sandpaper.

Her eyes say We Are Connected. Her body housed the man who
 fathered my mother, the
man who wanted sons.

She fingers flowers trapped in stars locked on squares and sighs
 I Can't Quilt Them
Anymore. But I know what she's getting at and it's another way of
 pinning me down.

To continue the threading and pulling together, the binding of
 people to myself with
nearly invisible threads.

THREAD

Jan Villarrubia

We were all there, Grandmother, talking.
The second you dropped the spool of thread,
the right side of your mouth
fell, your cheek, your eye.
We all knew what it was,
seeing it over and over in sisters,
fathers, mothers.
In a buggy as a child, you watched your mother,
opposite you, as her face changed, suddenly.

It's something that happens
deep in our heads. A thickening
of the dark red life-flow,
an explosion.
Little vessels too thin and frail,
like the thread you used
to take up our hems on Sundays.

Probability

Marian D. Moore

In this land, she said proudly,
all of our statisticians are expert
seamstress.
Their diplomas display their emblem—
a hand as it expertly threads a needle
with a frayed edge of spun fiber.

Rachel's Children

Martha McFerren
    for Rachel Maines

Across the fabric of America
she opens wide her arms, a Rachel
sobbing for her children, for they are not.
Pelisse, antimacassar, comforter alike,
all worn to nothing, no scraps left alive.

Such is the virtue of women's art.
A useful beauty for both seamstress
and her work. Since Eve spun
women were meant to give themselves
to thread. *Make it, use it, wear it out.*
Needlework, though transient, is factual.

Surely Mrs. Browning spoke for them:
We sew, prick our fingers, dull our sight,
producing what? A pair of slippers, sir.
Stump work, tatting, crochet, patchwork,
orphaned samplers long turned yellow,
drawn work, netting, beadwork, embroidery,
sachets, lace and doilies. Why?
No more of that, dears. A world's unraveling.

Rachel has searched that world,
found much, saved many:
and when a quilt was lost, there was
a weeping and a great mourning in her heart.
May she recover them at last—
those lost anonymous scraps—
in the baskets of thrifty cherubim
who braid the rugs of heaven.

THE VIOLET ROOM

Malaika Favorite

I am stitching a dress
for the room to wear
a dress of violet and cream.
The dress will cover the room,
a virgin girl walking down a path.
All the men are watching
wondering if she tastes like grapes
or more like flowers after a rain.

It is not a girl; it is a room
a room dressed in violet

The men are watching
wondering how it would feel
to slip between her sheets,
light green sheets with small purple violets.
The room smells like violets and rose water
The girl sleeps with one foot uncovered.

The moon enters her room,
through the window and plays with her toes.

It is not a girl but a room

The moon tries to crawl up her leg
but the lavender comforter protects her.
The moon glazes the bottom of her foot
and kisses the soft spot of her ankle.

The girl stirs and turns under the covers
of light green and small violets.
The room shifts its weight and purrs.

The moonlight falls asleep between her
smallest toe and the one next to it.
The girl never knew what the moon did.

Figure 4.7. *Pepper Cayenne*. Malaika Favorite, 2011. Mixed Media, 54 x 27 in. From Favorite's series: "The Garment as Muse." Courtesy of the artist and poet.

SEWING FOR THE HOME
Malaika Favorite

Use a seam ripper to gut out your old self
remove all the parts you no longer need.
Cut away unnecessary dreams, bury them
in a diary and burn the book in a fire
kindled by internal combustion.
Measure the width and height of your walls.
Find a piece of cloth large enough to cover
your inner self. Spare no expense on color,
decorate your being with hidden ambitions.
Mark your personality out with tailor's chalk.
Stand in the mirror of your soul and pin
your personal reality on with quilting pins.
Don't be ashamed to add decorative trims
found in your mother's sewing box.
Sew your new self on by hand with assorted
needles, size should vary according to
the depth of your wounds. Do not be
embarrassed by female stigmatas,
the suffering of life to re-stitch itself
requires long threads of red blood unwinding
from a spool inside your life womb.
Use this red thread to embroider life patterns
on your inner sanctuary; holy symbols
that only you can interpret and understand.
These are codes of memory, used
by your ancestral tribe, growing new
meanings with each generation.
Use straight stitches to secure your walls
with a heavy lining. Cover the lining
with zigzag stitches around the quilt squares
of your history. If your history is not square
use abstract patterns to define your self.
Employ gathering stitches in your family room

to pull your clan together, wrap them around
your goodness scented with crushed
petals saved from all your spring gardens.
Fold the hem of your home and stitch
in place with a French seam. When
life is cruel use the ruffler attachment
to crease cruelty into a book of blank pages.
When necessary use a blind stitch
to hide images not suitable for public view.
Cover your windows with sheer curtains
to allow visions of changing seasons.
Weave a welcome mat for your door,
require shoes to be left on the porch
and give out white socks for visitors
to tiptoe across your Persian feelings.
Sew buttons on your heart
unbutton only to friends and family.
Interview strangers before allowing
them to see the lining of your slip covers.

Figure 4.8. *Address for Rita Dove*. Malaika Favorite, 2014. Mixed Media, 30 x 13 x 6. From Favorite's series: "The Garment as Muse." Courtesy of the artist and poet.

Mending

Karissa Kary

You were walking ahead of me and have finally turned back to see why I am not with you. I have found an old table sitting on the curb and upon closer inspection learn it is a sewing table with an old Singer machine inside.

I fold the machine out of and then back into the clever table. Old spools and rusty needles sit in the small compartment under the sewing table. Someone took great pains to make sure they would have the tools they would need to be able to keep mending whatever needed fixing. Inside the side drawer of the table are aged and darkened instructions along with bits and pieces of equipment. You watch me pull the thread out of the spooled machine and it keeps pulling and pulling. It stops. It is stuck. I stop too, careful not to do any more damage.

My mother loves her old sewing machine, and I think that perhaps, I could love this one. My father, a craftsman, could recondition the wood . . . I could fix the lock . . . replace the old hinges that swing the machine in and out.... Though there is much work to be done, perhaps it could sew again. Perhaps I could set a chicken pin-holder on top of it like my grandmother did on hers, the red hen roosting over her multi-colored pin eggs.

I want to explain to you my mind and the picture of us that was crafted a stitch at a time, here and there, day by day until it was a part of me.... This us became something I wore with me every step. All these interactions. Hand to needle ... Needle to thread ... Threadto fabric ... Fabric to body ... Body to body ... And me to you....

I ask you to help me carry it down the street to its new home. As you lift the machine, it occurs to me that I sewed the button on your shirt. I wear a skirt that years ago I mended along the seam and a scarf that has pulls up and down its delicate weaving. I have on a shirt I purchased with you on holiday and there is a small run in the shoulder that needs to be fixed. This shirt is my next sewing project. You think I should get a new shirt.

I explain that everything worth keeping needs mending from time to time.

Inside I have been feeling something pull and pull, down deep a thread is knotted and stuck. As we carry the machine you tell me how you think it is a waste to keep this old machine that has no use. It doesn't work. Why would I want to create such a big project?

I realize just how much we have unraveled. There was a snag here, no time to mend it. A pull here and then there. Threads were loosed only to see they no longer kept anything together. I don't think it is a waste, this old machine. I do sew. I want to believe that it can work again, that something that has been abandoned and left on the street can make things better.

You don't sew. You don't mend.

I want to believe in mending.

My Only Golem

Rebecca Black

> *Cursed be the one who makes a carved or molten image,*
> *the work of the hands of an artisan, and sets it up in secret.*
> --Deuteronomy

Miss Nobody, sister
twin, I bequeath red plastic
funnels for breasts, hair
from the four corners
of my bed. For your shoe
a stone that bruised
my heel, razored blood,
a dram of jealousy. I'll
mortar you with muck
from the River Flint, fixident,
a jigger of my lost
drawl. Everything
I hate about myself.
The eighteen-year fever
coiled in my bones, a hitch
in the lungs, left ear mole.
In your stomach, brick
of cornbread, capers.

For your nethers,
a mollusk shell, fly
trap, only part
of the story.
You're the ache
& the cavity. Wire
helix of hair, willow
furl rigged with polyester
thread, taffeta rags,
shredded energy bills.
I'll feather your brow
with mystical letters,
Kabbalah kitten, my
golem. Marionette,
my maker and mask,
I name you Mephista.

The Loom

Peter Cooley
   after the painting by Vincent Van Gogh

Unless light be applied to it like a poultice
sex will not heal in us.
It is a wound less scabrous than any.
Therefore, invisible, Vincent set down here
the landlady's daughter, then the widow, then the whore,
within this little gnome upright over a thread
and composed the man in himself he must have lost
to lust for three women in succession hopelessly.
Or did he sit his ghost inside this frame
and spin out Margot who threatened death after he fled?
Whatever, the facts wash off in this clear air,
reduced to a clean Dutch radiance
which sets all things at such rigid angles to each other
they assume the attitude of prayer.
Kneel down, little weaver, in the falling light,
your heart is a bobbin, it cannot stop
thrashing and trembling even if the shuttle stop.
The loom is a cage. Our bodies are another.
The light falls, a man and woman trade their threads in it.
The light fails and they stumble, fall in it.
They move through each other, they touch and separate.
They find themselves raveled in the expanse of a great cloth.

V. Telling Stories of Cloth, Needle, and Thread

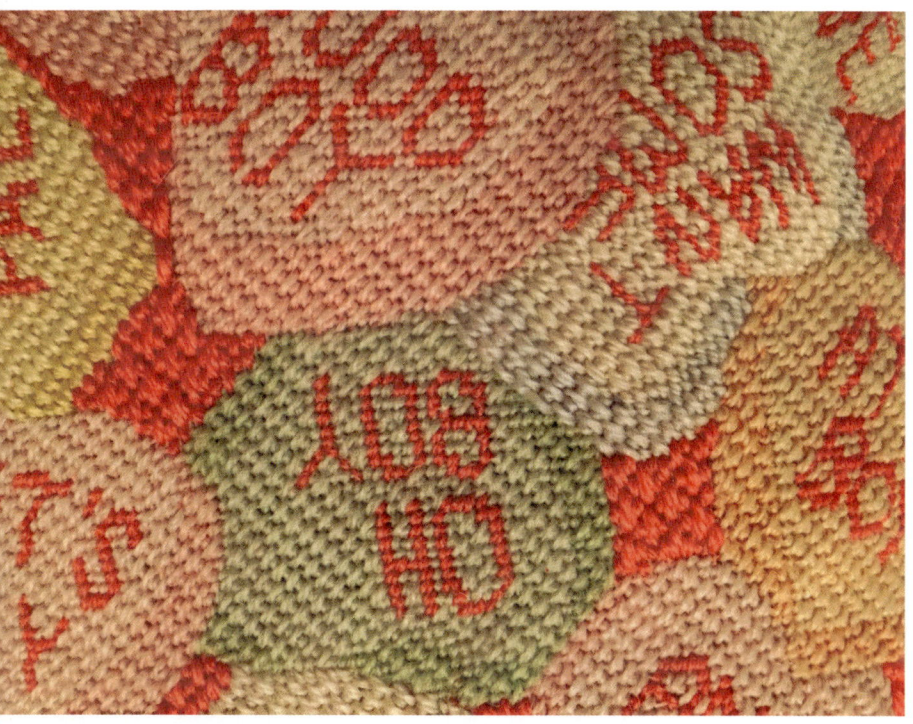

Figure 5.1. Detail of needlepoint piece created by Bobbie Malone based on candy hearts, created as a Valentine gift for her husband, Bill, 1978, completed the following year. Photograph courtesy of Bobbie Malone.

Figure 5.2. *Irish mannequin in a store window during Mardi Gras, New Orleans, Louisiana.* Photograph by Carol M. Highsmith. January 6, 2008. Library of Congress, American Memory Project. Permission of the photographer granted, October 27, 2016.

BELOVED STORMY, BELOVED TORCHY

Lee Meitzen Grue

This is story based upon people I once knew, or came across, when I lived in the French Quarter during my teens and my twenties. Because it was long ago, some of the names are imagined, but others are real. I came to write this when I was given a book once owned by Stormy and Torchy. Not much about their lives ever has been told and I tell my memories here with the same spirit that I witnessed in the French Quarterites then: a sense of excitement with living. In retrospect, one can see too how much of the life of the Quarter intersected with sewing.

You would have thought there was a party at Mink's Café. Much talk and hooting laughter. The interior decorators from Hadrian's Villa were there for coffee. After they left, Raymond marked the bottom of their coffee cups with the dishwasher's red fingernail polish.

"So now we'll know their cups from ours and you ladies won't have to drink after them."

The saleswomen and seamstresses from the Liberty Shop were flattered. It was a gallant gesture on Raymond's part. He's been looking after them. But they aren't too sure why they shouldn't drink after the decorators.

And Mink's not telling them. It's a taboo subject. All he'll say is, "Something you ladies shouldn't have to put up with."

But the decorators are only part of the buzz. Mink has thoughtfully provided them with a copy of *Look* magazine. Inside there's a full-page picture of Stormy, dancing on top of a bar backed by a band. A couple of people from the kitchen are watching. The spread in *Look* has made Stormy a celebrity overnight.[1] The women at Mink's huddle over the magazine. Stormy's dark hair falls past her high buttocks. Even in a picture they can tell the hips are swaying in one direction, the silk panels and the hair in another. The decorators are

---

[1] Stacie "Stormy" Laurence appeared in *Look Magazine*, April 1, 1947 and in *Life Magazine*, March 15, 1948.

nothing compared to this! "Who cares what those sissies do? I never saw a woman shaking herself like that in front of a bunch of waiters. I can't believe it."

Ione Theriot and Maureen Shaugnessy have spent their entire lunch hour poring over the magazine. They've read every word. Studied the picture. The audience of white men can't be seen. Out of sight; out of mind. To Ione and Maureen the photographic evidence is inconceivable. The multiple shades of New Orleans people might suggest to others that somebody in the past has been doing more than looking but Ione and Maureen don't think about that. All they think about is Stormy on a bar with the kitchen help watching. How would it feel to be Stormy? Exciting. Scary.

"It's time to go back to work," Maureen said mournfully.

They came to Mink's because Raymond always has something for the "girls." Some joke or astounding piece in the *States-Item*. Something to make them come back to Mink's Café rather than go over to one of the other places for their roast beef po'boys.

"I'm sick and tired of seed pearls, Ione."

"Better seed pearls than sewing sequins. I'll take seed pearls any day," sniffed Ione.

"It's a shame the Pratt girl's not prettier. Seed pearls show up your complexion and that poor darling's got bumps all over her face." Maureen likes pointing out the deficiencies of the homely debutantes: the ones with the big bellies, large noses, pimply faces.

"Well, you know what? You get tired of sewing Carnival gowns, you could go to work for Stormy. You could run up that cheeky little black number on the sewing machine in half an hour. Bet the money's good," laughed Ione.

"I wouldn't work for nobody does what she does."

"You're right about that, Maureen. Carnival works is tops. Don't we get invitations to sit upstairs at Proteus?"

And they do get invitations to the Proteus ball. Upstairs at the Municipal Auditorium, in rusty black evening dresses they've worn for the past five years, they watch as the nineteen-year-old queen glides around the room with her sixty-year-old consort. She's wearing a dress that would have bought a small house in the suburbs for either of them. They note each whispering rustle of her gown—the graceful fold of the fabric as the queen curtsies and inclines her scepter toward the non-dancers, the women who sit upstairs without any hope of even one call-out to dance. Ione and Maureen bask in reflected glory as the queen bows and sweeps around the room in a white silk creation covered in seed pearls, each one of which they've sewn on by hand. They envy her nothing. She is their Queen.

***

Torchy Wilde opens at six p.m. for the after work crowd. It's early and La Lune is a late night bar. She works a double for extra cash and downtime. Nothing happens until eleven p.m. when the dancers drift in. Torchy greets each one by name, including the women in dresses that tilt and swirl around their thighs when the slick looking men fling them out onto the dance floor. Sometimes Tony Almerico plays; the music has a Latin flavor. The room is more Parisian then American. Any Friday night you could see the tango danced exquisitely at La Lune by a woman with red hair, a lantern jaw, and a slim hipless figure. She always dances with the same partner, a man so handsome that the people at the small tables seldom look at her face, remembering only two slender bodies twirling in tango fans as the musicians play "La Cuparsita." His face is passionate, as if the tango is the real act of love. And the patrons seeing them dance believe that any other act that human bodies engage in is only a gross approximation of this beautiful coupling.

Torchy doesn't dance at La Lune, although her look is as dramatic and slick as any of the men. She dresses her short body in black slacks, ecru silk shirts, and the short bolero jacket worn by the men. Her black hair is combed back in a perfect ducktail; in front, one lifted strand dips across her left eyebrow. There is always a cigarillo dangling from one corner of her mouth, one eye slightly closed as the thin trail of smoke climbs upward.

There is a woman sitting in the corner at the end of the bar drinking champagne cocktails. Occasionally, when the glass empties, Torchy slips behind the bar to lift out the bottle sitting in a bucket of crushed ice to shake another cocktail. Torchy is always aware of the woman and the glass as she sets up and tends to the others in the room.

Someone says to no one in particular, nodding toward the woman in the corner, "You know a corner of the room is where the power is."

The woman wears high heel black sandals without hose and a black sundress slit up the side. Her dark hair is swept up in a French twist. One long, fine leg crossed over the other swings in time to the music from the jukebox. Her skin is very white, pasty, as if she's never in the sun. Luminous, she is a striking figure in the semi-darkness of the room. The faces of the men turn to her attentively. Like toreadors, they observe every movement she makes, but none of them moves in her direction.

Torchy finds reason to walk outside the bar to say a few words.

"Another drink, Miss Stormy?"

"You pouring? I'm drinking."

"I'm pouring my heart out and you know it."

She did know. Stormy had just come back from New York and this was her first stop. The gossip had already run up and down Bourbon Street, "Stormy is leaving Jack Lester. She's back with Torchy. Yeah, she's at La Lune's right now."

Torchy had not asked the obvious question: why are you here when your husband is there? Instead she plays Anita Ellis on the jukebox and mixes champagne cocktails. She will continue to mix champagne cocktails until Stormy stops drinking them or is too drunk to drink them and has to be taken home. Torchy mixes drinks as if Stormy has always been sitting in La Lune, as if she'd never left New Orleans. Never been Jack Lester's wife.

"I have to go back to work," Stormy says. "Somebody told me Frank DeSalvo's wife just had a kid. She can't work. Maybe he needs a dancer."

"I don't know if you could work for Frank DeSalvo. He's not your class."

"What's my class? I never liked that word. You're whatever that word ought to mean, Torchy. You always will be."

"Always is a pretty long time. You're the one goes on trips."

"That's the last one. It was a big mistake."

After the spread in *Look*, she'd married the photographer. He was obsessed with her, taking hundreds of shots of her while hanging at the bar at the club drinking Jack Daniels on the rocks or hanging at the edge of the stage. The camera was an extension of himself, and she began to feel he was making love to her with the camera, that he saw her as she saw herself: powerful and beautiful, striding up and down the stage.

Stormy wasn't really a dancer. She wasn't a dancer the way Kalantan or Lilly Christine was, and she didn't take much off. She had presence. Her walk owned the stage.[2] Her face, always impassive, ignored the audience and she never drank with the customers. Sometimes she'd go into the back bar and send Torchy or Alice Brady a telegram a couple of doors down.[3]

One night when she came off stage, she said, "How you doing, Jack Daniels?" and that was the beginning of it. She knew his name was Jack, and she knew what he drank, which was more than she'd bothered to know about any man who'd come into the club.

The pictures he took of her were black and white studies. They went past the mask. In Jack Lester's pictures, her luminous face was surrounded by a living darkness. He was not like the other Johns who came to the club every night to see flesh. The photographs he took made her a star, or maybe it was the time she went up to Baton Rouge and let the football players dunk her in the fountain after they won the big game that made her a star. Maybe Jack's picture of Stormy coming out of the water dripping sex was what made her a star. Anyone who came to Bourbon Street had to go to Stormy's Casino Royal to see Stormy.

Jack's persistence was exciting, and finally sexy. He was a mirror. She could see herself full length as she'd never seen herself before, and when he came to the club one night with two one-way tickets to New York, she went with him. She said, "Jack, everything's going to change in New York."

It did. They were featured in the gossip columns. Walter Winchell wrote about Stormy the beautiful exotic dancer—the toast of New Orleans seen at Twenty-One with her new husband, fashion photographer Jack Lester. They went everywhere. She no longer worked. She read everything. There weren't enough books in the world to satisfy the hunger she had to know things. Pretty soon she knew more than he did. During the day she liked to pad around the apartment barefooted, listening to the latest rhythm and blues from New Orleans: Johnny Ace, Johnny Adams, Shirley and Lee, Chuck

---

[2] Exotic dancers of note included those mentioned here, as well as Evangeline the Oyster Girl, Alouette Leblanc the Tassel Twirler, Rita Alexander the Champagne Girl, Blaze Starr, Linda Brigette the Cupid Doll, and Tee Tee Red. Kalantan was called Kalantan the Heavenly Body; Lilly Christine was called Lilly Christine the Cat Girl.

[3] Alice Brady (1928-2012) ran Alice Brady's at 514 Ursuline Avenue, and Mr. D's Hide-A-Way at 700 N. Rampart St.

Willis, La Vern Baker, or people she'd worked with. Sometimes she'd dance for Jack, which made him romantic. For a while it was all romantic. When she got lonesome for home she'd write to her mother who worked on Bourbon Street and never wrote back, or to Miss Willie, who raised her and still worked at Maison Blanche making curtains for rich people. Mostly she wrote to Torchy who always wrote back: Torchy sent Stormy something she'd copied from a Gideon Bible years before:

> *Entreat me not to leave you or cease following you. Whither thou goest I will go, and whither thou stayest I will stay. Your people will be my people and your God will be my God. Whither thou diest, I will die, and there will I die, and there I will be buried. May the Lord deal with me severely if I allow anything but death to separate us.*

In her letter Torchy wrote, "It's what Ruth said to Naomi. It's the way I feel about you." The letter made Stormy homesick and she stayed in bed most of the day. She thought about her wedding day. The Justice of the Peace who'd married them was a fan. He blushed when he told her he'd seen her picture in *Look*. "I thought the pictures were beautiful but I'm glad you've turned your life around."

It did seem that way at first. Jack was gentle—intelligent. His eyes saw everything through the camera lens. He'd married a sophisticated woman who stalked the stage. If he took her to nightclubs everyone wanted her and ignored him. He wouldn't let her work because everyone wanted her. "You're my wife," he said.

The woman at their apartment was someone else: a shy girl from Mississippi who liked to walk around without shoes, who didn't wear makeup, who cooked fried chicken and greens, who sometimes cried for her Mama and Torchy all night, and who, when she was sad wanted him to "put your mouth where it will do some good." It was a place where he'd never put his mouth before. When he didn't, she bought stacks of postcards to send to the strippers at the club in the Quarter to tell them how wonderful her life was in New York.

After two years—after almost two years to the day, she wrote to Torchy. "I want to come home." Torchy sent her a train ticket. After eighteen hours on the train, with nothing to eat but the chicken she'd fried before she left New York, it was Torchy who met her at the station. "Where's your bag? Did you check it?"

"I don't have a bag," she said.

Now she was back. It was the same, but not the same. Everyone knew who she was—Stormy, and that meant something. She was heavier now. Had come into her woman's body—voluptuous, older. She could have lived forever on the adulation of a few rich, gay men who saw her as the ultimate woman—the woman they would like to be—not too differently from the way Jack Lester had seen her as she danced above him, when she was the most beautiful dancer in New Orleans.

After the first week, she left Torchy's apartment. The physical part of their affair was over. It was like that line Anita Ellis used to sing from *The Four Walls and One Dirty Window Blues*: "I'll call up my used-to-be. He'll straighten out my affairs." Stormy had called up Torchy to straighten out her affairs. It was time to move on.

Stormy moved in with a younger woman. Jeanie had come to town wearing a sharp business suit to work as a buyer for Kreeger's department store. Now she was working as a barmaid at Wanda's on Bienville Street wearing black slacks, a man's shirt, and a ducktail haircut, staying with Stormy in a slave quarter apartment on Ursuline Street.

Jeanie looked like a clean-cut young boy. One Saturday night she lost a cap on a front tooth in a fight with a male customer. It was not obvious—not worth having fixed. She seldom smiled and would rather drink than look good. The books she read were by e. e. cummings. She tried to write like him: all small letters. Stormy smothered her with mothering. In the six months with Stormy, Jeanie had four bar maid jobs but couldn't hold one. "It's because I won't sleep with the bosses." Word was she did sleep with the bosses for free booze and they tired of her quickly.

One Sunday morning about 3 a.m., Stormy came in from the club. She found Jeanie lying on a white chenille bedspread covered in blood from twenty-seven hesitation cuts she'd made to her face, arms, and breasts. Stormy knew there were twenty-seven because the doctors had documented twenty-seven: one for each year of her life—three more than her father had made when he ended his.

Now that Jeanie was residing on the third floor of Charity Hospital in the psychiatric unit, Stormy was able to reexamine her life. The doctor said that Jeanie was a great danger to herself and should stay in the hospital for an extended period. Stormy knew from the bruises she was wearing around her own neck that Jeanie could be dangerous to others.

Torchy gave Stormy the money to move and moved her. Stormy moved while Jeanie was in the hospital tending to her new love, a woman who smoked a pipe and looked like Ernest Hemingway without a moustache. The woman was undergoing a series of shock treatments, and when the orderlies dumped her back in her bed like a slab of cold beef, Jeanie cared for her.

Now Stormy was back with Torchy, painting oil portraits of Quarter people she'd known or worked with. Torchy gave her a one-woman art show at La Lune. One wall was plastered with portraits: Ruthie the Duck Girl, Ivan from the Disgusting Group, Lucita, Mary Collins from the Galley House, Aggie, Louise from the Starlet Lounge, Alice Brady, and Galatea. Bill Christy cooked a huge buffet. Everybody came to eat and drink and buy their portraits. The show was a huge success. After the show, Stormy quit painting.

Stormy was older—they were both older. Stormy said she'd never leave again. Torchy was the one constant in her life, but they both knew she was restless, never quite satisfied with life if it stayed too much the same—she loved change—a new woman—a new man.

Once when the real restlessness hit her—when she wanted to shake up everything, she flew to Chicago where Jack Lester was working for the *Chicago Tribune*. He'd married again and had kids, but he went on a week-long tear with Stormy. They flew to New York and visited as many of their old haunts as still existed. She knew he would probably leave his family if she asked him to, but she could only be the woman he wanted for about a week.

Torchy picked her up at the airport in a new Cadillac convertible.

"Where'd you get the car?" Stormy asked.

"From my new old lady."

"New or old—you better hold on to her. She's a live one."

"And you, Miss Thing. Did you get New York out of your system?"

"For now. Did you miss me?

"You know I did, but I didn't lose any sleep."

"God, it's good to be home! There's no light like this anywhere else in the world."

"How would you know? You got a shuttle going between here and New York. You don't even go back to Mississippi."

"I like the bright lights."

"Baby girl, you haven't missed much even if you haven't been a lot of places." Torchy in her black sunglasses didn't smile, but Stormy knew her eyes did. She took Torchy's hand and held it.

Stormy was back at DeSalvo's dancing on stage. The sign out front still said: STARRING STORMY. It stayed up whether she was in town or not, but the sign had weathered. DeSalvo, who was renovating the club, had the sign taken down.

NADIA THE MERMAID WHO STRIPS UNDERWATER was more of a draw. DeSalvo had modified the stage for Nadia's tank, and he always got his money's worth. The big tank limited Stormy's area to stride. Made her act smaller. When the new sign went up it read NADIA THE MERMAID, NUDE UNDERWATER, and underneath, STORMY, A BOURBON STREET LEGEND. Nadia wasn't really nude; she ducked behind rubber plants or fake coral and gave the illusion.

Stormy's mother Enola worked on Bourbon Street in a blue comedy act. She was the farmer's daughter in a short, pink gingham skirt and pasties. Enola had been working the street for thirty years. She always sent her money home to Mississippi where her Daddy had been a sharecropper, where her mother still eked out a living with a garden, and where four other daughters, none of whom had stayed married but had a mess of kids, lived. When Enola went home, it was to Mississippi; when Stormy went home, she went to Torchy or sometimes to Miss Willie.

One Sunday Torchy said, "Come on Baby, let's take a ride."

They went to Metairie. To the other side of Airline Highway to look at JIM WALTERS MODEL HOMES. Stormy was excited. It had never occurred to her that anybody she knew might buy a house. It was a finish-it-yourself house. Not too much bigger than a trailer.

"How are you going to do that—finish it?" Stormy asked. "You don't know which end of a hammer drives a nail."

"Watch me."

And when it was finished—Torchy's house in the suburbs—she took in anybody off Bourbon Street with a hard luck story: Drying out? Can't make the rent? Name your poison. Torchy could feel sorry. And she didn't badmouth them when they left complaining of the food or the uncomfortable couch. She said, "They're good people."

The year Stormy got sick—no one thought she was really sick. A look of profound sorrow had always been part of her allure. There was a deep note to many things she said, although she didn't talk much. In spite of her voluptuous figure, men and women both thought of her as delicate and treated her that way, but she'd been amazingly healthy. She danced five nights a week, five shows a night for twenty years.

Her quick humor—a belly laugh—would break out of any quirky little happening, but she didn't like dirty jokes—too many nightclub comedians.

It began as a light head on stage; whirling the silk panels to show her legs became an exercise in caution. Caution made her feel old. She thought it was her eyes. "I'm going to look pretty silly on stage in granny glasses."

None of the imperfections of her body had ever bothered her, and she laughed about this too. There was always someone who wanted her. It was like being too rich: out of sheer animal vitality, she'd been wasteful of her looks.

Stormy's skin was flawless, unlike Marie Cavanaugh, who at fifty looked eighty and stripped in the dark under black light, swooping around the stage to *Claire de Lune* in iridescent butterfly wings and glowing scarves, which she removed slowly, stripping down to a luminous G-string and pasties. In the dark Marie Cavanaugh was the moon. Men in the audience never noticed her age or scars. The illusion worked and they were horny.

Stormy made few concessions for her heavier figure. Bunny Gay (Costumer to the Stars) constructed what he called an "industrial strength bra" with black French lace over a full-sized brassiere. The bra concealed her breasts except for an extravagant cleavage in the front. Bunny, who worked for Art and Tony, dressed all the strippers. He always called her "Mama." He told anybody who came the shop, open from 10 p.m. to 5 a.m., full of crazed coke queens sewing at flying machines, "Mama is the prettiest dancer on Bourbon Street. Only a dumb fuck like Frank DeSalvo would headline a drowned rat over Stormy. But you know how it is: rats run together."

The eye doctor, when Stormy finally kept an appointment, told her it was not her eyes—something deeper—something he couldn't fix with a pair of glasses. The other doctor she went to couldn't fix it either—it was past fixing.

At Torchy's insistence Stormy quit working and moved back in. This time to the country or to what Quarterites considered the country— Metairie. It was not Mississippi; she'd never liked Mississippi. Here there was her little dog and coffee in bed in the morning with Torchy who brought it in for both of them. They had always slept late, had breakfast around two in the afternoon. Now Stormy wanted to get up early for fear of missing any part of the day. Each day was like a semiprecious stone. Slight imperfections made it unique. Time did not seem to be going too quickly. Torchy had saved a little money and they let her off from La Lune with the promise of her job back any time she wanted it.

Stormy said, "Doesn't this remind you of summer vacation when you were a kid? The summer goes on and on."

The days were like two lifetimes.

In the past, Torchy had known writers who lived in the Quarter: Lyle Saxon, Tennessee Williams, and others. Sometimes they'd come into La Lune. Tennessee gave Torchy a book with a personal inscription. More often, she bought the book and got the author to inscribe it.

"Hey, listen to this, Storm." She'd read a passage from Elizabeth Barrett Browning or from "This is My Beloved." Torchy was partial to love poems. Stormy would listen and play with Alouette the toy poodle. "Yeah, that's great. Just like you and me, Torchy." Torchy would laugh. She knew Stormy liked ribbing on the square.

No one in Torchy's family had ever been to college. She had worked since she was fourteen. In the Jim Walters house, Torchy built bookcases in every room. Stormy would show her books to friends and say, "This is my Tulane University."

For the first time in her life Stormy was not restless—not looking for change.

"Mama," Bunny said when he came to visit, "You're still the prettiest dancer on the street. Forget the Cat Girl. Forget Blaze Starr. Forget Kalantan. Mama, you're the one."

"She's the happiest I've ever seen her," Bunny told Torchy. Exactly what Torchy wanted to hear.

Stormy said, "You know Bunny, everybody thinks I'm being brave. It's not that. Now I know what my life is all about. I can see it. It's all of a piece, and it's not bad. Not bad at all."

When Stormy died there was a short obituary in the *Times-Picayune*. Ione Theriot couldn't believe it. She immediately called Maureen Shaugnessy, who remembered. "Like it was yesterday," she said, "those pictures of Stormy in *Look*."

And to them this was a memorable death—like Roosevelt dying. They would remember what they were doing on that day for the rest of their lives. Stormy was important, although they were never quite sure why.

Torchy had a burial policy she'd taken out on Stormy twenty-five years ago just like she was family. The policy paid for a metal coffin and the burial, but it didn't pay for interment—finishing off the tomb. Torchy had to do it herself with concrete blocks and Quikcrete. While the Quikcrete was still wet she wrote on it: BELOVED STORMY. And she later had it put on a stone.

In all those books in the bookcases she'd built, Torchy found a book Stormy had given her. It was a paperback, Penguin's *Book of Sonnets*. She read the inscription, "To Torchy, Love Always, Stormy" and thumbed through. She found something she'd never seen before: a note from Stormy on the blank page facing Edmund Spenser's sonnet called "Amoretti."

Torchy-Darling sometime accidentally you'll discover this, you'll pause and read it. Perhaps (God forbid), you will have forgotten me. You'll have to concentrate in order to remember me, but believe this—wherever I am, at whatever time you read this, I'll be thinking of you;

at anytime, at any distance, your name will be on my lips for your name is in my heart.

Stormy

The Spencer poem read:

> *Happy ye leaves when as those lilly hands,*
> *Which hold my life in their dead doing might*
> *Shall handle you and hold in loves soft bands,*
> *Lyke captives trembling at the victors sight.*
> *And happy lines, on which with starry light,*
> *Those lamping eyes will deigne sometimes to look*
> *And reade the sorrowes of my dying spright,*
> *Written with teares in harts close bleeding book.*
> *And happy rymes bath'd in the sacred brooke,*
> *Of Helicon whence she derived is,*
> *When ye behold that Angels blessed looke,*
> *My soules long lacked foode, my heavens blis,*
> *Leaves, lines, and rymes, seeke her to please alone,*
> *Whom if ye please, I care for other none.*

Some years later, when Torchy died and her will was read, her main request was that she be buried beside Stormy, with BELOVED TORCHY inscribed on her tomb. Her old friend Alice Brady took care of the funeral and the inscription on a granite block. She set the concrete blocks but before she could spread the Qwikcrete, her right knee gave out and she had to have an operation. Torchy's tomb is not quite finished yet.

Stormy and Torchy are buried in Greenwood Cemetery at the foot of Canal Street where the bus driver always called "Cemeteries-End of the line."

Figure 5.3. *Patsy Jordan sewing in the living room of her daughter's home at La Delta Project. Thomastown, Louisiana.* Photograph by Marion Post Wolcott for the U.S. Farm Security Administration, 1940. Courtesy of the Library of Congress, American Memory.

Casting On

Lee Barclay

"Saving the world?"

"I'm just sitting here."

"If you say so."

"You can read my mind now?"

"I don't need to. I can see it in your stitches."

I stared at the yarn balled neatly on her lap, clean white against her navy blue skirt. I followed the string up to her hands, where she straightened my stitches on the knitting needle. "What are you talking about? I cast on exactly the way you showed me. Those stitches are perfect."

Mammaw wrapped her arm around my waist and inched me closer to her hip on the couch. "That's not the point, baby." She smelled like gardenias. "You're not back at graduate school. This is the one place where you don't have to be perfect. Look here—your stitches are so tight I can't work the needle through. The whole point of casting on is to make a chain down the needle to hold your knitting stitches. The needle has to fit through each stitch."

She carefully pulled the yarn off the needle, gathering each loop in between the red fingernails of her thumb and middle finger.

I grabbed the needle. "What are you doing? Just shove the needle through. It'll go."

She cupped her hand over mine and squeezed it gently. "You're going to pull out as much as you stitch. You don't have to push."

I grunted.

"How attractive." Mama in her voice.

My stitches pooled onto her lap, the crimped yarn unraveling. I stared at her fingers and choked back the fresh swell of the funeral. Our reaching arms, the succession of hands inside the casket— Mama's, Mammaw's, mine. Those three hands, identical.

Mammaw snipped the frayed yarn, wound it around her fingers, and placed it on the coffee table. She placed the ball of yarn and needle on my thigh, covering the rip in my blue jeans.

I whispered, "I miss her."

"I do, too." She stared at her rose garden through the sunroom's back wall of glass. Pruned, bare branches. Raw mounds of earth. Each rosebush freshly transplanted across the river to Monroe. Redolent buds once bloomed in banks of green in her daughter's fertile North Louisiana soil. Red, lavender, yellow. Orange, cream, copper. "Now cast on, Caroline."

I blinked at my left hand. As if reflected through the glass, a field of tattooed red roses from wrist to fingertips gazed back at me. I couldn't remember what to do.

"Caroline, you just did this." Her face, our stories worn into the patchwork of crevices. "Out to in."

"Maybe I'll move in with you."

The steel wakes beneath her lashes, magnified in the lenses of her glasses. "Maybe I have my own life."

"I'm just saying—"

"Honey, I know perfectly well what you're saying."

"But I love you."

"I love you, too. I love my life. I love your life. Now where is your tunnel?"

I held the needle in my right hand so that a tunnel fell between two falling strings of yarn.

"But if I'm not here you'll—"

"Once you really get going, baby, you can take your knitting everywhere. When I was really into knitting, I always had it with me. I just sat and knitted and tuned out all the noise around me. I only heard the clacking of the needles."

I touched the thumb and forefinger of my left hand together and inserted them into the tunnel from the backside toward my chest. Opened my fingers. I wrapped my middle, ring, and pinky fingers around the dangling tunnel of yarn. The tunnel opened into a diamond as the yarn stretched around my thumb and forefinger. My finger pointed like the imaginary pistol I fired in my cowboy games as a girl.

"Good. Now pull the needle down toward your palm until the yarn makes a pair of scissors. Remember?"

"Maybe I'll just stay for a little while. I don't have to go back to school until fall. I'll take care of the roses until they get established."

Her eye twitched. "You're always welcome, Caroline. I love your company. But they're not your roses."

"Maybe you should have given me some! You don't need forty! It's absurd!"

She reached for my hand and drew the tip of the needle down a few inches. A pair of scissors appeared. "Now use the tip of the needle and grab the yarn. On the far left: out to in."

I bit my lip and pulled the tip of the needle to the left: out to in. To the right: out to in. I continued the motion through the left handle of the scissors. I pulled the yarn through until another loop found the needle.

Through the tangle of white yarn, cut blood roses bloomed. Mama's hands in mine. Mammaw's. Tiny rivers washed the powder from Mammaw's cheeks as she watched her roses. Red, lavender, yellow. Orange, cream, and copper.

I reached for her face. "Mammaw—"

She stopped the spilling stitches with her fingertip. Took the needle from me and untangled the excess yarn.

"In knitting, Caroline, there's nothing you can't fix. You can always pull it out and start over, unless the yarn is totally frayed. And even then you can cut it and tie on a new thread. But knitting is knitting, and there are rules. If you're breaking them, it's just not knitting. Would you like to try?"

"That's what I was doing."

"No, baby, you've been casting on. It creates your foundation, but knitting starts with a very different stitch and has a rhythm all its own. You'll use two needles for that. For purling, too, which is an entirely different stitch altogether."

"Just forget it. What's the point?"

She glared at me over the rim of her glasses. "Excuse me? Knitting is the point."

She held the dressed needle in her left hand and lined the remaining stitches along the underside of the needle into one short row. She looped the trail of yarn around her right pinky and laid it over the forefinger of the same hand. She picked up the free needle with her right hand and tried to insert the tip beneath the uppermost stitch. The yarn squeaked as it pulled taut against the plastic. "Do you hear that?"

I nodded.

"That's not supposed to happen."

"Why are you grinning like that?"

She tried to loosen the stitches with her fingernails, but the yarn wouldn't budge. "Because your stitches look just like mine when your mother taught me how to knit."

"What?"

"Too tight, just like mine. The needle won't slip through. You're going to have to do all of this over."

"Mama taught you how to knit? I thought—"

"Mother worked to raise other people's children while I stayed home with my brother and sisters. There was no time for knitting. Your mother taught me much later when she was an adult. I was hopeless."

"Then who taught Mama?"

"Books."

She laughed. No sound came out, but her shoulders bounced the way I once did on her knee. "The two of us—"

I held out my hands to her, red roses. "Here," I said, "show me."

FLIGHT PATH

Janis Turk

I dressed Isabella like a doll, brushed her wispy brown hair. Covered her in besos. Absolute adoration I felt for her. So tiny, her perfection. So I dressed her in the most beautiful clothes.

As a child, my little sister would brush our little dog and dress her in her Baby Tender Love's pink doll clothes. I dressed my daughter like that—with a care she could neither consider nor comprehend any more than my sister's doggie had.

We lived in Metairie. My baby's father played in a band on Frenchman in the Marigny. Bongos, if you call that playing, slapping a stretched, tanned hide—thump, thud—if you call that playing.

He slapped. I worked.

I stayed up at the kitchen table late at night while he slept.

"Carolina," he would call me, angry, down the hall. "Carolina, come to bed!"

But I had scraps of paper to go over in the night. I'd sit in the kitchen making lists of all the bills: gas, light, rent, baby food, diapers. We had no health insurance. No car insurance, either. I would lay it all out, trying to find a way to afford to finally leave.

As poor as we were, Isabella was a Baby Gap kid with blue jean skirts and jackets, size 0-XS, and she had a purple Laura Ashley coat and hat at Christmas that I could ill afford. She was a fashion plate in kiddie *couture*. I remember best an Easter dress my mother made for her with a Peter Pan collar, white lace, ribbon edges, rosebuds.

My mom was the kind of mother I thought that I should, but never could quite, manage to be. She made pot roasts; she baked pies and bread. Her pancakes never burned.

She decorated beautifully. She cared about clothes and shoes.

She knew what mattered.

And she could sew.

I knew some of it. My pies are unparalleled. My *pan perdido*, perfect. My gumbo better than at Dookey Chase, bread pudding and even baked Alaska to rival Antoine's.

And our camelback house was immaculate, lovely, and tasteful— hiding how appallingly poor we were, in money and in spirit.

Figure 5.4. *Mary Protects Jesus.* Malaika Favorite, 2011. Mixed Media, 54 x 27 in. From Favorite's series: "The Garment as Muse." Courtesy of the artist and poet.

But I did not sew.

I knew deep down that I wasn't like my perfect mother who could do anything, who knew everything.

No, she did not know *everything*. She didn't know he pushed me, shoved me into walls, pulled my hair.

My *Leave It to Beaver* life and *Father Knows Best* fairy-tale childhood hadn't prepared me for this or prepared my mother to talk about such matters over Breakfast at Brennan's or Friday Lunch at Galatoire's—over mimosas, Eggs Benedict, and toast points, Trout Nancy or Crab Meunière—when she'd take Isabella and me out sometimes for a special treat. And she didn't know how tight finances were in my quickly unraveling universe—oh, maybe she did a little, I guess. She always picked up the bill after breakfast.

He didn't beat me, really. I can say that now, and it's true. But he left me shattered and broken in a million tiny, almost imperceptible, ways.

He held a loaded gun to my pregnant belly once. That counts, doesn't it?

"Why did you stay?" they all ask me now. "Why didn't you tell me?" asked my mother over brunch, years later—and every year since.

I tried, I did. Every night I'd sit in the kitchen and try to add it all up. No "pros and cons" lists needed. It came down to simple arithmetic: one car and who would get it, and, then, how I'd get to work when he did. How I'd keep the house or get together a deposit to rent another. How we'd live, my little daughter and me.

And then I'd throw away all the papers and sit in the kitchen in the dark listening to the airplanes take off and land.

We lived in the flight path of the Moisant Field airport. Planes flew overhead till 11 p.m. and started up again at six. I'd sit in the kitchen smelling the jet fuel fill the night air outside while the whole house was asleep. I heard them take off.

I knew I wasn't going anywhere.

And so, it was on a night like that, that I began to sew.

I'd borrowed the neighbor's Singer sewing machine and got $2-a-yard fabric at Wal-Mart on Veteran's—white cotton with little red strawberries on it.

I decided my first attempt would be a little jumper with a balloon bottom and elastic holes where Isabella's chubby, little brown legs would stick through.

The only thing I'd ever made in my life was a big, ugly mauve circle skirt with a pocket in it. At St. Martin Junior High in Biloxi, we all had to sew something for a Home Ec project. I remember I cried as I made this skirt because I had to rip it all out, all my stitches and seams, because it came out all wrong when I tried to do it. My mom had to finally stay up late at night to fix it for me so I could wear it to school the next day in order to get a grade. In the morning, it was as though the elves had visited the tailor in the night. The skirt was laid out, making a perfect circle on top of the dining room table's thick felt pad. My mom's nice sharp scissors and a shiny never-used ripper lay next to her masterpiece. That's all I remember about sewing except my tears.

I never put on that skirt again after I wore it to school that once. I hated it. I've never liked the color mauve. I don't know why I decided to make that skirt, anyway, or why I picked that fabric or that pattern. I never would have bought an ugly skirt like that. Do you ever notice how people tend to make things they would never want to wear or use? Christmas trees out of folded pages of Reader's Digests, crocheted potholder squares, quilted placemats, tie-dyed T-shirts, Christmas breads with dry candied fruit. Why is that? Did they think they wanted those things when they began, or was the *making* "the thing" and the having part an unpleasant, unexpected consequence?

Mom remembers the whole skirt incident quite differently.

She says, "You *can* sew. Don't you remember that skirt you made in Junior High?" she says, as though she's forgotten who really did it all, when she knows perfectly well it wasn't me.

This time, I was more hopeful as I began to sew for my little daughter.

I was sewing with an overwhelming love for Isabella, with my desire to make her comfortable, to have her see that she was beautiful and well-cared for all at once—sewing with an honest, raw desire to put a life together for her in tightly stitched pieces with a real pattern. I loved her so. I still do.

I'd say, "Do *ojitos!*" and she'd bat her black, spidery Spanish lashes at me, and I would marvel at the power of someone so small and so fabulous, so tender and so timid in a world so hard.

I sewed late into the night. I no longer needed ledgers of my entrapment. I needed a project as I served my sentence in marital hell. I thought just maybe sewing would turn out to be something I could do, something to make me feel as though I were a good mother. Something even he, and his mother, and his sisters would allow and understand.

And so, one night I started sewing.

I started at nine when he went to bed.

By midnight, I was making progress.

I loved best the starting part, with patterns and pins and those wheels you roll through an ink-like paper and then roll over the fabric, making choppy lines to trace with scissors as you cut. I loved the hopefulness of pattern pictures. I loved to thread the machine, especially the hidden bobbin wheels below.

By three, it was not working, but I would not stop.

I felt compelled to finish what I'd started, no matter what—to persevere past my damp eyelids and heavy heart—to put it together somehow, see it through, just as my mother did.

By 3:30 a.m., I was almost done. I was hurrying a lot—my buttons were sloppy, and uneven were the jumper straps. Threading the elastic through the tunnels of fabrics at the legs felt good, though. Tight, taut. It might just work.

He called out for me at 4:30, "Carolina!"

"*Calmate*, I'm sewing," I said with mama-like authority.

At four, he got up for water and grunted toward the kitchen.

At five, there were no airplane sounds.

Around 5:30 Isabella cried out. I ran to her crib, but she was sleeping. I sat in the rocker in her room, the lights from the airport parking lot throwing shadows on her walls through the plastic mini-blinds.

I went back to the kitchen.

The sun would be up soon. I was so completely spent.

I picked up the jumper, my most perfect creation after Isabella, I thought aloud—pleased with myself.

Until I held it to the oven light.

It was all wrong. All uneven. Clown-like—one strap longer than another on the jumper top. I went to button it up anyway, but the buttonhole was shut—sewn tightly together.

In Spanish they call the time of day just before sunrise the "*maldrugada*"—badly drugged, it seemed to me.

I took the ripper and began tearing out the tight, mean stitches that held the buttonholes together.

I began to cry, my own *ojitos* dripping wet with weariness.

It came apart more easily than I'd ever imagined, more quickly than I'd have ever guessed. It came apart in my fingers.

And so, without taking account of all I'd done up until then, I kept ripping and tearing, pulling, crying, coughing until I heard the first plane take off, the morning red-eye flight.

I kept on ripping, taking apart every stitch. Every thread. Every thing I'd ever done.

Each tiny tie that binds.

Weaving Together
(FROM THE NOVEL *DREAMERS*)

Donna Glee Williams

There. The Dreamer recognized the weaving porch perched above a saddle-blanket shop. And there: The Weaver in a blue-striped tunic, working at her loom.

"Good morning," the Dreamer called up to her. She didn't know what to say, exactly. "I came back."

"Just a minute, please." The Weaver took a few more passes with the shuttle; the Dreamer could hear the rhythmic thwack of the beater from the lane below. After a minute or two, the loom went quiet and the Weaver turned to speak to them, resting her elbows on the weathered wood railing of the little porch. "Sorry—I have to finish the strip I'm working on, or I'll lose track of where I am. But I can take a little break now. Welcome back, Dreamer. It's good to see you. You've come to check on how our work is coming along, I'd guess. And you've brought some different Ladies with you today, I see."

"Barley, Hearth, Gem, Sparrow: this is the Weaver I was telling you about. These Ladies helped me find you. I'd forgotten the way. And, I'm embarrassed to say, I couldn't even remember your name."

"Bur," the Weaver said. "I'm Bur, and you are all welcome. Just go around to those steps there and come up onto the porch. I'll show you what's become of all that threading you helped me do."

The Dreamer and the Ladies filed up the narrow stair and crowded around the loom, admiring the fine checked cloth without touching it. The Dreamer was confused.

"I thought…. I mean, the warp-threads we put on the loom were in stripes, saffron and white stripes. But this cloth is saffron and white squares. When you wove it … it came out different."

The Weaver laughed out loud. Her laugh was big. It filled the porch and spilled over into the street in a way the Dreamer was not used to. "I'm sorry," she said. "It just tickles me sometimes how little people know about each other's crafts. Here, let me show you. If you think about it, it makes sense. If the warp is striped and then I make the weft that crosses it striped too (which I do by changing shuttles,

Figure 5.5. Woven cloth from the Amuzgo ethno-linguistic group who lived in a village called Xochistlathuaca in the State of Guerrero, Mexico, ca. 1979. Photograph courtesy of Bobbie Malone.

going back and forth between saffron, peach, and white thread just like in the warp), what happens? Watch."

She swung back around on her bench, stopped talking, and began to send a shuttle wrapped with pale peach thread back and forth across the loom. It moved so fast that it blurred in flight. After each pass, she beat down the new-woven thread with a bar that packed it tight against its neighbor. The visitors watched over her shoulders without speaking

After she'd woven about a finger's breadth of the peach (which became a row of brighter and paler squares of color as it crossed the warp-stripes), she turned to face them again. "You see how it works?"

"It's wonderful!" The Dreamer hesitated. "Can I try it?"

The Weaver looked uncomfortable. "I'd be grateful if you wouldn't. I'm sorry, but…."

"That's all right. It was just an idea. It looks…easy."

The woman laughed again. "It's easy enough to throw the shuttle, I suppose. What's hard is to keep the rhythm so the tension stays exactly the same. Otherwise the cloth will pucker or the edge will pull in." She showed them the ruler-straight edges. "It takes a steady hand, the same hand from beginning to end. If I let anyone else, even an experienced weaver, take up the shuttle now, you'd see a change in the cloth. Sometimes, even a mood can change the weave. You can't hide anything from the loom. I hate to say 'no' to the Dreamer…. But here's an idea for you: I have another loom, just like this one, really, only much smaller. It was my grandmother's. It's for weaving those bands that the tailors love to sew around hems and sleeves and collars for contrast. Like what you have around your wrists and hemline, only with patterns. And color. Not gray. Anyway, I learned to weave on that little loom. If you'd like to learn a bit of the craft, we could set it up for you. If your edges don't come out perfectly (and they won't; they never do when you're just starting out), then no harm done." Bur smiled and made a little tossing gesture with her fingers, like setting something free.

The Dreamer was astounded by the idea. "You mean, you'd teach me? To weave? You'd teach me to weave?"

"Well, yes. Why not? Magpie taught me; why shouldn't I teach you?

If you'd like to learn, I mean. And," she looked at the Ladies, "if it's …
acceptable. If it fits with…your other duties."

"They give me my afternoons for myself," the Dreamer answered
excitedly, not noticing that some of the Weaver's "if" had been
directed at other people. For a moment, the Ladies beside her had
ceased to exist. "I could come after lunch and work for a few hours. I
usually take a long walk in the late afternoons—to help me sleep, you
know—but there's time for both. Oh, I would love to learn—if you
really mean it. I don't want to be any trouble."

"No trouble at all. Only…." The Weaver looked uneasy again. The
Dreamer liked this about her, that her face spoke the truth about
what was going on in her mind. Most people were hard to read. The
Dreamer was beginning to realize it was because they were telling
their faces to say something different from what they really felt,
because they were telling their faces to lie. The Weaver didn't lie with
her face and, right at this moment, she was blushing a little.

"It's only, and I wish I didn't have to bring this up, but times are,
well, not exactly hard, but they're not easy, either, and I'd like to be
able to make the Dreamer a gift of it, but the truth is, I can't afford to;
I would need to ask you to pay for the thread for your loom."

The Dreamer's face fell. "I don't have any money," she said.

"But you're the Dreamer."

The girl shrugged, looking at her sandals. "People feed me. They
give me my clothes, everything I need. But not money." Why did it
make her feel so naked to say that?

"Not money," the Weaver repeated sadly. "Nobody ever gives
you money. There must be a lot of coin coming in and out of that
compound, one way or another, what with the Garden and the
Council's fees. I don't suppose you could ask for some?"

The Dreamer blanched. Ask for money? Ask who? The Scribe? She
doubted that his hand ever touched a coin. The Keepers? They must
have something, she supposed, to see to the needs of the household,
but she had no idea how that worked, and it was probably all doled
out by the Council of Interpreters anyway. She couldn't imagine
asking the Council for money. It was unthinkable. It couldn't be done.

But just before she opened her mouth to say that it couldn't be
done, the Weaver offered her an idea. "There may be another way.

What if I buy the thread for you?" The Dreamer started to demur, but the older woman went on. "An investment, you see, not a gift. I'll buy it, and help you set up the loom and guide you through getting started. In return, you'll let me sell the weaving as 'made by the hand of the Dreamer.' That would bring us a pretty price, no matter how raggedy your first piece comes out. There would be something in it for you, too, for the work you put in."

"Oh, I couldn't take anything; all my needs are provided for."

"Nonsense, girl. I happen to have strong feelings about this. Weavers don't work for free; we get paid. And a girl needs a little money of her own, even a Dreamer. You never know what might come up."

So they shook hands on it, the Weaver and the Dreamer. Some linen thread would be purchased. The Dreamer would come in the afternoons and learn to weave.

VI. Learning About Ourselves and Others Who Sew

Figure 6.1. Memorial Wedding Cloth.1897. Photograph. Courtesy of Sally Reeves.

FASHION AND POWER

Arthur Pfister
  to Momma

R oy Rogers was the King of the Cowboys, Lash LaRue was the
King of the Bullwhip, and Jax, Dixie, Regal, and Falstaff were
the molasses of the masses. The Cisco Kid was a friend of mine.
Four o'clocks, chineyball trees, and giant swarms of mosquito hogs
(my cousin from over 'round London Avenue by St. Aug called 'em
mosquito *hawks*—anything but "dragonflies") were in abundance
then.

A two-parent household was the norm, "Please" and "Thank you"
hadn't gone outa style, Catholic school kids ended the Pledge of
Allegiance with "One God, one country, one flag," and tourists were
callin' New Awlins "New Aw-*leens*." My gran'ma ate her chickens
"fresh off the hoof" from Miss Beaulah's yard next door ('cross the
basin on Iberville Street) and Fury was "the story of a horse . . . and
the boy who loved him."

Mr. Cassidy was hoppin' along, Bugs was doin' the Bunny Strut,
and Aaron Neville was sho' 'nuff tellin' it like it was. Miss Ginny was
stompin' and 'rompin' 'round the room, Morgus and Chopsley were
performin' fantastically frightful experiments involvin' all parts of
the inhuman anatomy, Gene Chandler was the Duke of Earl, the
Three Stooges were committin' malice in the palace, and Dorothy
was off somewhere chasin' a Black & White rainbow.

Parents terrified and titillated their children with local lore and
tall tales of The Bugar Man and The Gown Men (them mens in them
white gowns up 'round Charity Hospital who were rumored to whisk
children away to some distant, bedeviled haunt where they would
execute all manner and mayhem of unspeakably atrocious acts on
their bodies, youth, and innocence). It was a wonderful world.

It was a time when thongs were sandals and upwardly mobile
men (and some wimmins) of color were longshoremen, electricians,
bricklayers, carpenters, plumbers, teachers, preachers, nurses, and
mailmen (wasn't no such thing as mail*wimmins* back then). Lionel
trains, Fanner 50s, Robbie the Robot, and Chatty Cathy were the

Christmas gifts of choice, baseball was played with wooden bats (and real balls), and Roy Campanella was an eternal thirty-nine. I was the # 1 fan of Sandy Koufax (and what he didn't do on Yom Kippur). Nelliebelle, Bullet, and Trigger were all in the family (c'mon, baby, the good times was rollin').

It was also the time of "race movies" like *Imitation of Life, I Passed for White, Pinky,* and *I Crossed the Color Line* (at the Carver, the Circle, the Clabon, and the Gallo). The Incredible Shrinking Man was the only "shorty" we knew. It was a time when the guv'nuh rode a white horse up the capitol building steps 'cause they didn't wan' buy him a Cadillac (*You are my son, Shine*). Pontchartrain Beach and Pontchartrain Park weren't "open" yet. Jessie Hill's *Ooh Poo Pah Doo* was out there creatin' disturbance in yo' mind and high schools were named Carver, Lincoln, and Washington.

It was a time of shotgun weddings and shotgun houses. It was when the vejitibble man unroutinely snaked through the twistin', shoutin', animated streets of the city long unremembered by care, euphoniously hawking his everfresh wares. Al Johnson's *Carnival Time* was all over the airwaves and *real* New Awlins cooks were makin' goo-gobs of gumbo until they were too pooped to pop. Champion Jack Dupree was a boxer, a spy boy for the Yellow Pocahontas, and barrelhouse piano professor (*Momma, move yo' false teeth; Poppa wanna scratch yo' gums*). New Orleanians were drinking in (and regurgitating) the sweet wine of their long-revered tradition of gaiety and merrymaking. Mardi Gras Day, the most fabulous and fattest of Tuesdays, was approaching. For twenty-four hours all would be disremembered and forgiven in the city that care forgot. It was Carnival time, just befo' Mardi Gras Day, and all my momma did was *sew, sew, sew.*

My momma sewed. She was a master (mistress?) seamstress. A dressmaker. She learned how to sew from her mother who learned from her mother who learned from her mother (and I really cain't remember back no further than that). She "took in" sewing befo' colored wimmins of her particular pedigree could even *think* about workin' at Haspel's.

She was a lady of lineage, delicate in her language and skillful in her craft who knew mo' stitches than a combat medic. She sewed for some rich white lady writer who had a big house in the French Quarter and who used to always ask momma what some term meant when she said something (and then wrote it down); the racketeer man' wife (she had the first Mercedes-Benz I ever saw); Mrs. Moorehead, the wife of an old beer, bourbon, and balls general (Momma and 'em used to always laugh when I called her husband a "Frigidaire General"); and a buncha other fish-white wimmins with names like Amber, Elspeth, Pilar, Penelope, Zoe, Heather, Phoebe, and Chloe who used to take the dresses and stuff she made and have her sew in the label of some faraway, fanciful, fashion designer so they could front 'em off, sashayin' and promenadin' at the segregated balls and charitable affairs they would grace with their charming Southern presence.

Although formally unlettered and informally schooled, she mastered the complexity of the most demanding and exacting Simplicity patterns, humming softly while surrounded by a sundry assortment of cloth-covered tables, cedar robes, and chiffarobes. Her world was one of thimbles, pins, needles, tape measures, rulers, ribbons, scissors, spools of thread, yards of material from bolts of fabric of all patterns "on account" from Mr. Levine (the rag man), zippers, buttons, and notions of all manner and stripes that she got from Krauss, McCrory's, Woolworth's, and Maison Blanche Annex.

Her Singer sewing machine sang sweetly as she sewed curtains, Carnival costumes, formal Mardi Gras ball dresses, prom dresses, plastic book covers, beautillion dresses for a mélange of debuts, elaborately bejeweled crowns, doilies, drapes, slipcovers, foundations (whatever that was), sportin' gals' and fancy wimmins' outfits, flannel baseball uniforms, patches on Boy Scout uniforms (the Beaver Patrol), denim satchels for chinees ("marbles" to the uninformed), moo-moos, First Communion gowns, liturgical and ecclesiastical vestments, baby doll pajamas, sequined turbans for Oliver and Charles Brown of the Royal Dukes of Rhythm (which always assured momma and daddy the most prominent, boo-coo good seats at Carnival balls and an assorted array of their gigs), wedding dresses, bridesmaids' git-ups, christening gowns, death shrouds, cassocks, surplices, (and eventually and inevitably) bold, blue, paisley print dashikis, and a pietistic patchwork of all things delightful and delicate. My sisters just enjoyed stringing the spent spools of thread and making shoestring necklaces.

Local legend and common gossip held that a notorious lady in red, a fancy woman who used to ply all kinds of trades on Orleans Avenue, had her wake right there next to where momma sewed by the Magnavox console stereo in the front room of the late Victorian two-bay, camelback, shotgun clapboard house, its tripartite window cornices crowned with pierced-work cresting and gaily-fluted window frames as ornamental devices. Right there on Dumaine Street it was—two blocks from where Fats Pichon, the piano professor, used to live. They say this lady was laid out right there in the livin' room—all in red—restin' on a bed of pink satin and all decked out in her favorite red Carnival gown. They say she was the prettiest colored woman you ever saw.

Light and shadow were amplified by the house's jigsaw surface variations above its green, slime-covered, slick brick alleyway. Momma always liked to work by the front room's project-green hurricane window because the light there was so good.

Inside the house's front room, poo-brown French slidin' doors (my uncle in the Seventh Ward called 'em "pocket doors") opened to the next room where a pitcher of Jesus stared solitarily above a lamp by the bed. First Communion and Confirmation photos, graduation portraits, baby pitchers, photos of WW II veterans, assorted ribbons, fadin' plaques, and images of long-dead ancestors hung on the mantelpiece above the unused fireplace's iron grate.

My momma's longtime client and friend, Miss Rosa Belle Boudreaux, sat on the plastic-covered, imitation French provincial sofa under the window's beatific light and genteel gusts of riverfront breezes that stirred the billowing, gold and green Fleur-de-Lis curtains my momma had made. It was *some* airish in there! The ornate floral print of the well-worn linoleum floor covering's pattern was a vast canyon where unbroken-backed cowboys and the creepiest of critters roamed as I crept and crawled, absorbing all that was around me. Miss Rosa Belle Boudreaux, and my Aunt Sweet (Aunt Sweetie's eldest daughter), and my momma discussed the wisdoms and wonders of their universe. How my gran'ma once rode a horse bareback on the bayou (I always thought "bareback" was about the horse not havin' a saddle), about that time my uncle was gittin' off the troop ship and got all tangled up in the scramble net on the side and spent half the war in the hawspital. (They said, knowin' *him*, he probably did that on purpose.) They also told about how Mr. Tee-*Tee* was a good provider because everytime he'd come home from runnin' on the water he'd pack the icebox and pay up all the rent.

And they told about how just 'cause people is old that don't make 'em no classic; about how "All yo' skinfolk ain't yo' kinfolk" (and other age-old adages); about that time my *parann* and *nanann* was tryin' to git work in the aircraft factory in California during the war and my *nanann* turnt around in the diner and saw she was sittin' next to Nat King Cole (and fainted); about the time they was out in California and they didn't want to hire my *parrann* because my *nanann* was bright-skinned and my *parann* was dark-skinned (and they thought he was married to a white lady). The colored lady at the table pulled my *nanann*'s coat and told her to git in the other line and they hired her on the spot.

There were other short and tall tales of Sixth Ward (Tremé) New Awlins' sewin' and conversatin' in that precious, precocious age. They talked about knowns and unknowns and the things that they knew that they knew (which were the known unknowns)—which is to say that there were things that they knew they didn't know. But there were also unknown unknowns that they didn't know they didn't know.

I thought about these things as the City Park bus shook, rattled, and roiled the unadorned splendor of the tiny half-a-shotgun house, as the bus's timeworn, rusting, aged hunk perilously made its way up the one-way vaginal thoroughfare that was Dumaine Street to the end of the line at the park, where, I knew, it would idle near the former plantation's swampgreen, oak-laden expanses.

Miss Rosa Belle Boudreaux was a flame-haired, pink pedal pusher-wearin' beauty with canyon-deep décolletage, well-coiffed hair, flashy gold jewelry, sensible shoes, seafoam green eyes, and a sky-blue, knitted pillbox hat, who liked to make grand entrances like Loretta Young. She was *some* shapely! She was living proof of my (usually drunk) Uncle Sleepy's sayin' that "Wimmins rule and mens drool." The room's light kissed her gently on her gingerbread skin.

She was always all dolled-up and had a megawatt smile that would overload any straight-up man's circuits. The mens said she was so fine—she put the last three letters in class. She was always all gussied up and had a face (and chasmic, cosmic cleavage) that could make a grown man weep and a newborn baby cry for mo'. She would always say some politician named "McKeithen" could kiss her kitten, but I don't remember her ever havin' no cat.

My Aunt Sweet was a gentle, loving, scapular-wearing, plainspeaking, matronly soul who would give you the smile off her lips or the socks off her feet. She predated Miss Rosa Belle by a generation and enjoyed the veneration of our entire extended clan. She was mother confessor, confidante, familiar friend, and intimate to any who were blessed enough to encounter her sacrosanctity, for she wasn't just wunna them wimmins who party they whole life away runnin' the streets and then find Jesus when all they looks is gone.

She was a homespun philosophress who seemed to have a saying for everything, from "The Lawd don't like ugly" to "*Everybody* happy on weddin' day" to "Don't rock the boat— 'specially when you sittin' in it" to "If they wasn't no losin' they couldn't be no winnin'" to "A hard haid make a soft behind." Then there was "It ain't what people call you; it's what you answer to"; "The dog that *bring* tail—*take* tale"; "Better a educated *fool* than a *un*educated *tool*." Or "Don't shoot all the dogs 'cause one of 'em got fleas"; "You find yo' bottom when you stop diggin'"; "Never compare *yo'* insides to somebody else's *outsides*"; and "If you wanta see a rainbow you gotta put up with a li'l rain."

She also made the best pecawn candy (certainly not *pray*-leens) in New Awlins and had a big-old pecawn tree right there in her back yard on the corner (she always said "cornder") of Johnson and Lahopp (across from where them nuns used to live). We would make a pit stop there with our bikes on the way to baseball practice in Gentilly, pick pecawns from the tree in her yard, and have fresh pecawn candy and the world's greatest red beans & rice waiting for us after we returned and checked books out at Nora Navra Library over on Prieur and St. Bernard.

My world on the floor next to the rich cherry woodwork of the sewing machine's bottom drawer was dominated by a Kit Carson covered wagon set, squads of green army men, a Luzianne coffee can fulla chinees, and a cookie can fulla gaily-colored buttons of all sizes, shapes, designs, and surfaces.

That day, as I played in my brown playsuit with the blue bear momma had stitched on, it was the green chinees vs. the blue chinees. First, second, and third base were round white buttons and home plate was a BIG, BLACK button. I think the green chinees won that day while my momma was sewin' some Chinese "coolie" costumes for her, daddy, my uncle, and my aunt for an upcoming Carnival ball. (Can you imagine Uncle Bubby in a yellow and black coolie costume—complete with conical sedge hat and long, black platt in the back?)

That Mardi Gras my sister wanted to be a "snow girl" (a figure skater) and my momma was workin' feverishly tryin' to complete her costume, too. That afternoon I interrupted my mother's anointed tasks and reproached her, bawling, "You don't love me no mo'. You just sit there all day and sew. That's all you do is *sew, sew, sew*. . . . But yo' baby still love you 'cause you just so pretty. . . . You a glamour girl, a bathin' beauty, a movie star, and a nun. . . . You prettier than Matty Monroe and Jayne Mamsfield. Mammy Van Doren ain't got *nuthin'* on *you*, girl," I bullshot.

"Lawd, 'outa' the mouths o' babes . . ." remarked Miss Rosa Belle Boudreaux.

"Well, I'll be John Brown!" Aunt Sweet declared. "That take the cake! Lawdy-Lawd! I ain't never heard nuthin' like that in all my years o' livin' on this-here green earth! He sumthin' else! Did you hear what that boy said?" howled Aunt Sweet. "Jayne Mansfield? Mamie Van Doren? What he know 'bout that? That boy some ticklish!"

"Truth be told—he just like his paw," my momma said. "That boy just like *Big* Ernest. He like his wimmins top-heavy in the bust. He know mo' than you *think* he know. He was *borned* with it." She laughed. "You oughta see how he spread them *JET* magazines all over the kitchen floor and look at them middle pages all day long. That boy cain't *wait* to see a Tarzan pitcher— with all them li'l girls jumpin' up and down with nuthin' on top. He just like his paw. Just like him."

"The chineyball don't fall too far from the tree," my aunt offered.

"You the prettiest lady from here to Er-leens Avenue," I continued as my momma reached down from her work, extending me a hug and a smile as she laughed. She held me tightly for a moment, then placed me back on the floor to my world of cowboys, army men, chinees, and the cookie can burgeoning with buttons and baby boy fantasies. (It didn't take much to satisfy me back then.)

"That's all he want, is for you to hold him for a minute and then he go right back to what he was doin," my momma said. "That boy some sperled." My aunt and Miss Rosa Belle Boudreaux howled with laughter, marveling at this curious thing.

"I wish Tee-*Tee* was like that," said Miss Rosa Belle Boudreaux. "I wish *he* was that easy to handle. That man ain't nuthin' nice," she sizzled. "I don't know what that man' malfunction is! Lemme tell you what he done done *now*—'cause he done cut his water short with *me!*" she shoo-shooed. "I wanted to bust him up side his haid with a Daniel Green slipper the other day. That old helmet-haid man *some* kah-*goo*! Here he got *me* and don't even know what he *got*— and *he* livin' the life o' Riley! That man got a halfa dozen, brand new, Banlon shirts—every color o' the rainbow!"

"—He sittin' up in the baker' shop cryin' for bread!" my aunt suggested.

"Everything he need is right here—and he don't even see it," crabbed Miss Rosa Belle Boudreaux. "He couldn't even blow his nose if he had dynamite for brains. He so fulla cah-cah— his eyes is brown! He still makin' a BIG TOO-DOO 'bout nuthin," she sneered. "That man used to be the hand I fan, but now he out there galavantin' with You-Know-Who—"

"We all sin and fall short. . . . Who gon' love her when her looks is gone? No matter how pretty she is there's some man somewhere who cain't stand the sight of her. When you love a man and he act a fool—let him," Aunt Sweet offered, lickin' her chops at the trauma of the drama. The intoxicating sound of a practicing trumpet player pierced the air, serenading us, its bewitching aura radiating exotic enchantment and unhurried intimacy.

"Sweet—" Miss Rosa Belle Boudreaux began "—you can be so heavenly-minded you can do no earthly good. . . . I done caught him out there right in the middle of Dooky Chase Bar with Buttercup— that li'l low class, no class hussy with the bubblebutt be over there in the Green Room all the time—and over on Rampart Street – on the 'Ramp'!?! That li'l hoochie-coochie momma' behind hot as a truckload o' fresh cayenne peppers in the berlin' hot sun in the middle o' August! That li'l woman sumthin' else! She just young enough to be his daughter and smart enough to be his dog! *I* knows *that!*—and I don't know Miss Thing from Adam's housecat! He can hit the road, Jack! That man must be out his mind if he think *I'ma* keep on singin' that same old-same old, sorry, sad song. Then he gon' lie and tell *me* what *I* done seen! Gon' tell me what *my* eyes done uncovered! I know Tee-*Tee* was havin' ideas with that woman. I knowed it soon as I was crossin' the Er-leens Street neutral ground goin' over to Dooky's from the Lafitte! I don't need no leftovers! I don't need no constellation prize! Don't be givin' me no pitty party! Tee-*Tee* grease ain't hot 'nough! He keep doggin' *me* around—he gon' be a gone pecawn 'cause he best be done learnt—'Ain't nuthin' kill you faster than a old man or a young woman.' He ain't gon' just kick Miss Rosa Belle Boudreaux to the curve."

"Well, you know you can catch mo' flies with honey than you can with spit," my aunt proposed.

"Honey—he done bought that li'l strumpet from up off the Ramp a brand new washer-dryer and a color television set!"

"No he *didn't*??!!!???" my momma said, the hum of the sewing machine pausing a bit. "He bought her a television set? A color television set? A *real* one?"

"He been givin' her money she cain't even spend. He done made Miss-Lookin'-Like-A-Elephant-Comin'-Out-The-Boxcar-Backwards well si-tu-a-*ted*," Miss Rosa Belle Boudreaux stacattoed.

"Uh-huh," my aunt said. "What don't come out in the milk gon' come out in the rinse. Sumthin' in the milk ain't clean," she suggested. "You know—you cain't throw just anything in the pot and call it gumbo. . . ."

"Yeah-ya-right!—Talkin' 'bout how he saw me kissin' Willy 'cross the fence and heard me tellin' Willy he didn't have no sense! He think he done put me in a trick bag, but I'm ti-i-i-i-i-me 'nuff for him," Miss Rosa Belle Boudreaux seared. "Always talkin' 'bout a splinter in yo' behind when they got a telephone pole up *theys.*"

"*Oh-oh-oh-oh-oh...*" my mother dragged.

"Yeah," continued Miss Rosa Belle Boudreaux. "He all 'bout snatchin' and grabbin'. Tryin' to put some sense in that man' haid is like tryin' to drink water with a fork! But he ain't gon' be rainin' on *my* parade no mo'. I don't wan' make no big blah-*yay* 'bout it, but I'm serious as a hungry crab walkin' over a bare behind!

"Tee-*Tee* act like he done just got off the plantation! Actin' a fool—and here it is almost Carnival Day! He sho' done outdid his self! He act' mo' of a fool than Anus and Andy! Out there with that gold teef, tackhaid, bugarbat, ill-formed, streetwalkin' hussy . . . with her floozy, tart-brown hair! It ain't my fault! All that meat and no potatuhs!

"Then he was at that other woman' funeral last week—that li'l red woman from 'cross the river—and did he *perform*! All over the casket like a fool—and me sittin' right there in the church with everybody under-eyein' me up and down—like *I'm* the other woman! I didn't know that li'l heffer from Adam's *daddy*' housecat, but I *do* know he done footed both they bills. I know he was in cahoots with her. He always gotta have a woman between him and his mattress! He ain't got no skeletons in his closet! He got the whole graveyard! That man got mo' mess with him than Mesopotamia—and I got the right to sing the blues 'bout it 'cause he sho' nuff think he in high cotton!

"Talkin' 'bout he look like Major Lance! I'll Monkey Time his behind! Back there in the project livin' like some kinda hermit—older than Noah—and *he* was 400 when the flood came! Like—like I done told him—'If you cain't take it—don't bring it!' He can put me *out*, but I ain't gon' *let* him put me *down*!

"Talkin' 'bout me and him gon' go to California and git some work in the shipyards. I ain't goin' to no California—to Los Angeleez—and no kinda points inbetween—not with *him*! He ain't gon' be havin' *me* sleepin' in no Murphy bed the resta *my* days!

"I don't like no California anyways. Them people out there drinks you under the table— and don't feed you nuthin'. He ain't gon be takin' *me* way out there and flyin' the coop on me! Talkin' 'bout I don't know my role as a woman. I knows my role as a woman. As long as he can walk in from work—or wherever he done been—and have some food cooked and some clean clothes and some good lovin' . . . that's my role. . . . That's my role as a woman," she wailed.

"Baby," my Aunt Sweet admonished, "'Don't set the blanket on fire for a flea.' You fattenin' the frog for the snake. One monkey don't stop no show. You much too young a woman to be with that foolishness."

"Foolishness?!? Foolishness!?!? Y'all ain't *seen* foolishness 'til you done seed Tee-*Tee* git pissy drunk! Law-aw-aw-awd, that man did some clownin' the other night. He was *some* clownish! That man clown-ded mo' than Bozo!"

"*Whu-u-u-u-u-u-ut*!?!??!," chimed my momma and Aunt Sweet.

"We out there the other night ridin' up Canal Street—rollin' right up from the river—I'm drivin' and he juiced-up-tore-down drunk," she started. "We right there in fronta Maison Blanche and Lover Boy decide to start upchuckin'. Got vomit all over his pumpadoo hair. Tee-Tee had done drunk a gallon o' Gallo, a whole halfa G o' Thunderbird and two whole quarts o' Bali-Hai (regular *and* pineapple). Here I am tryin' to git us home—and he actin' a fool! Out there like some character! All out the car window throwin' up from the fronta Maison Blanche all the way down Canal Street to Krauss. He *did* some cuttin' up! He was *some* stupid! Then he gon' be callin' his self gittin' salty with *me*.

"Tee-*Tee* was tore up from the floor up and needed a checkup from the neck up! He was in rare form! That man almost brought my Injun' out! They needs to put him in a home for the feeble-minded! He so fulla his self! Gon' call me 'country'! Got the nerve to call *me* 'country'! He need to watch how he waggle his tongue! He ain't gave Theodora all that mess when *they* was married!

"My daddy ain't raised no fool! I'm Mr. Buddy B. Boudreaux' daughter! I'm Miss Rosa Belle Boudreaux, and chile— I'ma tell it like it is, 'cause I'm here to tell it *to* you! Then he just blew a fuse! Callin' me everything but a childa God! Always talkin' 'bout I'm always diggin' in his haid—like I'm gon' mess up my nails in all that pumpadoo hair! Like he the Count of Monte Crisco—all that earl up there!" she said, a smile erupting across her face. "Tee-*Tee* ain't got a pot to pee in—or a window to throw it out," she blabbed.

"Whoop-dee-*doo*!" Aunt Sweet sang. "When you throw a rock at a pack o' dogs, the one it hit is the one that holler."

"I'ma put the hurt on him. He ain't gon' be treatin' me like some popcorn, sucker John. I thought it was about beans, but it musta been potatuhs," Miss Rosa Belle Boudreaux simmered.

"Ain't that a shame!?!!" my momma said.

"I'm gon' git up, make my groceries, git on that Roper stove, and do my li'l cookin," Aunt Sweet said, rising from the couch as red bean smells wafted gently, smoothly, through the window. "I think the City Park bus done just 'bout made it back 'round from Er-leens Street. Lemme go haid on and git on the backa that bus. Baby—" she cautioned Miss Rosa Belle Boudreaux as she was leaving "—you better leave that poke chop sandwich alone." She then bade us farewell and went out into the world as she knew it, far from immaculately manicured Uptown lawns.

"But I love him. I love that man. He's the man I truly, truly love," said Miss Rosa Belle Boudreaux to my momma. Her face seemed drawn, sullen, and sad. A teardrop teased her left eye. "I love that man mo' than anything. I don't know why I love him like I do, but I sho' does love that man. If he would just be true to me . . . I know he didn't come into my life by accident. God don't make no mistakes. The last thing I wan' do is be a old, broke, lonely, colored woman when I kick the bucket."

I looked up at her from my universe, contemplating what I perceived, crept over to her, climbed on her perfumed lap, huddled close to her sweet-smelling, talcum powdered, warm, pecawn brown bosom, and slept to the sound of Miss Rosa Belle Boudreaux's heartbeat and the soothing music of my mother's Singer sewing machine at the end of a long afternoon of existential discontent.

Figure 6.2. *Mardi Gras Indians.* Photograph, ca. 1960. Box 1, Folder 4, George Longe Papers. Amistad Research Center, New Orleans, LA.

SEW, SEW, SEW
Arthur Pfister

There was another member of my family who sewed . . . my cousin, Brickhead Red, an appellation bestowed upon him by our family and his (usually criminal) associates due to his shaggy, crimson head of hair that matched the color of the bricks of the Lafitte Project. They always said his head was about as hard as a project brick, too. We usually called him "Red" or "Brickhead" or even "Brickhead Red" as opposed to Prickhead Red, Dagoe Red, Cherry Red, Icepick Red, Brickhouse Red, Trickhouse Red, Bugar Red, Boogie Red, Panama Red, Tampa Red, Uptown Red, Ninth Ward Red (the original), or Red Red. Yeah. He was my head-smashin', teeth-crackin', buck-jumpin', hardhead, humbuggish, in-and-outa-jail, always-fightin'-the-police-in-the-street cousin.... "Brickhead Red...Kill 'Em Dead!!!!!"

They say he was so mean he'd pop a cap in Jesus while He was on His way to Calvary—and stick a shiv in Mary for cryin'. That boy loved the jailhouse—he'd rather fight than switch. The only thing unarrested about him was his social development and his chronic halitosis. When he came by yo' house you had to always check the medicine cabinet to see if he had snatched up summa yo' momma' and daddy' pills.

He'd fight anything walkin' and cut anything breathin'. He was a character, a young toughie from by the basin who was livin' his adulthood in his childhood and his brief life was testimony to the adage "Bad niggers die young." They say he started that club they called the Halfa G's—where you had to drink three halfa gallons o' pluck in one day to join (one for breakfast, one for lunch, and one for dinner)—and not throw up. He drank three *full* gallons befo' 12 o'clock noon!

His past wasn't checkered. It was chessed. He was the *white* sheep of the family. He got in so much trouble that his favorite record was *Old Man Trouble*, his second favorite record was *Nobody Knows the Trouble I Seen*, his third favorite record was *I'm In A World of Trouble*, and his favorite movie was *Trouble In Paradise*. If he had ever held a job he woulda been a troubleshooter. If he woulda had an eventual choice, his favorite song woulda been Marvin Gaye's *Trouble Man*,

179

but suffice it to say that his favorite song actually was *Jailhouse Rock*. When he went to jail they'd say he was "away at school" (Scotlandville Junior College or Angola State University). He was "away at school" so much that he had to be the most educated human being in New Awlins history. He was living proof of the aphorism "If you don't want a nigger to steal something—put it in a book," but knew mo' versions of *Shine, Stagolee,* and *Shoo-Fly—Don't Bother Me* than the Signifyin' Monkey. He knew every word and nuance on the *Gene Chandler: Live at the Regal* album and was the only person besides the Duke of Earl who could hold that note on Part 2 of "Rainbow '65."

His favorite sports were bullshootin', robbin', stealin', fightin', and goin' to jail where his motto was "Blood on my shank or shit on yo' dick" (and other sayings unrepeatable in polite company).

If he had finished high school he would've been voted "Most Likely To Go to The Penitentiary." He thought Hai Karate English Leather-Lime was expensive cologne, and once told me, "Life is like ridin' in the Zulu parade every Carnival season and bein' on the same side of the float and seein' the people gittin' older and older a li'l teenantsy bit every year until you don't see 'em no mo.'"

I *still* don't understand what he meant, but that's what he said to me in the springtime of my youth, for in spite of all he did and all that was said by and about him, he was my spiritual teacher and guide, propagator of the faith, and keeper of the flame. He learnt me how to pull my pants over my knees when I sat down so they wouldn't "bend in"; how to walk in green slime-slickened, New Awlins brick alleys (*Don't walk natchally...**pat** yo' feet and walk*); how to pour beer (*Tip the glass to the side, bruh—so it won't foam over*); how to put a box together; how to keep my hands outa my pockets when I grow up and walk the streets (*Always keep yo'hands out yo' pockets 'cause you never know who or what might be comin' at you*); and all kinds of hip things to say like:

> *Niggers and flies I do despise*
> *One bring disease; the other bring lies.*

and: *On my honor I will do my best*
      to take what they give me – and steal the restz...

and: *It's Howdy Doody Time*
       It make yo' booty shine…

and: *Ashes to Ashes*
       Dust to Dust
       Yo' momma got a ass
       like a Greyhound Bus…

and: *Fat and Skinny was layin' in the bed*
       Fat rolled over and gave Skinny some head

and: *I went downtown (Too-way pocky-way)*
       to see Miss Brown (Too-way pocky-way)
       I gave her a nickel (Too-way pocky-way)
       She sucked on my pickle (Too-way pocky-way)
       I went uptown…

and: *My nigger, my nerve, my jelly preserve*
       You my ace boon coon, my pride and joy
       You a ugly muddafugga
       *But you **still** my boy…*

and: *I was walkin' thru the jungle*
       with my dick in my hand
       a bad muthafucka from the Congo land
       I looked in the tree -- and what did I see?
       -- a black muthafucka tryin' to piss on me…
       I picked up a rock and hit him in the cock --
       You shoulda seen that muddafugga run 24 CITY
       BLOCKS!!!

and: *The monkey chewed tobacco*
       The elephant ate grass
       If you don't be-leeve me
       you can kiss my big black --
       *-- **ask** me no question*
       I'll tell you no lie

If you don't be-leeve me I'll
I'll fuck you 'til you die…

and even: *I took my girlfriend to the show*
             and sat her on my knee-ee-ee-ee
             That girl FOT so hard she split her draws
             —and shit all over me.…

He learnt me how to Second Line and buck jump, how to give somebody a knife (*Handle first, bruh*), how to give somebody a light (*Give THEM the match and let THEM light it. Always keep yo' hands free*), how never to put after shave on my privates (*Ouch!*), how to pick up boxes by bendin' my knees so I wouldn't rupture myself (*Lift with yo' legs, 'cause yo' legs is the strongest part of yo' body*), how to work with a Tandy leathercraft kit (like he did in jail), how to sing a halfa dozen versions of *Li'l Liza Jane* (he picked up on that in jail, too), how to sword-fight with a garbage can top and a broomstick, how to make a baseball outa string and paper, how to clean the "dead man" from a crab (*Don't eat that yella part*), how to throw a knife, how to buy cheap wine, how (and why) a man should always put his big bills on the inside (*Let 'em see yo' ONES—not yo' TENS*), and how to build a skatin' truck (my cousin 'cross St. Bernard called 'em "skatemobiles").

He even cold-slapped me in my politically unastute brain with an explanation as to why I couldn't be in the Soapbox Derby (*That's for them **white** boys—not **you!***) and told me that "Just 'cuz you go to the Celebrity Lounge—that don't make you no celebrity." Yeah. He schooled me in a whole lotta ways.

He was raised up in the Sixth Ward and lived right there 'cross from the Lafitte Project on the corner in a small house with an oyster shell alleyway. (It's a grocery store now—Hung Wang had it, then that A-rabb, Brother Muhammed, got it.) It was on Er-leens right down the street from the award-winning Willie Mae's Scotch House and up the street from the world famous Dooky Chase Restaurant and Bar.

His world was one of cowbells, whistles, tambourines, Second Lines, fire water, handclaps, jumps, shouts, hollers, fried chicken, gasoline, wine, rum & coke, Kool Filter Kings, all kinda bars (cordner and jailhouse), the Nightcap Lounge, the Dew Drop, the Cozy Corner, Prout's, the Green "O" Liquor Store, swaggin' on berled strimps and crabs, joints, go-cups, scars, scams, schemes, secret stitches, sewin', cursin', stealin', robbin', shuckin' and jivin', doin' the Alligator, tellin' Injun' stories, smoke, drums, calumets (peace pipes), shanks, stocking caps, doo rags, day-old doughnuts (from McKenzie's on St. Bernard and Galvez—right 'cross the street from Corpus Christi Church), Ray Charles, jailhouse slippers, gold teeth, Hush Puppies, fistfights, dope, hypodermic syringes, and a plethora of injection site reactions (tracks). He was indeed a character, one of those social incorrigibles that St. Aug didn't want goin' there—or anywhere near there.

In spite of that, in spite of his sins, assorted mayhem, and too-numerous-to-mention criminal offenses, there was a light that shone in him. Three or four Mardi Gras seasons after the shoo-shooin' sewin' session I talked about a li'l earlier . . . about three or four Carnival seasons after that I was allowed to enter Brickhead Red's inner circle of joyous, festive sew-ers and reapers as they set about finishing their Injun costumes for Carnival Day which was less than a week away.

It was that time of year when all they did was sew, sew, sew in their annual effort to "mask Injun." Most of 'em carried the flambeau flame and picked up that li'l change in the night parades befo' Mardi Gras Day, but their main delectation and delight was to dance and prance in the flashing, regal, brilliant plumage of their radiantly-colored Injun costumes on the day of days that was the culmination of the Mardi Gras season, that wild, unbridled day of fun, frolic, and festivity.

Red always said he liked to sew by oil lamplight or candlelight (he probably had to inasmuch as the bill wasn't paid). That night, as I sat in my Hopalong Cassidy sweatshirt, black ten-gallon hat, and two-gun holster while perusing my cousin's needle & thread handiwork, his band of cutthroat (and sometimes comical) characters and creatures from the Sixth Ward Lagoon were solemnly sewing their colorful Injun costumes ("suits") along with him.

It was around the time right befo' Mardi Gras Day when Red had busted my cousin in the pool hall over on Claiborne Street (it's a church now) when he was supposed to be at the football game and Red didn't even tell his momma and daddy on him. On the pool table Red himself was a master of the three-cushion shot and an eight-ballin' ace his self, but his main racket in life was sewing the splendorous, colorful costumes with great virtuosity and veneration on those holy days of obligation right befo' Mardi Gras Day.

Every year, 'specially 'round Carnival time, all Red would do was *sew, sew, sew*. It was a solemn and (sometimes) hallowed event. Every year he and his tribal comrades in flash and feathers would sew a new suit as a means of outshining other Injun tribes and as a way of honoring seemingly ancient traditions. Every year at Carnival time he made a new suit, as did his father befo' him, his father befo' *him*, and his father befo' *him* as far back as anyone living could remember. If he was a character, then his fellow tribesmen comprised a cast of characters who probably embodied the most notorious sewing conclave in the history of the craft. His sewing circle consisted of Sixth Ward Lagooners such as Snake, Darkhorse, Turtle, Bulletproof (who had mo' holes in him than a strainer fulla water), and Blood & Wine. Everybody had a nickname. Everybody wanted to git into the act. A *States-Item*-covered white enamel slopjar sat in the cordner near the rickety door as the wind howled wildly, wickedly, outside. It was so cold that Mardi Gras season that you could take a leak and lean on it.

The light of a green kerosene lamp and several strategically-placed candles danced hellishly off the room's bare walls, illuminating the work of the men as they stitched their secret stitches, each and every one unique to its task. My cousin sat workin' on his headdress at a table with a white sheet thrown over it, a shoebox top fulla herb, some wine bottles, and Blackie, his old cayoodle, sleepin' at his green Army Surplus Store tennis shoe-clad feet (my cousin from over by the London Canal called 'em "sneakers"). He was raggin' in a purple Banlon shirt, brown iridescent tailor-made pants, a near-toothless grin (with one shiny gold tooth complete with diamond star) and his (usually) obligatory stocking cap and pumpadoo hair slickened down by Murray's Hair Pomade. They always said his long platts made him look like a *real* Injun. Six tattooed teardrops hung menacingly on his cheek just under his left eye. A big brown New Orleans roach took its good sweet time scurrying back and forth 'cross the table in the room's lusterless light.

He was busily, sensitively, gracefully sewing, his "LOVE - HATE" tattooed knuckles caked with tiny beads of sweat, a cigarette wedged behind his ear as he delicately concocted the elaborately-colored suit that he would proudly don on Mardi Gras Day—that day of mirth and merriment on which they would all be transformed into dazzling, shaking, swirling, whirling, stuff-strutting, befeathered, bejeweled, orange-purple-green-gold-yellow-blue-red, sartorially resplendent peacocks of all that is, was, and would be their pain, passion, and pleasure.

Snake was standin' behind a chair in immaculately-pressed jeans givin' Darkhorse a linin' (that boy always liked to keep his hair nice) with his dirty, dexterous hands while Turtle, Bulletproof, and Blood & Wine busied themselves with the demands of their craft and tellin' Injun stories.

They say Darkhorse's claim to fame was that he held the world record for the longest version of *Shoo-Fly—Don't Bother Me*. Blood & Wine was makin' a Bone Man outfit with a goo-gob o' dried turkey bones and a big hambone. Every year Blood & Wine was a Bone Man. He used to always go 'round scarin' every li'l child in the Sixth Ward singin' "Ashes to ashes, dust to dust—You best straighten yo' life or you gon' see *us*...." (That was when them kinda cats used to tell the children in the neighborhood to stay in school and don't end up like them.)

Bulletproof and Turtle were workin' on something the likes of which I'd never seen befo'. All I remember was that there was a lotta sequins, rhinestones, and stitches so teenantsy you'd think that a newborn baby roach made 'em.

Snake, who was the Wild Man one Mardi Gras and worked for years as an oyster shucker at H & K Oyster House (over on Claiborne and Dumaine), was widely known as the most adept bladesman in the Sixth Ward with a straight razor or a beechwood oyster-shuckin' knife. They say he learnt how to do hair from the legendary Joe

Mitch the Barber over in the Seventh Ward and how to shuck oysters from his daddy.

"Bruh—my haid *still* hurtin' me! I got hit by a truck the other day on Er-leens Street!" Snake said, standin' in a white sweatshirt and anklewhipper, high water pants, his thin fingers skillfully handling the straight razor at the base of Darkhorse's neck, a wicked smile pasted to his lips displaying a grill of cigarette-stained gold teeth. "The nurse tell me: 'It *oughta* hurt! You done got shot in the haid!' But I told her I *ain't* got shot in the haid! I got cut and hit by a truck on Er-leens!. . . I been broke up and messed up 'most all over my body! I done just had chemicals in both my eyes from tombstone cleaner. They operated on me and was talkin' 'bout they wanted to spearmint on me and gimme some kinda corny transplant. . . .

"I'm leavin' from over there by my momma and 'em house . . . I gits to Er-leens and Prieur, gits cut, gits hit by a truck on Er-leens and Johnson—that plate in my haid saved me—and gits picked up by the po-leece on Er-leens and Galvez! I had a syringe in my sock, cocaine in my system, and a unopened halfa G o' wine! All I heard was ZOOM!!! And had blood all over my shirt! Next thing I know I wake up in Parish Prison! I gits there and *they* tell me I didn't git cut—I done got *shot*! You cain't win for losin'!"

"Here he go. Now he gon' start talkin' 'bout his paw! That boy was the worst cellmate I ever had," mumbled Blood & Wine as he stitched away.

"My paw had a 'scorched ass' policy," began Snake as he deftly used the scissors in the candles' odd glow between swigs out of a paper cup fulla wine. "He didn't take NO prisoners. My paw' favorite tune was *I Gits A Kick Outa You*, his favorite drink was punch, and his favorite 'musement park was *Punch*atrain Beach – even tho' we couldn't go there. His favorite game was 'Truth or Consequences.' If you didn't tell the truth—you paid the consequences." *Laughter.*

"My paw used to talk to me in Morse code," he said, shadow-punching the air, "DOT-DOT-DOT-DASH. . . DOT-DOT-DOT-DASH. . .. My paw even had pet names for his punches—the Backhand Slap, the Delaware Punch, the Hatchetchop Killer, the Nut Buster, the Ass Buster, the Punches Pilot, and the Stay-Still-While-I-Kill-You-Son." *Swig. Laughter.*

"One time I asked him about my rights as a chile. 'Rights?' he said. 'I'll give you some rights—and some lefts, too!' Yeah, he was mean. He whipped my ass every day—*every day*! When I was bornded and my momma was layin' up in the hawspital holdin' me in her arms he came in, looked at me, and hollered, 'Wow! Thanks, Bessie Mae!—A new punchin' bag!'" *Swig. More laughter.*

"I ain't had no 'daddy'! I had a '*paw*'! The difference between a 'daddy' and a 'paw' is that a daddy build *mens* and a paw kill *boys*! My paw whipped my ass one day—said BAM! 'That's for what you did last week!' Then BAM! 'That's for what you did yesterday!' BAM! 'That's for what you did today!' and BAM! BAM! 'What's them for, daddy?' I asked him. 'That's for what you *gon*' do tomorrow!'" *Swig. Boo-coo laughter.*

Suffice it to say that all Snake's father ever gave him was a daily asswhippin', an empty safe deposit box (when he died), and a proclivity for alcoholism

There was a knock at the door. "Who dat?" queried my cousin. "Who dat?" he shouted again. "Who dat bammin' on the do' like dat?" Gittin' no response, he arose from his tenuous task, went to the door, opened it a teenantsy bit, and peeked through. It was Yum-Yum, wunna them nighttime broads, wunna them nocturnal, painted birds of easy virtue from offa Claiborne Street.

"Hey, baby! Where y'at?!?" said Darkhorse, lookin' up from his chair. Silence. "You can say 'hello.' I ain't gon' eat you," he ignified.

"Well maybe I shouldn't say 'hello,'" the soiled dove of the night cooed.

"Look, bruh, we up in here sewin—and *that* got to go back where it came from," Red said, indicating the woman in the crack of the door. "Plus—all that cold air gittin' in here. . . . She cain't be comin' in here, anyway. We sewin'! She cain't be up in here! I don't want nobody—'specially her—to see our colors and my stitches!"

"*Yeah* ya-right!" said Bulletproof.

"*Sho'* ya-right!" affirmed Blood & Wine.

"I know *that's* right!" assented both Turtle and Darkhorse.

"Bu-u-u-u-u-ull*shit*!" objected Snake defiantly, the straight razor poised menacingly in his rail-thin hand. "All the broad wan' do is come in and cop!"

"The bitch cain't come in! We sewin'!" shouted Red. "She can be Eleanor Roo-ze-velt! She can own the whole Roo-ze-velt Hotel—

but the bitch ain't comin' up in *here!*" yelled Red, still blockin' the partially open door.

Blackie stirred uneasily, got up, and quietly sauntered to the backa the house as though she knew what was comin'. "The bitch cain't come in," Red repeated. "She ain't comin' in here and bogardin' *nuthin'*. That's just my personal idiotsyncrasy. No bitches in here while we sewin'!" he barked as he loomed forward, leanin' on the door.

"I ain't no bitch! I'm a hoe!" the hoe protested in her state-of-the-profession, tartish git-up.

"I can smell *that*," murmured Darkhorse, lookin' up momentarily. Laughter.

"I'm tellin' all y'all studs—I ain't *sellin'* no dope tonight," Red explained. "I'm *sewin'*. We sewin'. Y'all know what we gotta do. The Chief ain't gon' like it if we ain't ready Tuesday moanin'. The bitch—" he started.

"Why she gotta be a 'bitch'?" Snake challenged. "I know that broad. That's Yum-Yum. She from Backatown. I know her people," he said. "I feel to believe you bein' too hard on the hoe—callin' her a bitch and all, bruh."

"She a 'bitch' 'cause them hoes is always bitchin'—bitchin', bitchin, bitchin'! Bitchin' 'bout *this*, bitchin' 'bout *that* – bitchin' 'bout my stitchin', bitchin' 'bout my kitchen—bitchin', bitchin', bitchin'! Then the first thing they wan' do when they gits 'em a *real* man—they wants to make *him* a bitch! Ain't *that* a bitch?!?"

"The bitch ain't comin' in here—not for all the vagina in China. Let the bitch stay out there on the hoe stroll—the bitch!" For a moment there was silence. One could almost hear the ships rollin' on the river, for when Brickhead Red talked, *everybody* listened. Then—

"*I know who actin' like the bitch*," mumbled Snake. Stillness. Silence. No one in history or farflung memory had ever signified, ignified, nignified, intimated, or outright stated that Brickhead Red was a "bitch"—and lived. The six teardrops under his eye attested to that.

"Say *what?*" asked Red, slammin' the door and walkin' over towards Snake as he backed away from trimmin' Darkhorse's hair. Red tensed, swept me out of his path with a gentle hand, and approached Snake.

"Bruh—I'ma 'bout to put so mucha you on the flo'—they gon' think it's the blood bank up in here," he said as he reached in his sock for his favorite (ergonomically-designed) shank. "I'ma cut the black off yo' ass!" he threatened. Me, Darkhorse, Turtle, Bulletproof, and Blood & Wine froze forthwith. We knew what was comin' next. "*Mawfiddice*"—he began, "You let a li'l gum-smackin' skankawank piece o' trim git us off what we supposed to be doin'—all 'cuz you smellin'up on a li'l twat—wan' git up in a li'l piece o' crack—a li'l poonanny—when you knows what we gotta be 'bout doin'. . . *Mawfiddice!*" he repeated. In the world's whole wide creation he wasn't gon' bow down, not Red.

"Who?" Snake asked provocatively. "Mawfiddice? Who? Who?"

"'Who?'" mimicked Red. "'Who?' You got feathers in yo' ass?"

"Huh?"

"—Feathers in yo' ass! Is you a owl?—'Who? Who'?" Red signified. Muted laughter. Nobody wanted to git into the act. No one wanted their static to cling.

"Say, bruh—" protested Snake.

"Look here, stud—I'm 'bout to put my foot in yo' stinky, black, alcoholic ass—I'm 'bout to put a big piece o' 13 Triple E foot dead up yo' prison wallet," Red threatened, displaying his weapon of choice. I felt like I was in a Shane movie as I peeked over the shoebox top fulla herb by the album cover, the half-empty wine bottles, and the paper cups atop the white-sheeted table.

"Don't be draggin' on me! I ain't no alcoholic," Snake protested. "I'ma dope fiend!" he nignified. "I'm sorry, bruh—I don't have the itch to fear man, woman, child, ghost, beast—or bitch . . . so if you feel like a frog—*jump*! You ain't puttin' *me* on no tip!" he undereyed as he brandished the straight razor in his long, killer fingers. "I'ma shave up that red haid o' yo's!"

"I ain't no erster you gon' be shuckin'," menaced Red, steppin' closer.

"Look, bruh—" Darkhorse cautiously chimed in at that crucial moment. "I know this yo' house, Red—and I ain't disrespectin' that," he said, slowly movin' aside. "But we gon' have a *real* problem if y'all start humbuggin' in here and mess up all we done done so far. Why don't y'all go on 'haid and settle this outa range where the blood don't spill all over the material. We done put a lotta time in this," he offered.

"If you cain't git along—git it on," instigated Bulletproof.

My cousin thought a second, looked over at me, and ordered me to git a large bandana from the chiffarobe in the next room, which I dutifully did. "Y'all gon' settle this right—Injun style," said Bulletproof.

Red and Snake agreed. I followed them as they went to the neutral ground (that island of grass, banana trees, palm trees, and other native flora in the middle of the two-way thoroughfare) on Er-leens across from the Lafitte where Bulletproof tied their left hands together. It was on. They sweated, bled, cursed, cut, and slashed each other (with extreme dispatch) like it was goin' outa style. There was a whole lotta hoopin' and hollerin' during the butchery and bloodletting of the profane, protracted, running orgy of stickin', slicin' and stabbin'. You wouldn't think that much blood could come from a human being' body! They fought all the way down Er-leens, leavin' a lake o' blood all up from Dooky's down to Prieur Street where they say the paradegoers had tore up the float for souvenirs back in 1949 when Louis Armstrong was the King of the Zulus. They was knife-fightin' out there 'til 'fore day in the moanin'—right there in the middle of the neutral ground with people all crowded around like it was Mardi Gras Day on Claiborne and Er-leens. My uncle said they *both* was stupid and shoulda sold tickets insteada fightin' for nuthin'. Eventually, the po-leece (who cared little about the spectacle of two natives cuttin' up each other in the middle' o' the street) finally arrived in a coupla prowl cars, dashboard lights flashin', si-reens blastin' through the droves of people, and whisked 'em away off to Charity where they patched 'em up, then brought 'em *both* to jail. I don't know if they took 'em to the Pink Palace in the First District or to Tulane and Broad, but I *do* know they went to jail. I didn't see my cousin again 'til I came home one summer from college.

I'm not gon' be the judge of his deeds and dastardly decisions. That's not my role as a man. All I know is just befo' every Mardi Gras I think about those remarkable spirits and souls I grew up around who protected, nurtured, cradled, comforted, and counseled me in my life's infancy and youth.

Every year I remember them and pay them homage—their often undearly departed souls; their joy, pain, sunshine, and rain; their long-suffering fears and tears; their moments of loving, madness, and mirth; their humanity and insanity; their jocularity and imagination; the humility of their prayers and the futility of their struggles; their yesterday hugs and kisses; their deferred dreams; their blessings and bereavement in sadness and sorrow; their sewing and reaping; their laughter and weeping; their fashion and passion; their halo of protection and affection unbound by the restraints of time.

And every year around Mardi Gras, around Carnival time, all I do is sew, sew, sew.

Background and Center, Sewing for Our Culture: Words from Herreast Harrison, Interview with Cynthia Topsey-Ellis

In the following narrative edited from a March 2007 interview, Herreast Harrison, a fifth-generation quilter with a background in Museum Studies, speaks informally of the incorporation of art from different cultures, beading both for traditional women's gowns and for suits worn by Mardi Gras Indians

Herreast Harrison:

I was born in 1937 in a town in Louisiana called Lecompte. I stayed there till I was about seven. I was young when we moved here to the New Orleans area. My mother and I moved to Metairie with an older sister. Then, later, we lived in another house in the metropolitan area.

You ask how I learned to sew. My mother was a seamstress. My grandmother also sewed. My great-grandmother, my grandmother, and my mother were quilt makers. That's what they did in their spare time and leisure time. And as a child, too young to actually sew, you were the go-fetch person. You picked up the scissors or if a thread dropped you picked it up. Or you had to sit and put all the patterns together for them. The women would sit around the table and sew. You were too young to sew so you had to do other things.

If they were making a beautiful quilt and it had a lot of different patterns in it, well, you know, you would stack them. And then someone might say, "I need a green triangle." I would run around there and get a green triangle. So it was that introduction for me into sewing.

My mother made most of our clothes. When I became a teenager, I made my clothes. In high school, we had the proms. So I always made my own gowns and Mother helped and then sometimes she would make gowns for the other girls. People didn't have a lot of money, and I will never forget a girl—I was very, very friendly with— didn't have money to get a gown. So I worked at a drugstore as a counter girl or whatever, and I bought the material for her gown and my mother sewed it. We made her graduation dress, too. She looked so beautiful. She was so happy in that dress. Mother, she would fit the dress to the body. That is the way you do a good job.

There were always fabric stores. And then you would have the Jewish people that would go around in automobiles, you know, in the Forties and sell fabric too. But there was Dryades Street, which is now Oretha Castle Haley, where they had lots of fabric stores where you could go into and purchase material. I think there was a store, Kaufman's, that I remember as a child.[1] I had that background.

Next I used to see the Hollywood stars come on television and they often had little beaded tops. So I started beading, beading gowns for people that went to balls. People who liked to involve themselves in nightlife, they would see the top, someone else's top, and then they would contact me.

I got all my customers by word-of-mouth. One was Leah Chase, the singer. I beaded a top for Leah when she was a young girl. I beaded two for a woman whose husband owned a nightclub at Galvez and Washington Avenue. It was called Charlie's Corner. My husband's niece, Gilda, I remember beading an *entire gown* for her, not, not just the top, the entire gown. And I remember another gown I made for a woman who used to help me with my children. I don't think she had enough money to do it or something but I liked her a lot because she used to babysit for me whenever I had to go someplace. So she wanted this gown. So I was going to make it for her. The crystals were very expensive, and Greenberg's was the place where they bought a lot of stuff. So I went there. I must have purchased $500 worth of crystals and beads. I would extend them to make a chain of beads and then the crystal was at the end of it. And so when she walked, by the crystal having the weight, the beadings would all shift. It would shift, and she said she was just a hit.

I did a lot of beading. All this I did, and later, when my husband who turned out to be interested in masking and the Mardi Gras

[1] Segregation ruled that African Americans could shop in many stores but were prevented from using the fitting rooms. The Jewish merchants on Dryades Streets, as well as the Jewish-owned Krauss on Canal Street, were possibly among the first to change these policies, as noted in the essay here, *Decorative Cloth*. See Civil Rights Movement Veterans, Timeline: "Sit-Ins Background & Context," http://www.crmvet.org/tim/timhis60.htm# 1960nosmb, accessed September 6, 2015

Indians, that *beading knowledge* came in handy. It was *a different kind of beading* but the transitioning to what he needed went easier because I had knowledge.

When I married my husband, Donald Harrison, Sr., I had no idea of this culture of the Indians. There was actually a man that masked as a Mardi Gras Indian who lived around the corner near where I lived as a young woman, on Shrewsbury Road. But we didn't pay any attention to him because we just didn't know much about the phenomenon. I knew the whole of the Harrison family, and they too, especially his parents really didn't care very much for masking, especially his father. His father was a Mason and he had other traditions that involved processions, that involved Carnival. To him, Mardi Gras Indians were violent. He never wanted any of his children to mask, I understand. Also, I don't think his mother was into the traditional culture of New Orleans as it is practiced here very much at all, like the second line or things like that. I think she would watch it but it wasn't anything that she participated in.

There was less emphasis on sewing then. It was different then, the masking. From pictures that I've seen of the fifties, they were not as elaborate. Going back, looking at pictures from earlier times and listening to the men talk about how the suits were constructed during that period of time, we can see how it has evolved from then to now.

So, the creative part was not part of what my husband's parents saw. On the other hand, my husband's mother did have a brother who masked. Joseph King. And later on, several of her children were quite involved with those traditions. She has a son Edwin who's quite involved in the second line tradition. Edwin Harrison. He owns Sunset Cab Company and he is quite involved, quite active with Tambourine and Fan.

My husband, too, always loved Carnival. He was in the service for eight years, stationed in Buffalo but as I understand from the years before I actually knew him, even when he was there, far away, he would come back to New Orleans for Mardi Gras and he would mask.

He was a mapmaker. That was the Korean conflict but he didn't go to the front. He made maps of gun targets and everything. He did that the whole war.

When he came out, you know that was when I met him and that was the end of that tour of duty. At first, he wasn't involved directly in Carnival. He was one of those people that left the tradition as far as *masking* every year for twenty years. We had to send our children to school. I sat down with him, and I had a talk because that's an expensive enterprise.

I was sewing in other areas then. I always worked at the dining room table or the kitchen table. You put the pieces someplace or, you know, you had a place where you stored them, so when you got ready to sew you could. It was always leisure time. After dinner you're sitting around, you know, you pick up, you know, your piece and you sew.

Eventually, my husband began to mask again. My earliest recollection was when I helped him construct the apron for a suit. Now mind you, they don't call them costumes. A costume is something that you put on to pretend that you are something else. This is more involved than that. It is a way of life. It's a philosophy. It entails multi-layers of things. So it is not, it is not, a costume. They don't put that on and pretend they are anything. They are not pretending that they are Native Americans. They are giving tribute to Native Americans for helping our ancestors when they decided that slavery was something that they could not handle, that they wanted no part of someone enslaving them. The men who ran away and sought refuge with native people or indigenous people, were given that help. They were taken in. I understand they even intermarried. They were shown a way of life along the bayous and rivers and were shown how to live in this climate and in this environment. So this is what these men are doing, they are honoring that help. The two groups, the Africans and the Native Americans, they had a lot things in common and this honors that common thread. They worshipped nature. They did not take more from the land than was necessary. They did not misuse the land and things like that.

True, you'll find some practitioners who will use the words "costumes" and "suits" interchangeably because they know that whomever they are speaking to may understand better if they say "a costume." But practitioners in their hearts, they are not going to say "a costume." They are only saying that so you will understand what

Figure 6.3. Big Chief Donald Harrison, Sr. (1933-1998) of the Guardians of the Flame; Suit designed and created by Donald Harrison, Sr. and Herreast J. Harrison; Photograph, 1992, by Herreast J. Harrison. Courtesy of Herreast J. Harrison and Cherice Harrison-Nelson.

Herreast Harrison did all hand and machine stitching to assemble pieces beaded by her husband, Big Chief Donald Harrison.

they are talking about. They call them suits. It is almost like a second skin, another skin to be who I am and what I am. *It's me.*

The construction of the suits for me tells a story. They start with the apron, and whatever beaded image is a narrative of whatever story they are trying to convey. And a lot times, people do not really look at the intricacies of the beaded image. Since it carries a theme, they see the big picture. It's saying something.

To make this, you bead the image on the canvas. Then there are spaces around that image and so they used to scale it. They call it "scaling" because it is done with sequins and it is like a fish scale.

I understand, in the early years, like when they first began, they used to actually use fish scales. So the term came from that: "scaling." They scale with sequins and with a bead on top. And that's what he did when I first met him and when I would be given that task. But he always beaded his patch, his piece, which would be a large piece. He would do it.

One suit I helped with, one of the first, had wings. I don't know if that was the first time someone wore wings but my husband introduced them, I think. And he had the wings on and he had aurora borealis crystals, drop crystals on those wings. My friend, the one I made the elaborate gown for, saw it, and that is how I came to make her dress, so it goes that way too: the beading for gowns to the suits, the suits to the beading for gowns.

He would tell you what he wanted. How he wanted it done because the men design their own suits. Sometimes they may be two years ahead. Because, for instance, my husband was projecting even if he was wearing a suit one year, he would be talking about what he was going to wear next year or the following year. "I want to have this theme," he would say. One of the suits that he was planning was going to be along the art technique of Picasso.

You see? And the last suit that he designed and wore was on the techniques of Salvador Dali, the surrealist. His figures were contorted. It was a trail of tears to show the injustice of that trek.

In the early years of the Mardi Gras Indians, the museums were not really interested. They did not value what these men were doing, which to me was very unfortunate, which leads into why I took courses in Museum Studies and earned a degree. My experiences

Figure 6.4. Herreast Harrison sewing mask, 1992. Photograph by Al Kennedy. Courtesy of Al Kennedy, Herreast J. Harrison, and Cherice Harrison-Nelson.

sewing and beading and especially work with the Mardi Gras Indians definitely led to that.

The first time that I knew of any suits being shown even here in the city, I think, was in 1964 and that may have been through the efforts of [civil rights activist] Jerome Smith. I really don't know how it came about but I did hear something recently that he was involved in it. I have the newspaper article where they talked about it. It was a tiny little article in the *Times-Picayune*. These suits were shown in the library and the article mentioned that exhibition. I remember the library right at Loyola and Tulane Avenues [New Orleans Public Library Main Branch], how the suits were displayed in those windows at the top. Then after that exhibit, they had something that came on Channel 4.

Now Mr. [Allison "Tootie"] Montana, one of his suits was bought by a museum, early on. I think it was a red suit. He probably is better known for the suit construction than all the others even though he did not stick to the traditional construction. He went to a different, completely different type of suit construction. His construction evolved into three dimensions. His is the Downtown style. Uptown is the style that has a narrative. It tells a story. It's flat. It's like paint on canvas. Either way, it is work and work and work to make. You had a whole year to do it so if you were working on an apron, you'd devote so much time. You finish that. You do the crown band. That's the stone work mostly. People like my son, if you look at his, he has some beaded portions to his, in addition to the stones.

You have to put it together. It has to be constructed. You do the different parts. You do the cuffs. You do the crown band. You do the apron, you know, you do the front of your shoes and just all different portions of it.

My daughter said that my husband always said that women were mere embellishments in the tradition. They were just there to make the Chief look prettier. They just walk alongside them. But I am quite sure they play other roles and especially now. They usually match the Chief. Most wives get involved in sewing and construction of the suits, always did. Now they do more.

Especially when you mask as an Uptown Indian. That style is more expensive than any style. This is controversial. People will get angry with me for saying it. But it's true. They use rhinestones. Rhinestones are expensive. My husband used to use aurora borealis. Those stones are expensive. You heard me talk about the teardrop crystals, aurora borealis: they're expensive. They also used plumes: they're expensive. They used boards. If you look at my son's headdress you'll see all types of fur; you'll see all manner of feathers on there. On that one, there's mink on there. There's all kinds of different types of fur. All that, all that's a lot of money and time.

But all work, especially all creative work, yields positives. There are positives surely and so when my husband wanted to participate again, and the children were older, I said, "Fine." It is a tradition, it is handed down just like they were in a university learning art. After they are taught the basics, then the person uses their own creativity, their own experiences, and their own ideas about creating something. It is supposed to change. It is supposed to evolve. I am always teaching about this history, this evolution. I do that with schools. My husband started initially going into the schools because he said he wanted to tell the young children about something they didn't know about. You see people, a lot of people who see it, even participate, stand on the side, they really need to know why. Why do these people continue to do this? Why do they get in the street and second line?

The answer is that they are freeing themselves through creative activity.

I have always known that but it is made clear to me not only when I see what happens to those learning to bead but also when I see other people recognize the value of creative work. For example, there was a woman who did a photography exhibition. She included a picture of my grandson wearing one of his Mardi Gras Indian suits. One of her labels said "Free" or "Freeing yourself in America" or "Freeing self in America."

I saw: "She got it." Because for an African American man, I don't care what heights he excels, he's really never free.

Now with the Mardi Gras Indians, also importantly, it is what they retained. Because if they had not started this tradition, then all of those African connections would have been lost. Because it was told to them as a people that you have to be assimilated no matter what. They retained this connection, underneath.

There's a book called *Hidden in Plain View* about quilting. The tradition and work of masking is like what is described by that title. Meaning could be presented and remain secret. Masking today is a way of life that has meaning, that persists in having meaning, that concerns those things denied that nevertheless remained and evolved as powerful statements about identity.

Figure 6.5. Herreast Harrison, seated in the middle, sewing with Dariel Thompson (right), Flag Girl with Young Guardians of the Flame, and Dana Roy (standing), parent of the Little Chief Kevin. 2009, Colton School Artist Studio. Photograph by Cara Harrison Daniels. Courtesy of Cara Harrison Daniels, Herreast J. Harrison, and Cherice Harrison-Nelson.

NEEDLES & THREAD/HAMMER & NAILS

George Koschel

Robert and Bill, two gay men who sew, are from the same generation. Bill is fifty and Robert is forty-eight. Tall and thin, Robert keeps his receding hair closely cropped. Barrel-chested, Bill has the body of a heavyweight boxer.

Robert grew up in the Midwest. At age ten he tried his hand at needlework. Later he made a caftan from two pieces of muslin which he sewed together. After he finished, he painted a picture of Bette Midler on the front of it.

His mother showed him the basics: how to read a pattern and how to use her sewing machine by spreading the material and moving it through the pressure foot. Asked if his brothers or father gave him a hard time, he said, "They knew I was a 'queer little boy.'"

Bill, a native New Orleanian, inherited his sewing expertise from his mother who made all her own clothes. She also worked as a seamstress on Carnival krewes for Momus, Athenians, and the Mardi Gras Ball in Washington, DC. Bill began sewing out of necessity. At age thirteen he wanted to wear a new pair of pants but couldn't because the hem needed fixing. His mother was too busy to help. He fixed the hem. In this case necessity was the catalyst that began his experience with needle and thread. Bill's family did not think it odd that he was able to use his mother's sewing machine.

At that point Robert and Bill's lives took divergent paths. In high school Robert knew who he was and went to the gay bars in his local town despite the bullying he endured from other students. In high school Bill dated girls. At age twenty-three, although "very naïve," he married. He questioned his sexuality before his wedding and tried to postpone it. Friends and his fiancée convinced him that his cold feet were just a "normal" reaction.

Seven years into the marriage and two children later, Bill was "not happy with myself and I knew I could not make a wife and children happy if I could not make me happy." A year later the marriage ended. His children, a son and a daughter, were four and seven respectively.

Bill did not explicitly come out with his children but was open about his first relationship with another man. They spent every other weekend with Bill and his lover and went with them on vacations. Bill says that his children were smart enough to know that he and his partner at that time were "family." Still he and his partner were discreet about physical affection in front of them.

He credits his children's acceptance of him to his wife who was supportive. He knows his wife had discussions about his sexuality, especially after the children had religious assignments from the Catholic Church that condemned homosexuality. Bill says, "I feel that her non-condemnation of my lifestyle was beneficial to my children and to our relationship."

Bill's wife could not sew. Thus, Bill made his children nightshirts as well as curtains, pillows, and a comforter. He was excited when his daughter asked him to make her a sweet sixteen dress. He knew that if he had any problems he could ask his mother for help. Bill made his daughter's Christmas formal after they initially joked about the expense it would entail to get someone to make it. Once again necessity was the mother of invention.

Bill says his daughter is "sentimental." Because of that and the success of the other two formals he made, she asked him to make her wedding dress. He was "very happy." He also hoped the wedding dress might be passed down to a future granddaughter. Bill is sentimental too.

Fear quelled the "excitement" of making the wedding dress. His mother had died and if he encountered any major problems, he had no one to help him. However, optimism reigned. He made what he calls his "test dress." He took a basic pattern from a sleeveless "A" line dress and incorporated it into a different pattern on top of one that had a sweetheart neckline with straps. The bride-to-be also wanted an additional panel on the front that gathered under the bust line. The panel is the same length as the dress on one side so there are just gathers on the right side of the dress. She has tried on the test dress. It fits, and now he says, "I'm much more confident."

Robert graduated from high school and migrated south to live in the warmer climes of Houston and New Orleans. In 1998, the hotel where he worked let him go. He lived in the Quarter and discovered the fabric department at Krauss. Of Krauss, Robert says, "They always had the neatest fabrics every week and you never knew what you would find." Robert's experience with Krauss was not unique. It holds a fond memory in the hearts of many gay men who did drag on a regular or occasional basis.[1]

At Bookstar he discovered the magazine *Burda* that had a new pattern every month. Either through the use of needle and thread or hot glue, Robert estimates he has created between twenty and twenty-five costumes. A black cotton jacket with lining and a pair of dress pants fashioned after a Calvin Klein design in *Vogue* are the two things he is proudest of making. Right now Robert is learning how to make quilt blocks.

Thinking in stereotypical terms most people would think it appropriate that Robert and Bill both possessed a deft hand in the art, or craft, of sewing. What at first glance would seem a bit more idiosyncratic is that both Robert and Bill are comfortable constructing things.

As a child, Robert built a few model boats and airplanes. The first thing he remembered constructing was a model of Godzilla or Godzilla-like monster. In junior high school, Robert studied shop. As an adult Robert helped remodel the other side of his house, the construction project of which he is proudest. He has also helped friends with small construction tasks.

As a child Bill frequently put together model cars. In addition, he enjoyed constructing and decorating kites. When he was a Cub Scout, he built a birdhouse.

In his first house Bill installed a fireplace by tearing out a wall and cutting a hole in the roof. With his father's guidance he was able to do the electrical work that the remodeling entailed. Every time Bill purchased a new house he says his mother would always ask, "What wall will you knock out first?"

He is proudest of the fireplace he first constructed. "It was a great learning experience," he says. "For example, always use gloves when working with bricks and mortar." By the time he had finished

[1] See essays in this volume by Tucker, Pfister, Pierce, and oral history of Nguyet Vu.

making his first fireplace the lime in the mortar had eaten away at his fingernails.

A great deal of similarity exists between sewing and building. With sewing, the seamstress or tailor uses a pattern. With construction, the carpenter uses a blueprint. The only differences are the tools of the trade and the material to which they are applied. In both crafts the tailor and carpenter can always ditch the blueprint or pattern and fly by the seat of their pants.

Girl on a Bridge

Marda Burton

Although the New Orleans French Quarter captured me for its own some twenty-five years ago, I grew up, married, and reared four children in Laurel, Mississippi, named for the bushes that once grew in profusion in the surrounding virgin pine forests. The bushes were disposed of because their gorgeous blossoms poisoned cows, which were the major source of income along with timber. There, I lived with my grandparents and my widowed mother, Grace, who worked as a secretary for a local oil company.

In those days, many of the ladies in Laurel did fine sewing by hand. My family was part of that tradition. They crocheted, knitted, hooked rugs, and embroidered; things they created with their hands and hearts are treasured heirlooms, although they themselves have gone on. Their various sewing projects lingered around in sewing baskets waiting to be taken up in spare moments.

The ladies of the town also painted and played piano; lessons in both were pressed upon me at a young age. But the genteel skills of sewing were customarily passed down from the elders to the young girls of the family, and the Eubanks and Thaxton clans were no different. Sewing was considered a fine art. Buying items that could be handmade was not popular—for reasons both aesthetic and monetary. Consequently for years much of my wardrobe was made by my grandmother, "Mama," who kept up with the latest styles. She used an old Singer foot-treadle sewing machine, which was off limits to me until I was a responsible teen. Mama also hooked rugs of her own design. My busy mother spent some of her free time embroidering and painting, and later added to her skills exquisite decoupage boxes which were duly exhibited by the local Lauren Rogers Art Museum.

My dolls also had extensive wardrobes. Scarlett O'Hara's clothes were carefully sewn by Mama to replicate the gowns in the movie—hoopskirts and all. Scarlett had an especially large selection of dresses, including the green velvet "curtain" outfit. I also had a beautiful

Madame Alexander doll I named Melanie, and Mama determined that she, too, should be dressed appropriate to her character.

At a very early age, I've forgotten precisely when, I was taught to embroider. When Cousin Grady brought a linen sampler back from Japan after World War II, my mother decided it should be saved for me to work on when I grew old enough to use a needle. The minute I saw the scene—a little Japanese girl in a kimono holding a parasol, standing on a bridge overlooking cherry trees in blossom—I began dreaming of someday traveling to Japan and other fascinating countries when I grew up.

In the meantime, I embroidered the sampler for what seemed like months. At first I found difficulty with the tiny stitches my mother insisted I make. As I grumpily pulled out and re-embroidered stitch after stitch, I finally finished it after many pricked fingertips, and not a little boredom. But I had also learned firsthand one of Grace Thaxton Kaiser's primary rules for living: "If you are going to do something at all, do it right."

Mother and Mama were busy too. They crocheted lace and embroidered the borders of luxurious Egyptian cotton sheets and pillowcases that they placed in my "hope chest," another custom of the day. The "hope" that eventually showed up—Lt. Richard Burton, my very own pilot back from the Korean War—seemed happy with my handmade trousseau. He especially liked the "rehearsal dinner" gown: a strapless cloud of flowered chiffon with a matching scarf to trail behind. An ivory satin gown was the "borrowed" part of the ceremony—from Cousin Betty, my Maid of Honor. Her father, my uncle Paul, financed my handmade trousseau and gave me away.

Marriage brought me terrific gifts from my husband, who generously enabled my long travel-journalist "dream" career headquartered in the French Quarter and also four fabulous boys, Terminex, and my own Singer Sewing Machine. Whereupon I copied Scarlett and pulled down our white dining room drapes to sew up a glamorous wedding gown to play Tracy in our Laurel Little Theatre version of *The Philadelphia Story*. Oh dear. Besides the unavoidable Southern accent—but this was Mississippi, and nobody seemed to notice—also, unfortunately, after dress rehearsal, I broke out in a rash. Again, nobody noticed but itchy me. Unlike Scarlett's velvet, my drapes turned out to be fiberglass, and I had not flat-felled the seams.

Many Vogue-pattern outfits ensued during the coming years, as well as family-made baby clothes for our fourth generation—another four boys. The first-born of these grandchildren were twins, adorable in matching handmade outfits, but nothing alike in other ways. The matching outfits were fast worn out by the younger two.

I have given up sewing now in favor of writing. I do my best to color black and white words as I embroider a story rather than a sampler. But I still treasure my very first embroidery effort. The little Japanese girl on a bridge is now a beloved and comfy pillow.

COSTUMES AND QUILTS

Alice Henderson

I grew up in a family that prided itself in its Scottish heritage. My parents took trips to Scotland for bolts of wool cloth woven in the various family tartans. My mother sewed jackets, suits, and kilts, which we proudly wore. I also enjoyed the costumes that she fashioned for Halloween and our school plays.

Many years later in 2000, my own son, Tristan Codrescu, started a theater company that he called "Madame Palmetto's Amusement Company." I did a lot of costumes for his circus about Cortez and the Mexican conquest, "Cirque de la Conquista." In addition to gold and leopard skin loincloths for the pagan gods, a goddess, Lady Hummingbird, metamorphosed into the Virgin Mary complete with cape and crown. This show had two runs, the first at the Contemporary Arts Center on Good Friday, 2002. The second adaptation was in September 2004. Hurricane Ivan cancelled the first week at the University of New Orleans (UNO) Downtown Theatre. The circus costumes needed to be form fitted so they didn't interfere with the movement. Many of the performers came up with their own outfits, either from the Goodwill or Army Surplus. This left me to do the specialty items like the feathered headdresses.

I also costumed Tristan's production of "Salomé." This was staged at the UNO Downtown Theatre (formerly a Masonic temple) in February and March of 2003. It required more elaborate ancient Middle-Eastern costumes for biblical characters. I would have liked making elegant, regal robes for King Herod and Queen Herodias. I did in fact make silken kimonos for Salomé and the Queen, but actors have other concerns about their images than proper costumes. Our King wanted to show off his legs, so a Roman-style tunic and chest plate were requested. Salomé also had ideas about what to wear and what to bare. I fashioned a unique top so she could tuck in her seven veils for her dance of the same name. Then she could twirl around flinging the scarves and voila, topless!

After Hurricane Katrina, my husband Carroll and I escaped to Michigan. My sister Liz and her husband Dave gave us a rental house

Figure 6.6. *Flooded Ninth Ward.* Quilt by Alice Henderson.
80 x 72 in. Photograph courtesy of Grevy Photography.

Figure 6.7. *Katrina in the Gulf of Mexico.* Quilt by Alice Henderson.
80 x 72 in. Photograph courtesy of Grevy Photography.

to stay in. It was September and already starting to get chilly at night. We were given Red Cross blankets of very scratchy white acrylic fabric. Carroll and I felt that since Katrina separated the citizens from the city of New Orleans, we were like the Oakies during the dustbowl. We called ourselves New Orleans Mother Earth Refugees aka NOMERs.

Katrina wrecked vengeance on many Gulf of Mexico oil rigs and platforms, some of them still leaking ten years later, since no official entity requires them to be sealed. We believed the hurricane was a lesson in global warning. I was the Talented Art teacher at Ben Franklin High School before the storm so I was always looking for art lessons.

Sister Liz lent me a sewing machine and I sewed quilt top covers for the scratchy Red Cross blankets. The first was an abstract-looking overview of the flooded city with a patchwork of rooftops and treetops. The second was a giant map of the Gulf of Mexico with a huge Category 5 Katrina spinning around like everyone saw on Google Earth. I have made more quilts since then, but the global warming theme seems to stay with me.

Figure 6.8. *Man's Struggle with Nature.* Quilt by Alice Henderson. 90 x 72 in. Photograph courtesy of Grevy Photography.

THREADS OF MEMORY

Nancy Alcalde

We cleaned the attic out, my son and I, an attic which had not been explored in decades, and surely must hold treasures. We climbed up with some trepidation mixed with great expectations. My parents had bought this old house many years ago, upon visiting New Orleans and then discovering that they could not leave. Now, since my mother's death, I am living in it, having also fallen prey to the seductiveness of this endlessly fascinating city.

We found no worldly treasures—just old doors, window frames, rugs, and such—but there indeed was a treasure, worth more than money could buy, in a little trunk. Here there were things that my grandmother had made—my first baby outfit and clothes for my many dolls (my dolls were always the best dressed in town). My grandmother had been a gifted seamstress. Needlework of all kinds was her life and her passion. In the bottom of the trunk, there were several lacy rosettes with needles still in them, which perhaps someday would have become decorative covers for the dining room table. Attached was a note from my mother, explaining that she had found this under my grandmother's pillow when she died. She had been so ill with a failing heart, so weak that the doctors had forbidden any activity whatsoever, including sewing. Somehow, however, she had sneaked this into her sickbed, working on it in secrecy. How cruel of them to try to take this away from her, and how defiant of her not to allow them to do so. When I picked this up, I felt that I held her passion in my hands.

My grandmother came to America from Yorkshire, England, when she was three years old. She grew up in Pennsylvania, met a handsome, charming Scot and fell in love. They married and became my grandparents. She had always been a rather shadowy figure in the background of my childhood memories—a quiet, shy woman—but now my picture of her has taken on another dimension and she has moved to the forefront of my memories. She has taken up residence and now lives inside of me, enriching me with her presence.

THE GHOST CROCHET

Moonyeen McNeilage

My mother came from a family of thirteen children. She was the second eldest. Her father and mother were share farmers and the children were expected to "pull their weight." For my mother this meant she always had a baby on her hip before and after school. She claimed that she had one hip lower than the other from this extra load. Her Aunt Lillie in Melbourne taught her to sew, knit, and crochet. When Granma announced one day that she was expecting again, my mother famously shouted "bloody rabbits," packed her bags and caught the train to Melbourne and Aunt Lillie, who arranged for her to become an apprentice to a famous Melbourne couturier called Madame Valerie. Mother was just fifteen.

The salon specialized in dragged silk chiffon cut on the bias and attached to fine silk lining. Madame had a clientele among theatre folk and several well-known opera singers were regular customers, as the draped chiffon was very well suited to the "fuller" figure. My mother's special talent was in *rouleau*, a thin tube of fabric cut on the bias and used as tiny loops for buttons, very fashionable in the twenties and thirties. A row of these buttons would sometimes stretch down the entire back of a garment, as well as fasten sleeves at the elbow. Brides particularly liked this look, and when my mother eventually opened her own salon she specialized in bridal outfits.

She used to tell a story about how, when I was about three years old, her sister sent me an elaborately smocked dress made from a warm English fabric called *Vyella* which was covered in small, pink, printed rosebuds. I was playing with my dolls on the floor of the salon, keeping very still while my mother was fitting a bride-to-be and her mother, as well as the bridesmaids. I was wearing the beautiful dress and sitting quietly behind the full-length mirror. When she came to get me to say goodbye to the nice ladies, she discovered that I had borrowed her large dressmaking scissors and had carefully cut around all the rosebuds on the front of my dress. She said that when I stood up it was like a shower of confetti. I still have those scissors and I don't know how a small child could even lift them. My mother said she knew that I would be good with my hands.

Mother's first love was crochet and she was so fast and creative that I really never learnt properly. She would get impatient at my slowness and finish it for me. At age eighty-three she started to lose her sight and found sewing difficult and her swan song was my daughter's wedding. She managed to make the bride's gown, two bridesmaids' dresses, her outfit, and mine, and then said, "That's it." The results were beautiful.

At age eighty-seven she was very blind and had lived in a granny flat at the rear of our house for about seven years. She also developed severe osteoarthritis and had to go into care. She was still "knitting by ear" and supplied everybody with enough covered coat hangers to last us all forever.

In my last conversation with her, shortly before her death at ninety-two, I told her that I was learning to crochet. I said that I realized I had been a very poor pupil and if I had listened to her properly I might be able to do as well as she did. By this stage she was in a fetal position, completely blind, and could barely hear, but I saw her hands moving rapidly as if she was crocheting again.

STITCHING AND SANITY

Bobbie Malone

For nearly a half century, I've used needle and thread or needle and yarn to deal with anger, despair, frustration, anxiety, hope, desire, and joy. I always have at least one incomplete project in my backpack, one in my tote bag in the front seat of the car, one in the bathroom, and a couple of more in the den. I find the process of designing and executing soft and useful textiles both meditative and meaningful. And I am sure that stitching is an integral part of my sanity.

As part of an Uptown New Orleans "young married" Jewish social circle in the early 1960s, I took up knitting. That's what so many of the other women were doing after newlywed friends tried out recipes for each other at small dinner parties. Husbands moved off to talk business and golf; women sat together to kibitz and knit. Knitting took the edge off the difficult transition of moving from being a nineteen-year-old coed to becoming a young matron in my husband's hometown. I loved the feel of the wool and other fibers, and I made garments for every family member, with yarn and instructions supplied by the Knit and Dress Shop on Maple Street where lovely, patient women initiated customers into the intricacies of working with various kinds of yarn. I recall the trouble I had learning to turn cables. I kept ripping out rows that didn't come out right. On one of many trips to the Knit and Dress Shop, one of the instructor salesladies told me that if I wanted a perfect sweater, I could purchase one at Maison Blanche. Handknit should look it! I relaxed, and I still own that sweater I made in 1964, and it still looks good, even with its imperfectly rendered cables. But when I got pregnant with my first child, I decided to learn to needlepoint. I bought a canvas with an already-worked center design (a nursery animal of some kind), and I filled in the background to make a cushion for the rocking chair. It looked good, but I got bored and didn't think it was much fun. Sometime after my older son Benjamin was born, I walked into the Louisiana Crafts Council, then located up in Carrollton, and saw a needlepoint wall hanging designed and worked by artist and philanthropist Sandra Freeman. It was a Noah's

Ark, and the entire composition consisted of bright colors in a wide variety of stitches. I had an epiphany! I had no idea that such stitches existed. I couldn't wait to learn how to compose in yarn.

For Mother's Day 1968, Benjamin's dad (Stephen Sontheimer) presented me with Hope Hanley's outstanding introductory book, *Needlepoint*, with the following inscription: "To my Mommy with all my love, Benjy (O.T. for Mommy)." I immediately made a small sampler (about 4" x 7"), which has hung on a wall in every home I've occupied ever since, a reminder of how essential this first foray into creatively manipulated stitches transformed my life. Although no doctor has confirmed this observation, I am sure that stitching has contributed to my low blood pressure and high spirits. It was also something artistic that I could accomplish waiting in line for the nursery school carpool at the Jewish Community Center (JCC), at board meetings of the National Council of Jewish Women (NCJW), and later at Little League games, where both Benjamin and his younger brother Matthew played every summer for Carrollton Boosters. Inspired by the work of nationally renowned graphic artist and activist Sister Mary Corita (later Corita Kent), I began introducing words into my work, a theme I later set aside, only to have it resurface unbidden, many years later.

By 1973, however, just shy of our tenth anniversary, Stephen and I separated. The marriage had failed, and I was totally unprepared for life as a single mother. I hadn't even finished my undergraduate degree in Art History at Newcomb College, and even as an outgoing overachiever, I had never contemplated being on my own. Needlepoint, Gussie Woodest—my babysitter and the boys' additional "grandmother"—my analyst, and my women friends kept me sane. This list may not be prioritized, but it is certainly accurate. Of course, separation wasn't easy for the children, and they displayed their displeasure with the newly divided household arrangements. I thought I was managing my life and theirs, but I was mostly mangling just about every situation encountered and, consequently, feeling guilty and raw. The only thing at the time that I seemed to be doing well was my stitching, and I was stitching up a storm. Stitching alongside every aspect of my slowly evolving maturity became the pattern.

I got my first "professional" gig at the JCC, teaching needlepoint several times a week to groups of young and older women who were anxious to learn. Needlepoint was trendy at that time, so classes were lively affairs. Although I eventually graduated from Newcomb, and earned an M.Ed. from Tulane, when I began at the JCC, I'd never formally instructed a class. I'd volunteered through the NCJW as a "play lady" at Charity Hospital where the organization set up and staffed an air-conditioned playroom for ambulatory children in the wards and had wheeled carts of toys and games to distribute to young patients too weak or disabled to come to the playroom, and I had been a docent at the Delgado Museum (now New Orleans Museum of Art) taking school children on tours. I hadn't yet developed a sequence of classes, where one skill built upon its antecedent. I found that I loved doing so. But the truly memorable aspect of those classes at the JCC was the camaraderie that almost instantly emerged among the students and the revelations that women shared about their lives, less guardedly than they would have allowed elsewhere. The Women's Movement was well underway in some parts of the United States, and I was painfully becoming aware of myself beyond the roles of mother-wife, but I knew nothing of the national nature of the rebellion. Through my work with the NCJW and service on the board of the Urban League in the city, I was still too focused on social justice in race relations to pay much attention to the Women's Movement. Stitching became bonding, and although I didn't recognize it at the time, a precursor of my own dawning feminism. I am still beguiled that holding a needle and yarn and canvas (or needle, thread, and fabric) can accomplish what no amount of group therapy can achieve. I am no psychology student, but I have since witnessed this experience in many settings and still marvel at the inherent beauty of the phenomenon.

While teaching at the JCC, I was also designing my own pieces and carrying around a passel of felt-tip art markers and a sketchbook. On a visit to San Antonio, the aunt of one of my friends asked if I would paint canvases from a couple of those designs and sell them to her with sufficient instructions and yarn to complete them—my first offer of this kind. Not far from my mother's house in Alamo Heights, I learned about the Yarn Barn, a large store that stocked

Figure 6.9. *Shep Scharlack's Stories.* Antique quilt top for which author and seamstress Bobbie Malone (left) created the borders and hand embroidered punchlines from some of her father's most memorable jokes to commemorate the 100th year of his birth, Spring, 2015. Photograph courtesy of Bobbie Malone.

Figure 6.10. Detail of *Shep Scharlack's Stories.* Photograph courtesy of Bobbie Malone.

excellent needlepoint canvases and Paternayan yarns, favorites at the time and not always easy to come by. Owner Bobbi Ravicz and I struck up a friendship and negotiated a process where I could order yarns in wholesale quantities to package and sell with my designs. I called my enterprise, "bobbie's creative design solutions," and began selling hand-painted canvases and stitching guides to customers all over New Orleans. Many clients wanted me to design something site-specific to complement a painting or a fabric already chosen for a living room or den. By the spring of 1975, I had designed and stitched enough samples to hold a show in the lobby of the New Orleans JCC.

In the meantime, I was teaching at my friend Mathile Abramson's home in Gonzalez one afternoon a week and volunteering at McDonogh 15, where both of my children were enrolled, doing art projects with children on Friday afternoons. One afternoon, principal Lucy Carmichael encouraged me to meet the recently hired artist-in-residence, Robin Halpren-Ruder, who was doing schoolwide projects with the students. We hit it off immediately. Robin had created a large needlepoint wall-hanging as part of her MFA at the Chicago Art Institute and was hanging a show of her work at the downtown New Orleans Public Library at the same time mine was going up at the JCC. After we helped one another mount our shows, we decided to go into business together, designing and executing murals, logos, and needlepoint. Having neither capital nor location to open a separate studio, we formed Artenvirons, working out of my apartment or her extra bedroom. I handled the needlepoint commissions, but we both designed the murals, and painted most of the walls ourselves—except a couple that were too high for two young women to work safely. For those, we hired professional sign painters. Robin's husband was in medical school at Tulane, and when he graduated about a year after I married Bill Malone, she and Danny left for the Northeast for his internship. I, in turn, returned to the Tulane campus for graduate school in education.

By 1979, I was teaching first grade at Trinity Episcopal School and designing on the side—Artenvirons had been fun and hard work, but insufficient as a second income for a history professor and wife looking for a house to buy. I found that I loved introducing young learners to reading and math as much as I had enjoyed introducing women to yarn and canvas. And for Mother's Day, I taught my first graders to make their mothers needlepoint bookmarks after I provided them with small rectangular plastic canvas pieces and yarn. About the same time, I had begun working on some quilt patterns, redesigned for needlepoint and counted cross-stitch.

Then, on my birthday in 1981, another seminal book entered my life. Close Tulane history department friend, John Boles, and his wife Nancy gave me *The Quilters: Women and Domestic Art, An Oral History* by Patricia J. Cooper and Norma Bradley Allen. That beautiful volume of photographs of quilts and women quilters and their testimonies in Texas and New Mexico unwittingly opened me to two new directions at once: becoming a quilter myself, even though I had never actually *sewn*, and eventually, becoming a historian. Once I read the book, I realized how much fun it would be to create something that had pattern (in the way only printed fabric can render) in addition to color and design. My friend and fellow native Texan, Loraine Purrington, and I decided to take a quilting class from Nell Singleton at The Salt Box in Metairie. Like the long-departed Knit and Dress Shop, The Salt Box no longer exists, nor do any of the shops Uptown that in those years and through the 1990s carried yarn and canvas or quilt supplies. Nell was a strong, no-nonsense traditional teacher, who believed in hand piecing and authenticity without too much concern for perfection. She kept reminding students that those antique quilts we so admired were valued for their handmade look and feel, not their perfect piecing of perfectly matched fabrics. This advice was not unlike the instruction I received fifteen years earlier at the Knit and Dress Shop. The geometry that had eluded me as a high school student now seemed irresistible for a quilter. If only I had realized that material application as a struggling sophomore! Loraine, another dear friend, Elaine Maney, and I quilted weekly at each other's homes, deepening our friendship as we dipped our needles in and out of whatever quilts each of us was currently creating. My neighbor, Kitty Rawson, often joined us.

In honor of my becoming a Bat Mitzvah at the age of thirty-nine in 1983, Loraine presented me with a biographical quilt top that she hand-appliquéed—still one of my treasured possessions. Then, in incredibly short order, a number of events occurred that ultimately set our lives on a completely different trajectory. The year of my Bat Mitzvah, Matthew, like Benjamin, chose to go off to boarding school just as their dad had done for high school. Suddenly, Bill and I were empty nesters. After visiting his brother who had retired from the Dallas area and moved to attractive Hideaway Lake, Texas, some thirty miles northwest of Tyler, Bill and I decided to sell our Metairie home and move to an apartment closer to Tulane. We purchased a lot and built a home at Hideaway—which I laughingly but honestly told folks matched the quilt I'd made in Nell's class—where we planned to spend summers and vacations with the boys. The quilt top that Loraine made for me included an image of the Hideaway house, and she encouraged me to quilt it freehand, rather than imposing a pattern. With Bill's sabbatical on the horizon, he applied for and received a Guggenheim fellowship, allowing him to complete work on a book he was writing, and allowing us to move to Hideaway the following school year. While living at Hideaway and teaching gifted fourth graders in nearby Lindale, I designed a quilt top for Loraine created from cross-stitched squares of Texas wildflowers I worked during Matthew's Little League games, which she then quilted.

Bill and I lived out the East Texas fantasy for a few more years, with his driving back and forth to New Orleans each week while I continued to teach elementary school in Smith County. I moved from rural Lindale to urban Tyler, about twenty miles away, now teaching gifted students from second through fifth grade in three elementary schools. Through Temple Beth El in Tyler, an older member, Maurine Muntz, and I cemented our friendship once we began talking fabrics and quilting. Maurine was an extraordinarily talented quilter, and she and I began spending one evening a week quilting. Her home in Tyler was near one of the elementary schools where I taught, and while Bill was teaching midweek in New Orleans, the quilting evening turned into an overnight. I would leave from her home to teach the following morning. We were like little girls, giggling and sharing our ideas and fabric stashes. Before I moved back to New Orleans in the summer of 1988, Maurine decided that I needed a friendship quilt to remember my Tyler and Hideaway friends. We chose fabrics from both collections, and Maurine gave me a number of muslin lozenge-shaped pieces on which to gather signatures. In earlier times, women would stitch their own pieces, but most of my friends did not sew, much less embroider, and I used a running stitch to work each name myself. Maurine placed them into the quilt. Since Tyler is known as the rose capital of Texas, she quilted roses between the blocks, entered the quilt into a competition, and won a prize before she gave it to me. Looking at the quilt or cuddling under it brings such fond memories of all the women whose signatures I gathered: some favorite students and fellow faculty members—others, nursing home residents or Hideaway friends whom I came to know and love when I lived there.

When we moved back to New Orleans fulltime in 1988, I returned to graduate school once again, this time to earn my doctorate in American history at Tulane. Although stitching slowed down somewhat during this intense period of reentering academia, Loraine, Elaine, and I got back together to quilt weekly, with friends Joan Hunter and Sue Woodward joining us when they could. When Elaine became pregnant with twin boys, Loraine and I selected matching fabrics but different subjects, trains for her and sailboats for me, for baby quilts, and when Sue became terminally ill, we took turns finishing the quilt she had designed and stitched for her daughter, reinforcing the bond we had developed as we stitched and listened to each other's stories.

While I was writing my MA thesis in the summer of 1990, I began to think about how much fun it would be to design a quilt for summer using faded-looking, slipcover-like fabrics, and with the central focus, tumbling tumblers of iced tea. I succeeded in assembling the quilt, but after many years (interrupted by more pressing and smaller-scale projects) spent quilting ice cubes and lemon slices in each "glass," the borders still await completion, a goal of the quilt's twenty-fifth anniversary in its basket by my chair in the den.

After I'd earned my Ph.D., I found a position at the Wisconsin Historical Society in Madison, writing and editing books on Wisconsin history and teacher's materials for elementary classrooms—

Figure 6.11. Section of friendship quilt, designed, hand-pieced, and hand-quilted by Maurine Muntz with names hand-embroidered by Bobbie Malone, Summer, 1988. Photograph courtesy of Bobbie Malone.

work that felt like it had been created just for me, since I had wished for similar resources available on Texas history when I was teaching there. I warned my supervisor that I *had* to stitch during division or staff meetings in order to pay attention. Thank goodness he understood, and I was able to participate in discussions and piece quilts simultaneously. To keep my office connected to the needs of educators, librarians, and local historians around the state, we formed an advisory committee representative of these constituencies. Through workshops we planned and performed together, one member, Bonnie Jancik, an archaeological educator associated with the University of Wisconsin-La Crosse, and I became friends. When we discovered that we both loved quilting, the friendship blossomed and included our husbands, Bill and Paul, when we began trading visits to one another. Both Bonnie and Paul have excellent visual ideas and are master craftspeople—Paul with woodworking. They especially encouraged me to be more experimental. Through Bonnie, I began using embroidery floss to quilt so that the stitches themselves form a more dramatic graphic statement.

After some fourteen years at the historical society, journalist Linda Brazill made an appointment to see me. I was editing the Badger Biographies series for young readers, and she proposed a title that she was interested in writing. Unfortunately, nothing came of that proposal, possibly because we almost immediately started talking about our mutual interest in fabrics, sewing, stitching, and designing. I pulled out the quilt I was piecing, and within the next few weeks, we had begun assembling a small group of congenial women with whom to stitch. Although the personnel varied and the meetings were inconsistent in the beginning, a lively Wisconsin coalition formed—Linda, Sara Golbach, Madge Klais, Rae Erdahl, Sally Wood, Karen Prickette, and me. We named ourselves "Second Saturday," the day of the month we chose to meet. At first we met for a couple of hours, but the mornings began to stretch as we shared ideas, informally critiqued or helped each other with individual projects, or introduced books or upcoming exhibits. Eventually, we planned field trips to art museums or lectures and added extra times to meet for coffee. The intellectual sharing and excitement probably pushed me to retire in February 2011—as I realized I did not necessarily need professional employment to keep me stimulated and creative. I still credit Second Saturday for my decision to push away from the office desk and shift to my laptop for my own research and writing, and to afford me more time for fabric-centric projects.

Coincidentally, just before I retired, I learned of a collaboration instigated in conjunction with the exhibit, "Handmade Meaning," created by the James Watrous Gallery, the University of Wisconsin-Madison's Material Culture Program, and the Wisconsin Decorative Arts Database. Interested community members were invited to pick up a small square of muslin, a tiny embroidery hoop, red embroidery floss, needle, and a selection of patterns, one of which could be chosen, modified, worked, and included in a group redwork quilt, to be assembled by and exhibited at a local quilt shop. The project recalled the quilts Victorian women created as fundraisers during the late nineteenth and early twentieth centuries and therefore used some of the same design criteria for today's DIY crafters to achieve an overall unified effect. I chose an image of a spool, thread, and needle, which I stitched in the red floss. Along the thread I also stitched in black, "Lifeline to Sanity," the first time I'd actually used embroidery stitches since I was a child filling in a design printed on a dish towel, and the first time in over forty years that I had incorporated words as a central feature in my needlework.

The next turning point in my adventure with needle, thread, and fabric occurred a couple of years later when I learned that, as an adjunct to the Triennial at the Madison Museum of Contemporary Arts, local artists Laurie Beth Clark and Michel Peterson were planning events under the umbrella name, Café Allongé. They had already contacted eighteen artists to hold "performances" in eighteen local coffee shops around the city. All one had to do was sign up online and purchase a beverage from the coffee shop hosting the event. As I scrolled through the list of artists and coffee houses, I noticed that Leslee Nelson, a noted textile artist whose work I admired, offered to meet several times. I signed up to hear her talk about the memory cloths she was creating. After about twenty minutes of her talking with four or five of us about her creative process as she shared several works of her own, Leslee spread out needles, embroidery floss, and fabric scraps, and asked us to begin to stitch our own memories—something none of us there anticipated. I worked on a small piece of denim, unsuccessfully trying to capture my deceased jeweler-father's diamond loupe, but relishing the idea of becoming a memory cloth maker myself. As I left the shop an hour or so later, I knew that instead of finishing the piece I had just begun, what I really wanted to do was to stitch the most memorable punch lines of my father's "stories" that he repeated in any given social setting. While visiting Bonnie and Paul, I had purchased an antique quilt top some years beforehand that was in terrible shape but in compelling colors, with large empty yellow shapes that called out to be filled. Now I knew how to fill them! Within the next couple of months, the Memory Cloth Circle began meeting every week at the same coffee shop. Almost every woman (the group probably has since swollen to about twenty regulars) focuses on memories—mostly recycling previously used textiles such as handkerchiefs or table lines—and we informally share techniques, ideas, thrift shop and yard sale finds. We've had shows of our work at our home base, Lakeside Street Coffee House, as well as an exhibit at the Artisan Gallery in nearby Paoli. Once again, women opened up to each other in intimate and completely unpredictable ways, establishing bonds that would otherwise go unfulfilled as they created work that surprises even the embroiderers themselves. No one's work duplicates another's, yet all involve and respond to the interaction of those in the group. The spontaneity feels positively magical, if not spiritual, as we have begun to consider ourselves sisters in stitches.

As I write about threading my way through my adult life, I marvel at the experience of doing the same thing that women have been doing for centuries, finding themselves and each other through the work of their hands, while enhancing both sanity and equilibrium.

STITCHERY

Phyllis Parun

The view of my life from New Orleans has changed very dramatically since the flood of '05. In spite of the devoted effort hometown people are putting into the "bring New Orleans back" campaign, very little of what was once my life remains intact. In place of my old life a new one is emerging, one with less leisure, less *joi de vivre* and fewer longtime friendships as people have moved away. It is in this time of disorientation that memories from my past vividly flash before me, bringing me comfort.

When my neighbor and friend Lee Grue asked me to write a little something about sewing, I really could not recall anything that would be worthy of ink. It took me weeks before I even entertained the idea at all.

The storm and flood left my personal economy damaged, so in January 2006, I went to work for The Road Home. A majority of people in the company had damaged homes or businesses or both. We all arrived on the job in desperate need of inspiration and so we each began to share some of our favorite quotes.

The first one I found was hanging in my kitchen. It was the Serenity Prayer. The one I have was passed down to me from my mother's family. It had a stitched vine and flower border on a brown fabric with red lettering.

I don't know if my aunt stitched it or if my grandmother did. It just hung in my mother's family home in Hammond, Louisiana, where I lived as a child. The work had been in my family since I was born and I can't remember anyone ever speaking of it. After they died, it passed to me.

Living in this stressful post-flooded city, this piece of family stitchery presented its wisdom to me. I remember having given photo copies of this poem several years before to recovering AA friends and to hotheads, and now it hangs in my office on Poydras Street.

That was in April of 2007. So I had at least one piece to write about but that did not seem to me to be enough of a story. So I didn't write anything for another month.

During that month, as President of the Louisiana Chapter of the Women's Caucus for Art, I was launching our local chapter into a National Tour titled "Katrina Diaries 2005-2007." In so doing, I was constantly looking for new materials.

Earlier, in January, I had been the kickoff speaker at the Arts Night series at the Bywater Alvar Library. My presentation turned out to bring back many memories about New Orleans in the 1970s. Many friends from that era attended and we had a wonderful time reflecting on the role of the New Orleans Public Library and the Artists Information Bureau for which I was the Visual Arts Coordinator in the development of community service at the public library.

In April, my neighbor Elizabeth Shannon was the guest speaker. When I first met Elizabeth she lived in an artist's coop they named "The Last Resort." It was there in that house on Esplanade that I had first met Jim Rivers.

Figure 6.12. Front and back of fabric and paper doll. 7.25 x 10 inches. Created by two sisters, Doris Catherine Wolters and Sophie Ada Wolters, ca. 1922. Photograph by daughter and niece, Phyllis Parun.

Jim was a weaver from South Louisiana. He was fond of growing brown cotton, which he would first spin and then weave into branches and reeds, creating unique natural wall hangings. His work was completely different from the traditional drawing and painting that I learned from Mr. John McCrady at his French Quarter art school. After that exposure I had a fresh approach to making art. I too began to collect twigs and branches for some future work. As Elizabeth spoke of her work in retrospective that day at the library, I began to remember that her found art of palm fronds in the late 1970s inspired me to collect palm fronds too.

As young girls, my mother's sisters had worked in the family business by caning chairs in Grandfather Philipp Wolters Jr.'s upholstery shop, which he opened in Hammond in 1905. It was in the shop that the girls developed a lifelong appreciation for texture, fabric, reeds, and stitchery. From their collection I have inherited many boxes of cloth scraps, which they had squirreled away to be used in repairing chairs, dresses, hats, and future projects. They were always planning ahead, using whatever found materials they could garner.

Years later my Creole Cottage is brimming with tapestry, cloth, reeds, stitchery, and all manner of natural and handmade textured fabric and materials. My collection of stitchery work left to me by my family elders covers a wide range of styles and techniques. I have crocheted blankets, afghans, *petitpoint* fabric chair seats, decorative pillows, and *macramé* window dressings.

This was how it all began for me. I was born into it. Almost all the materials which I have in my studio have been given to me or found. Though I don't stitch per se, I do make wall hangings. And I too collect found and saved materials. I especially enjoy collecting reeds and twigs that fall into my path. I tie or bundle these together making my own version of wall hangings by incorporating painted paper or cloth into them.

In my New Orleans Creole studio cottage the outdoors are so much indoors that often I feel like I should rake my floors and sweep my yard. Everything seems to be in reverse after the flood.

230

Figure 6.13. Petit point upholstered chair cushion. 14.5 x 14.5 inches. Created by Marie Philippine Wolters, ca. 1940. From the Wolters Family Archive. Photograph by her niece, Phyllis Parun.

THE FABRIC OF OUR LIVES

Valentine Pierce
dedicated to Carlota Theresa Houlemard, 1936-2013

Figure 6.14. Carlota Theresa Houlemard, ca. 2005.
Photograph by daughter Valentine Pierce.

If my mother had been an entrepreneur, she'd have been rich, a fashion designer of dream clothes. Until her final day, at seventy-seven years old, she was still sewing, knitting, crocheting. She rarely, if ever, bought anything more than underclothes or coats from a department store. For all of our young lives she made practically everything we wore. I remember one summer outfit she made for us five girls. Tab-top blouses and culottes (these days they call them skorts)—all exactly alike—white background, rampant orange and yellow, bursts of red, flashes of green, dabs of blue, bits of brown. Butterflies, bumble bees, birds, ladybugs, flowers filled our bellies, backs, behinds. We knew we were cute.

One year, as she set about choosing patterns for our Easter outfits, she asked me what I wanted. I didn't care, I said, so long as it was easy for her. "I'm not making it, you are," she said. I had been sewing since I was eight but mostly doll clothes and simpler items although I did take on a jacket once. I had to rip out the sleeves because I put them in backwards, and I had to blindstitch the hem because finishing was a cardinal rule. "Do it right or don't do it" was my mother's mantra.

The Christmas I turned eight, one of my presents was a small red cast-iron sewing machine with a natural wood base. You could hand-wind it or use batteries, a good thing because we never had

232

enough batteries. I put a yellow submarine sticker on it. (The Beatles were hot during that time.)

The first thing I made with that sewing machine was a pleated skirt for my other present, a Barbie. The lightweight plaid fabric boasted turquoise, gold, white, brown, and shimmering shades in between. I was so proud because I made it without a pattern, carefully cutting the small rectangle of fabric, pinning and pressing the pleats, basting the waistband, which I secured with a snap that was almost as big as the band.

Later, in junior high school, I had home economics. It was that era. All the girls had Home Ec; the boys had Workshop. I almost got into trouble with my teacher for not pinning my pattern the way she thought I should. What saved me was I had mine pinned, cut out, sewn, and hemmed before the other girls had theirs laid out. It was a spring green jersey knit dress. The teacher made me her assistant. Years later, a former classmate reminded me that I had taught her to crochet, and to this day, she still finds it relaxing. I don't remember it, but we never know how we affect others, do we?

Some years ago a friend pointed out that as a result of crocheting I had perfected a skill few people possess, one I took for granted. I can wrap anything—yarn, thread, twine—into a perfect ball from as tiny as a gumball to twice the size of my hand.

Anyway, my mom figured that since I was now taking sewing in school, I could make my own Easter clothes. I made a green jersey knit blouse (yep, it was left over cloth from the dress) with buttons and a yellow double knit tunic with matching pants. I can't tell you what it takes for me to make a buttonhole these days or repair a zipper, let alone put a zipper in. Funny thing is, when I was in the military, people wondered why my uniforms fit so well. I'd had a pair of slacks altered on the base. Instead of removing the zipper, they took in one side seam and the center seams and put a fold beneath the waistband. Naturally, the slacks looked and felt twisted. From that day on, I altered my own, ripping them from the waistband down— including the zipper—and modifying them to fit my body shape.

Later in life I lacked the patience to deal with anything more than a simple repair. I'd rather have my mom alter my clothes than deal with buttons, zippers, or waistbands. How many wonderful brand new clothes I've left in stores because they didn't fit quite right and I was too lazy to go through the trouble of altering them.

It's the same with all my "domestic engineer" skills. I had so much trouble with the first bedspread I tried to crochet, I cajoled my mother into making it for me. Good thing she loved me because it fits a king-sized bed with ease. And yes, I've bought some knitting needles. I finally misplaced them, still in their unopened packs.

When Hurricane Katrina devastated New Orleans in August 2005, my mother lost practically everything, even the sewing cabinet she'd had since I was a young girl. She had always spent her waking hours working part-time and sewing, knitting, or crocheting. Without these comforts, she would be edgy, unhappy. I remember talking with her that October. She'd bought some hand-held computer games "just to keep myself occupied," she'd said. I understood how she felt because I also had left all the things that bring me the most comfort—books, writing supplies, computer.

When we were finally let back into the city I had to move, and my stuff was going in storage so when my mother got settled, I gathered all my sewing, knitting, and crochet items, including my sewing machine for her. Mind you, I can't begin to compare my meager supplies with her seventy-seven years' worth but I had enough to make a decent showing and I had some really beautiful fabric just waiting for loving hands to turn it into works of art. I have to tell you, some of the yarn, needles, and crochet hooks already belonged to my mother. If she was crocheting when I visited her, I always begged some yarn or needles. I even went through her books, though I could barely tolerate reading the instructions. I can do more than basic stitches but have no patience for complicated patterns. Still, every once in a while I feel ambitious, daring, eager to brave the world of fancy stitchery. That bravado usually only lasted a week, maybe three.

I never actually made anything fancy, just hats, each of which I gave to any friend who admired it. Giving them away was so much easier than committing to making one. Crocheting, knitting, sewing—these are things I do only for me, restful hobbies. I did make a couple of very large "comforters" for my children. My daughter's turned out crooked because she wanted it before she went to college so I was rushing despite my limited abilities. Sweet child that she is, she said it didn't feel crooked when she was all warm and toasty beneath it. My son thought his was cool because I managed to crochet his initials in it. I must have ripped that thing apart a couple dozen times.

I made four lap covers, too, for myself, my best friend, and our mothers. It started as something to do, the one week of the year I get the urge to craft those homey things. When my girlfriend saw it, she remarked on how beautiful the colors were. Since I was in a lap blanket phase and we both have the same affliction—an aversion to cold—I decided to make her one. I'd had the foresight to make a mental note of her favorite colors and had so much "stolen" and thrift shop yarn, along with dozen of skeins I'd bought over the years, that I had every color anyone could want. When I showed my mom the one I'd made for my friend, I could tell she wanted one. It surprised me because she could make her own—a much better one—if she wanted but she wanted one from me. Moms are really good for boosting the ego, aren't they? My best friend's mom also liked hers so much, I made a fourth. That was the end of the lap blankets, although I dreamed of making not only more of them but hundreds of specialty items I could sell at various craft shows, flea markets, maybe even in the French Market or on the Internet. I've looked at many of the items sold in stores and know that most of the handcrafted items sold these days only require basic skills. Just think what I could do?

The odd thing is, by 2011, I was making things to sell and had gone through several books of new stitches. The truth is, I love the designs; I'm just not crazy about patterns.

My mom never actually taught me to do any of these things. My grandmother never taught my mom. I never taught my daughter. Somehow, we just learned it and we all find comfort in it.

My mom could make anything she or someone else could dream up, crochet any stitch, decipher all manner of instructions from complicated Vogue patterns to coded craft books. Plus, my mother was the creative type.

She readily modified any pattern to suit whatever she decided to create. She often mixed and matched patterns for her "private specialty clothing line." The same with knitting and crochet.

Remember that Barbie doll? It was the only one I ever had. My mom crocheted a dress, hat, and collar and sewed a can-can slip for her. She was so lovely she won first place in a contest. Years later, my mom did an entire bridal suite for several of my daughter's Barbie dolls and their grooms.

Figure 6.15. Crocheted jacket by Carlota Theresa Houlemard, date unknown. Photograph by daughter Valentine Pierce.

In 2012, someone taught me to tat. It is something I've wanted to learn since I was a teenager. When I told my mom, she'd wanted to learn as far back as she could remember. Neither of us knew this. As a result, my mother asked me to teach her. I did. And for that Christmas, I ordered her books, shuttles, and seventeen spools of the most beautiful thread I could find, from Istanbul, Turkey, because it is no longer made in the United States. At least a third were variegated, my mother's favorite kind of thread and yarn.

Like most people, after Katrina I went to my mom's house to see what I could rescue. One of the things I found was this incredibly intricate tablecloth. When I told her, she asked if I had also found the bedspread. I remembered that bedspread. I hadn't seen it in years. Unfortunately, I hadn't found it. That tablecloth is older than I am; the bedspread is only a few years younger. I hope she eventually finds it. She said I could give it to my daughter. My daughter said she would love to have it. My daughter admired her grandmother's skill so much. I had to send her home from California the summer of her junior year so her grandmother could find the pattern and fabric for her senior prom dress. Of course, I had to send her again at Christmas for a fitting.

My mom had closets full of clothes, ninety percent of which she'd made herself. Brilliant colors, fancy stitching, odd buttons. All of them, however, were, after Katrina, covered in mold, mildew, mud. I wanted so much to save them; it broke my heart to leave them. I'm sure we could have washed them but our family has health issues, particularly asthma, and my mother's health was not optimum. It was better to leave them and avoid the exposure so many are now suffering from.

I did manage to rescue several of her crocheted Christmas ornaments. We had a booth at an art market a few years later and my mom had her ornaments on display. Someone picked up one of the angels, which had been stained during Hurricane Katrina. When she told the guy the story of this little angel, he bought it—for his mother.

That year of Katrina, I gathered all the stuff I'd rescued and all the stuff I was giving her and drove it Shreveport, Louisiana, three weeks before Christmas. For us, it was like Christmas day as the two of us went through the boxes. "That looks like my crochet book," my mother said. "It is," I laughed. "Hey, remember this yarn?"

Next we went to the boxes of fabric. "Ma, look at this one!" I repeated as I pulled each piece from the box I'd chosen. "Oh, look at this!" my mother would exclaim as she emptied another box. Before you knew it, fabric was spread all over her dining room, and we were dreaming aloud about what each piece could become. Like my mother, I love fabric. Like to touch it, hold it, make plans for it, even smell it. I still remember the scent of the fabric my mother bought from many of the now closed five-and-dimes on Canal Street. I knew whether it came from Krauss, Woolworth's, Kress, Hancock's, or a half dozen others just by the scent.

I knew I would miss the cloth I was giving my mother, long for the creations I'd never make, but the truth is, I also knew I rarely had the time or the patience for it. I had so many things I liked to do that some just never got done. Besides, I found zippers frustrating, buttons outside my realm of patience, blind hand-stitching impossible to hide, and finishing too tedious. Still, I bought fabric and patterns in hopes I would actually make something. My mother, on the other hand, would spend hours, days, getting it just right. Carefully ripping away mistakes, searching stores for the perfect buttons, matching spools of thread to fabric swatches.

Even though Christmas was a few weeks away, neither of us was expecting to have any money anytime soon, so my mother wasn't looking for a Christmas gift (she never does anyway), and I wasn't planning to give her one—but I did. I gave her the fabric, yarn, needles, patterns, and myriad little things that bring her so much comfort. She, in turn, gave me the joy of seeing her smile and hearing her voice filled with the glee of a child who'd received that most wanted, most favorite present.

After her passing, I became the rightful owner of enough yarn, fabric, and supplies to open a small store. (By the time she returned home in 2009, she had nearly rebuilt her stockpile.) Funny thing is, my passion for crafting had been piqued with our endeavor to sell our work. That interest increased once I had every implement known in my spare bedroom. I finally had to go legit and buy shelves and containers to organize it all. Now it is my art room and sometimes I just walk in to look around, wondering how, in the time I have left on this earth, am I ever going to create all the things that come to mind.

Figure 6.16. Angel decoration made by Carlota Theresa Houlemard,
ca. 2010. Photograph by daughter Valentine Pierce.

Jan Gilbert, Interdisciplinary Artist, New Orleans: An Interview with Jan Villarrubia (2013)

Jan Gilbert: *I have used stitching many times; it's part of my artistic vocabulary.*

Background by Jan Villarrubia:

For the following interview, Jan Gilbert arrived at my house in her cherished car, an old, white Honda, laden with laptop as well as notebooks, scrapbooks, photographs, and postcards. She wore a black outfit which emphasized her oyster white hair and sea green eyes. As she opened the passenger side of the car, the pile began to tumble out, but her quick reaction prevented anything from falling into the gutter puddle. As she unpacked the car and handed me some of the treasures, she half apologized for the load, explaining it's easier to talk about her work if the visuals are at her side. We hauled the collection inside and got comfortable in my study, her documents in easy reach.

Born and raised in New Orleans, Jan is known for her intense energy, ability to juggle many projects at once, cultural activism, and mentoring of young artists. She just finished a stint as Interim Director of Visual Art at the Contemporary Arts Center and later this year will be awarded a Community Arts Award by the Arts Council of New Orleans. In her work, Jan combines installation, ritual, and conceptual and public art. Since the early 1980s, she has exhibited, lectured, performed, and curated around the world and has participated in numerous international art exchanges in Switzerland, France, Italy, and the Republic of Macedonia. Her funding credits include the National Endowment for the Arts, the Rockefeller Foundation, the Warhol Foundation, the Trust for Mutual Understanding, and the Ford Foundation. She has received fellowships from the Louisiana Division of the Arts, the Pollock-Krasner Foundation and Art Matters. In addition, Jan is a cofounder of the artist/writer collaborative the VESTIGES Project, During her three decades with VESTIGES, she has directed, produced, and participated as a core artist in a wide variety of public art projects that include video, performance, and site interactions. She received her undergraduate degree from the University of New Orleans in 1980 and her Master of Fine Arts in Painting from Tulane University in 1982.

...

Jan Villarrubia (JV): I have known you for years, love your work, and one of my favorite pieces is your banana leaf with stitches in it. Will you explain that work?

Jan Gilbert (JG): I'm delighted to. *Offering 1* was done in 1999, very organically, in keeping with the subject. I had been diagnosed with Stage IV breast cancer, and a friend of mine, Ellen Johnson, told me that she was going to be making a pilgrimage to the top of Mount Rainier. And she asked if she could take something to the summit for me on my behalf, as a talisman of sorts, but also to give her inspiration to climb the mountain. Of course, the two requirements were that it be light, because she couldn't be carrying a sofa (laughs), and that it be biodegradable, because she was going to leave it at the top.

I was very touched at that proposition, and I wanted something that reflected life, death, and really, my surrender to what would be. I knew that I wanted to do everything I could do, but I also knew that I had a wonderful life, and if this moment was meant to be, it was meant to be. And this really marked that moment.

I remember going to St. Louis Cathedral and making a little spiritual visit with prayer. I walked out, went into the Jackson Square right across the street and picked out a banana leaf right there. I took it home and decided that what it was going to be was this pocket. And, of course, in typical Jan fashion, I decided that if she was going to take this up there for me, that we were going to pack as much punch into this little pocket as we could. I had another friend who, almost the identical time that I was having my illness, he was going into rehab, which would be a tough journey for him as well. So, I gathered locks of his hair and mine, mine had fallen out, and the ashes of a couple of close friends who had died, one, a mother of a

Figure 6.17. *Offering 1* (front). Jan Gilbert, 1999. Mixed media, 10.75 by 8 inches. Photograph by the artist.

Figure 6.18. *Offering 2* (back). Jan Gilbert, 1999. Mixed media. 10.75 by 8 inches. Photograph by the artist.

As artist Gilbert notes: "*Offering* documents what was successfully brought to the icy top of Mount Rainier by a friend: a Jackson Square banana leaf turned pocket, full of tiny locks of hair (mine, my husband's, and Peggy and Charlie Bishop's) and equally tiny portions of cremains of my friend, Jamie Burks, and of Peggy's mother, Mary Jane Benefield, and Charlie's mother, Betty Bishop."

243

friend, and another friend of mine had died of HIV-related illness a few years before. So, I crammed all of our material intentions and the ash cremains, literally, of these people, little bits of it, as well as my hair and my friend's, and made this little talisman that I folded up in this banana leaf and stitched it to make it into a pocket. I have used stitching many times; it's part of my artistic vocabulary. But in this case, I liked the idea that the leaf itself had kind of a pendulous, breast-type shape. I slapped it right on a photocopier. And that's the image, because the original piece itself went to the ethers. I put a black background behind one side of it and a white background behind the other side of it, so it was front and back. It became a pair, just like a pair of breasts. And I used the sewing to represent some type of suture, of healing, sewing it together.

JV: I've noticed that many of your works involve some kind of stitchery or sewing. Your grandmother was a seamstress, right? Tell me about her.

JG: It's my pleasure to tell you about her. My grandmother Mary Azzarello Basilo …

JV: Is that your mother's …?

JG: That was my mother's mother. She was very close to us. She was Italian, Sicilian, lived in the French Quarter and had babies in the Quarter when it was an Italian ghetto. Later, she lived on Catina Street in Lakeview. She lived in the tiniest house imaginable. It was just teensy, teensy, teensy, like a doll's house. And I remember the fig tree in the backyard, and I remember going there all the time. She had been trained, along with her two brothers, a trade, where they could support themselves. One brother was a shoemaker and the other was a tailor. And she was trained as a seamstress. She studied, and we heard this all of our lives, studied with a French *modiste*. I looked up what a French modiste was, and it's a fashionable dressmaker or milliner from the French *mode*, you know, modiste. And, with the word is the indication that the articles reflect the current Parisian fashion. So, it was a high fashion person who taught her how to sew. I tell you they had no money, and, yet, her daughters were gorgeous. She could take a *Vogue* or a *Harper's Bazaar* magazine and copy anything they wanted to perfection. And she knew so much about fabrics and could figure out ways to get good fabric, even though they really were on a budget. But she sewed for many people. She worked at this machine, day in, day out, except on Sundays. She loved her day of rest, but she loved being at this machine. I've often referenced her as my absolute, number one creative influence, because part of it was the ritual and the reverie she experienced that was palpable to a little kid leaning over and watching this.

Figure 6.19. Jan Gilbert and grandmother Mary Azzarello Basilo. Photograph by Charlie Gilbert, ca. 1962.

JV: She sewed for your mother and…
JG: She sewed for all of us. She was a master tailor. She sewed coats and everything, everything, and the finishing of them was utter perfection and it had to be the highest quality fabric. She made my whole first communion outfit. Wedding dresses. She made my sister's. It was one of the last things. My sister's eleven years older than I am. She taught me how to sew as a young adolescent, and I sewed a lot of clothes myself. I remember her just loving sitting at the machine! She had some emphysema-type related thing as she was getting older,

and I remember her coming home from the hospital and us all being excited and putting out little roses next to her bed and being just so excited that she was home. I remember she was just berserk that they didn't want her to do anything. She would say, "What do you want me to do, just sit down and look at myself?" She was that sort of eager beaver who really enjoyed her trade with a passion.

JV: What was she like?

JG: She had long gray hair wrapped up in a bun. Do you think that might be one of the reasons why I like gray hair? (laughs) The fun thing about it was that she wore these little tailored, little old lady housedresses. And she would giggle if you'd put lipstick on her. She was so NOT sophisticated, which was what was so wonderful about her. But she laughed a lot and cursed like a sailor. And she was very religious. But, she knew about sophistication of design. My mother and aunt had a lot of flair and knew what to point her to as well.

JV: Did your grandmother encourage you in your work, Jan?

JG: My grandmother truly was such an inspiration. I think that the work ethic, the idea of the practice of art, the practice of creating, the ritual of creating. I always use the word "reverie," you know, when you are in a zone. She got in her zone and you could see her zone, and she wanted to be LEFT in her zone, she really did, not in a nasty way, just, let her do what she needed to do.

As I got older, I would work on kid projects. I did a lot of ceramics, a lot of collage. My mother always encouraged that sort of thing. As long as we were going to make use of a magazine or even an encyclopedia—we never had very expensive encyclopedias, we had old ones—we could actually cut them up, if it was going into a project. So I think it was real easy for me to translate, this is life, what she's doing. 'Cause that zone or flow where time is lost, you're happy here, doing something productive, and you're jibing with the universe, really.

JV: Do you remember when you first used sewing or stitches in a particular piece?

JG: I absolutely do. It was in college. Fashion became one of the things because of the family. We could excel in that. It was a tool of my mother's that she placed a lot of emphasis on. So, when I went to art school—I was taking printmaking at Tulane at night—my mother

246

bought me a Top Drawer work shirt that probably was very expensive, at the time, to use as a work shirt in a studio, which, of course, I thought was the most outrageous thing. First of all, I am very happily messy, you know, (laughter) so the idea of wearing something nice was terrifying to me. But I remember working on one of my early etchings. There is a technique for etching that's called a "soft ground" where you can actually run things through the press, and they will give an impression of whatever you run through. So, I took that little shirt and just ran it through the press, into the soft ground. Then the ink was stuck to this shirt, which made it okay for me to wear, because it was kind of "christened." It made this amazing impression, and it really became the torso or the heart of a person. I was always super influenced by literature and writing, and I had read a book by Kurt Vonnegut's son, which was really a battle with his mental illness, called *The Eden Express*. And I called this piece *The Eden Express # 2*. I made this kind of square piece of the shirt, and then I made a pocket of the same piece that was off to the side, at an angle, like this dislocation, this part of yourself or your identity that maybe you didn't understand or you didn't know, it was at an angle. When I printed it, it had a pattern. It was one of the earliest conceptual pieces that I did, where I actually would take a little period of time every day and do sort of an etching with a pen, into the plate, kind of taking my temperature of the day. And that's how I covered the surface. And I remember one day not putting, not doing any, and having the words *Without Weather* scrawled into the thing, and that came from another book I had read. When I really looked at it, it seemed like those two things needed to be joined in some way. So it was a creative act of looking at one part of oneself and one's identity and bringing it together. It was black thread, and I actually sewed two copper buttons onto the print as well. So, the idea became the threads as sutures to, again, heal something. I know that in my own awareness it was an homage to my grandmother, and it always has been, but I don't know that it was a conscious homage at that point. It was way more spontaneous. And only did I later learn that this was her creative influence, and it was my way of paying, giving her credit.
JV: But, she was already . . . ?

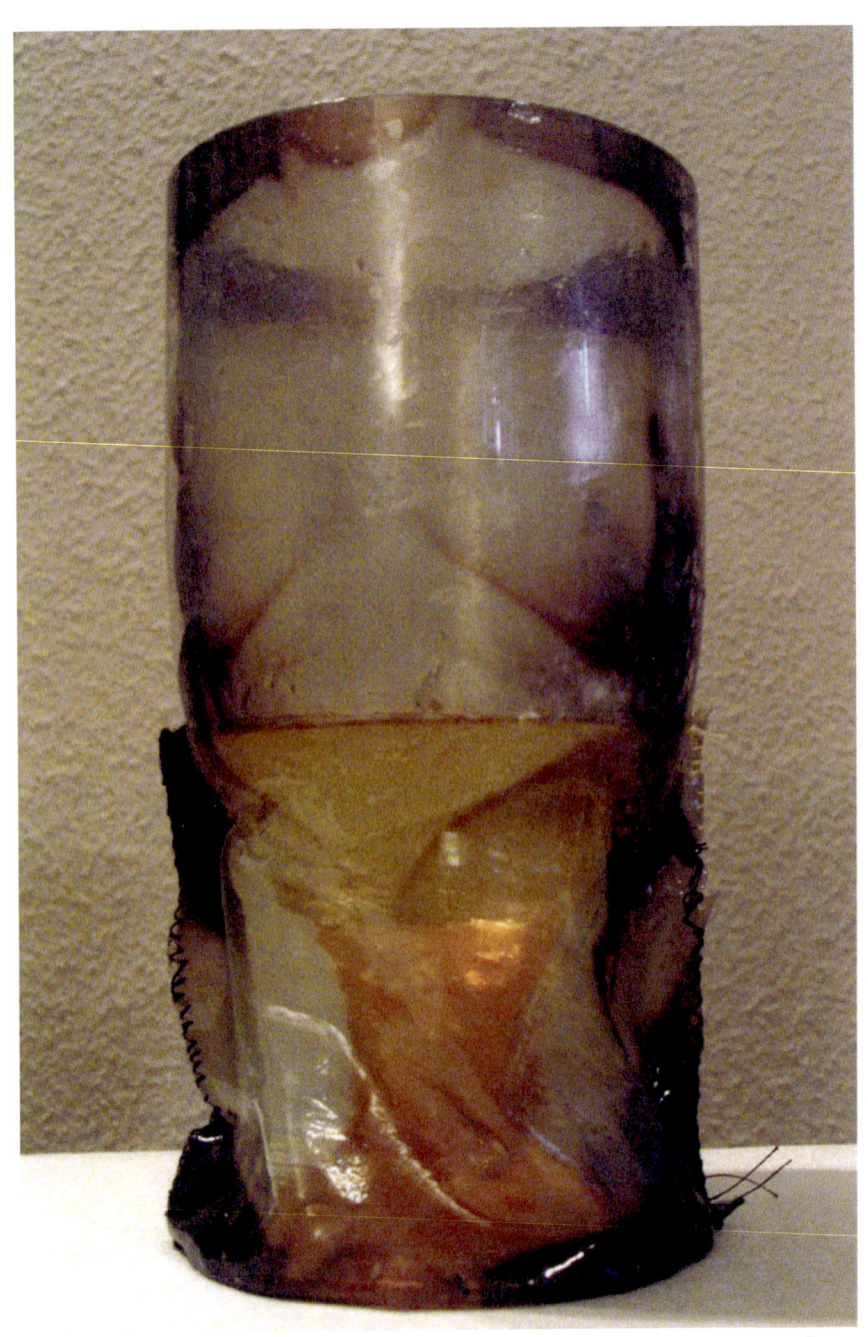

Figure 6.20. *C Cup.* Jan Gilbert, 2004. Mixed Media,
9 x 4 in. Photograph by the artist.

JG: Oh, yeah. She was dead. She died in 1965 during Hurricane Betsy. Yeah, she died that weekend in the hospital by herself. She was in the hospital during Hurricane Betsy. I was around twelve years old or so. This was 1977 by the time I was doing this.

JV: Will you talk about some of your other works of art that incorporate sewing?

JG: Yes. That was undergraduate school. I continued investigating printmaking, and I fell in love with painting. I loved printmaking and I loved painting. I took a lot more of those than necessary, by far. I went to graduate school at Tulane in 1980. I was there for a couple of years, and my work, though I was painting, it became more three-dimensional and even installation-oriented. I worked with these ideas of clothed torsos, where the pieces of fabric didn't fit. They had the shape of a person's trunk—shirt, belt, and hips—very abstracted. Then, towards the end of graduate school, I decided I wanted to do a self-portrait. And, what I did for my self-portrait, I built a closet. I brought pieces that my grandmother had made, that my mother had made, that I had made. I went to Wembley Tie Company and got tie fabric. The closet was divided, and it was kind of a male and a female side. I liked this idea of ourselves as the combination of the masculine and the feminine. So, I was using clothing and fabric, and that work shirt found its way into the closet. I got neckties from relatives and friends, and it became this self-portrait. That was where it was super conscious, and you know, giving the lineage of that (my grandmother's sewing) as a creative influence, saying that very directly.

At the same time, I was doing more abstract painting. The first one was *Tucked Lace* and these were folded pieces that were very much about fabric, and I started using patterns and I would do stitching in them, but they were all about layering and different surface interests, really, in a much more abstract way.

JV: So, let's hear about some of your more recent work.

JG: Okay. There was a series that I did right after graduate school that was one of my first professional exhibitions after my Tulane thesis exhibition. It was called *Framed*. It played with all the ideas of what frames, in terms of frame of mind, frame of body—that body, torso—even the framed format, bordering things. For that, I started using fashion images from fashion magazines that had been stockpiled at my mother's house. So this idea of recycling these images mattered to me. I was also intrigued, again, by this male/female idea. A lot of these fashion images, in my opinion, pretty clearly were done by men, and yet, of women. So the idea of reclaiming that was one of my *modus operandi*. I would take patterns, I would take images, and I would make these photo transfers that would often become transparent, and then layer them with patterns underneath, up over them, you know, newsprint, pieces of words, whatever. I would paint both under and over, but I often would use some whipping stitches. And sometimes I would blow them up really large. *Hathor* is about a nine-foot by nine-foot mixed media. Hathor is an Egyptian goddess, where she's kind of trapped in this web. It blends both the sewing as well as the patterns, and I would say they're all somewhat self-portraits.

Another image of the Hathor person, but a transparent kind of light box, is a piece called *Shift Back*, which, again, plays with these fashion images, patterns and stitching. Those are early, and I dwell on them because I was finding the tools and the vocabulary for my later work that's grounded it for years.

Later, in the '90s, I created a mixed media installation called *Auto/Biography/Charts*. Joseph Beuys was a very big influence here. He had done a series of works called *Dialogue through Time*. I found a very large auto mechanics manual that was a flip chart demonstration type thing, so it was largish, maybe thirty by forty inches. It's eighty-eight pages. I tried to pay homage to a lot of my creative influences, Joseph Beuys, Ed Kienholz, Eva Hesse, and other artists, but also digging up some of my earlier pieces and photographs, and it was an extracted version of that.

Another piece is actually a torso with my neck and breasts. *C Cup*. It's a glass, a vessel, very subtle and hard to see. That was done post breast cancer, as well.

And I always like to mention it's now many years later, and my health has been quite good and I'm happy about that.

JV: Whenever I think of your art, I think of repetition. So that's the influence of pattern.

JG: Patterns for me really have been so easy to talk about. I've never been able to follow directions. (laughter) So, even when I was a kid learning to sew, don't ask me to follow a pattern's instructions.

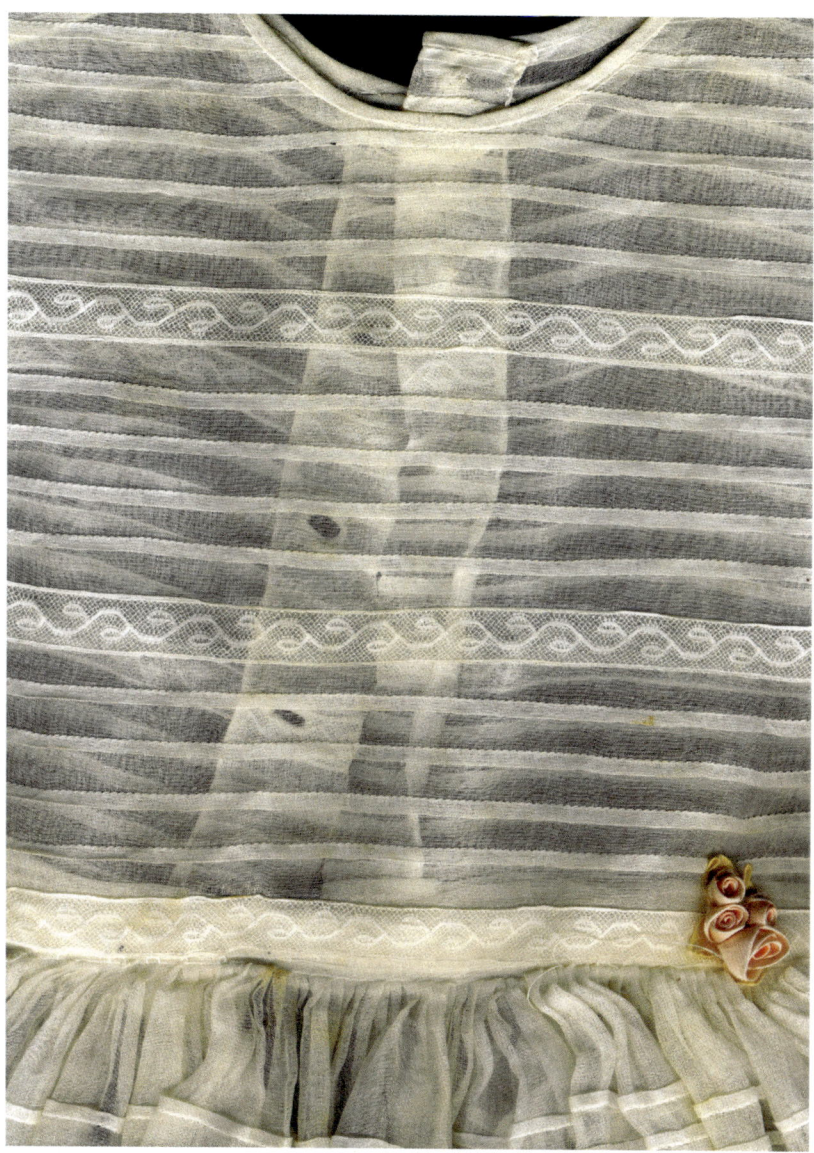

Figure 6.21. *Hand Tucked Communion Dress*, 2013. Jan Gilbert.
Photograph by the artist.

This image represents a scan of the 1959 dress, long saved in the artist's
sister's closet for safekeeping. Gilbert has since made other art pieces from
the scanned images, including wrapped blocks of wood.

And so I really always was, just do it! You know, I mean I would figure it out myself in my way. I could not go from one to two in this logic, supposedly, that to me is highly illogical. To me they represent conventions and directions that I subvert, and I just take on and then do completely the opposite things that you're supposed to do with them. (laughter) To me, it's very clear, it's very directional. I guess it's all about process. My grandmother and her sewing and tools just helped me learn how I was going to approach life and, without a road map kinda feeling my way in the dark. But with these tools, somehow it all makes sense.

Afterword by JV:
Typical of Jan, she couldn't end when we finished the interview. She sent me one last email the day I was planning to send the piece to the publisher. Attached was a giclée print of a new work of art. Simple and exquisite, *Hand Tucked Communion Dress 2013* is the result of Jan's collaboration with me in the interview process.

VII. Zigzagging Finishing Seams: Three Poems, Other Words, and Images

Figure 7.1 Detail of a huipil, traditional garment of woven cloth from the Amuzgo ethno-linguistic group who lived in a village called Xochislathuaca in the State of Guerrero, Mexico, ca. 1979. Photograph courtesy of Bobbie Malone.

Figure 7.2. Nine Patch Quilt, created in North Louisiana, ca. 1930.
Photograph by Dinah L. Rogers Photography. From the collection of Judy Walker.

This quilt was given to journalist Judy Walker in 2015. The family was not interested in keeping it and sought out someone with an interest in quilting. Considered by some a family heirloom, for others, quilts require the burden of care. This quilt was also considered not as desirable because it was a utilitarian one, although in perfect condition, hand-pieced and hand-quilted, in the classic Nine Patch pattern. Walker was told it was "from the family home place."

Figure 7.3. Star Patterned Quilt, created in Perry County, Arkansas, 1970.
Photograph by Dinah L. Rogers Photography. From the collection of Judy Walker.

This quilt was given to journalist Judy Walker as a high school graduation gift.
Walker today has over fifty quilts in her collection.

Figure 7.4. Teaching quilt, for quilt-as-you-go process, created by Judy Walker, 2016. Reproduction 1930s fabrics. Photograph by Dinah L. Rogers Photography. From the collection of Judy Walker.

after a long day

Celeste Delafosse

every stitch such simplicity
every stitch drawing the next
the mind calmed by a tonic of singular focus
just one more stitch toward completion
a meditation requiring so little effort
hold on despite eyelids falling
one more stitch
the needle pricks
1, 2, 3, pricks you're out
but just one more
a thread of no thought
such peace
a thread connecting the tangible to tranquility
nodding is indisputable
sleep must be answered

Memories—Oral History Excerpts

Lydia Eaves Trice, born in 1921, and Dotty Eaves Kostmayer, born in 1923, are sisters who taught sewing to generations of Uptown New Orleans girls. Here below they speak of what sewing means to them:

Lydia Trice: *Our mother taught us to sew. And our grandmother. Sewing was something to do together and it could help you. It could help others.*

Dotty Kostmayer: *Clothes were fitted. When we went out, before we left, Mother would come with her needle and thread and practically sew our dresses on to us. And then she would wait up to help us out of our clothes, to undo what she had sewn.*

Lydia Trice: *When my sister and I had children who were in elementary school, Mother gave us each a little Singer sewing machine. And we taught sewing with those machines, and of course, others we could use. Every summer, we taught sewing, for about twenty-five years to twenty or so New Orleans girls.*

Dotty Kostmayer: *Now we don't teach but we still sew. We make pillows, and purses, and place mats, other things for the Colonial Dames. We donate these things for their annual sale to make money for Indian Reservations.*

Lydia Trice: *Do you know others who in their 90s sew? We don't. People ask us to play bridge or do other things. We have learned to say no. We are better at sewing. We have a sewing room and it is a way to be together three times a week and yet also do what each of us likes. Sewing, in general, lets you focus. You can push other concerns to the side. You are not thinking about any bad things. You are there, watching the seam, watching what should happen.*

Marie Schuller, born on Java (now part of Indonesia), 1929, New Orleans resident since 1959:

In 1945, the former Netherlands East Indies Colony proclaimed its independence and called itself Indonesia.

All Dutch people and people of Dutch descent were forced to leave the Colony. This process took more than ten years. My husband and I left with our two children in 1957. At that time we and some other Dutch people were the last remnants of colonialism and we were forced to leave immediately. Some cruise liners were used to ferry us to Singapore. We stayed temporarily in Singapore then left for the Netherlands. My husband found a job but had a hard time adjusting to life in the Netherlands. Soon he applied for emigration to the USA and within two years we left the Netherlands.

We loved living in New Orleans from the start. We also love and treasure the freedom of speech that we have in the USA.... Being Dutch we still carry "colonial thoughts" and we grew up learning to keep our thoughts to ourselves. I did not realize how much it had become a trait of mine not to express my thoughts. In New Orleans I had to learn that it was alright to express your opinions. It is strange that it takes so many years to learn such a simple thing.

My husband found a job right away. We decided for me to stay home with the children. To earn some extra money, I accepted sewing work. I did this for many years. I had learned how to make patterns and to sew when I lived in Indonesia. An aunt of mine made my wedding dress. I could have made it myself, but according to old wives' tales it would bring bad luck to the bride if she made her own wedding gown. So my aunt made my dress and I made the bridesmaid's dress. Now you know why I have lived such a wonderful life.

When our son was a junior in High School my husband and I decided it was time for me to have a real job. Our son might want to go to college and we did not have the money to let him do it. I told my clients I was looking for a job and they had to look for another seamstress. The husband of one of my clients made an appointment for me to have an interview.... This is how I came to work ... for 19 years.

Lucille S. Ashburn, b. 1931, is the older sister of Sally Anne Smith (1929-2011) of whom she speaks here:

In the United States, Home Economics was a subject required of all girls. Many of the teachers were professionals. Some had been chemists and could find no other work but many of them proved the backbones of their communities.

My sister Sally Anne began her joy for sewing in her junior year of school. Following that, when she was a rising senior, the class was assigned to do a sewing project for the summer months. Sally Anne chose to make drapes for two large windows in the living room and a slipcover for a chair. The teacher would visit each week and when the project was completed, she made pictures of the living room, drapes and new covered chair. The pictures were sent to the Woman's College [North Carolina] Home Economics Department and kept on file.

Sally Anne also preserved a dress that had been our mother's, now over 100 years old. Imagine that Sally Anne used a special pair of scissors all these sewing years and had them sharpened by the Knife Man who came through the neighborhoods in New Orleans. She saved to buy that pair of scissors and a thimble that she also kept and gave to her niece. Sally Anne was able to sew until death.

Judy Walker, born in Dallas, Texas, 1952; New Orleans resident since 2000:

I have many quilts: those collected, those given to me, those I have made. My family now quilts together over four states. We collaborate via Facebook, phone calls and reunions. We mail one another quilt blocks so we can all have part in one quilt. It is a multigenerational group.

New Orleans has not an unusual quilting scene, but a vibrant one. There are quilting guilds and then quilting stores. The commercial ventures generally follow the lead of one person, the owner. When she retires, another person comes along and starts a new store. I have seen a slight increase lately in fabric stores, in an interest in all sorts of handmade items. I see this as a reaction to how much can be obtained now online, how we all, all over the U.S., can buy the same clothes, the same furnishings for our homes.

Nguyet Vu, born in Laos in 1956, New Orleans resident since 1979:

I learned to sew because my mom made me. She knew how to knit. She said that a lady should know how to sew for the family. Repair stuff. She said, "a career that you may need later on. No one take it away from you." Okay, I do for you, Mom.

I have been glad I learned. Never sorry, I learned. Could work in factory, could teach, could work for department stores and specialty shops, have my own business. Alterations.

Hardest part is finding helpers. They do not have talent. It's like art. It's a gift. You teach, some learn but many do not.

People today wear convenience clothes. No convenience clothes in Asia. Custom-made there. The fabric here too not as good. From most of the chain fabric store is not good. But the store-bought clothes have better fabric now. Doesn't make sense or does it? For money.

I shop now St. Charles, Promenade, and across the river: a hardware store: Ullo's, across the river. Fabric is beautiful. Remember Krauss. Fabric stores can be the best place in life: Everything beautiful.

Nicole Gibson, born in New Orleans, 1972:

I learned to sew at Kenilworth Mall in New Orleans East. The fabric stores all had sewing classes. I am not even sure they charged. Well, very little. You bought the pattern and the fabric and you used their machines. Three days a week one summer, when I was fifteen, I went there.

We made wrap-around skirts. Our moms had had something called Home Economics classes. They had made aprons. By our time, no Home Economics.

Figure 7.5. Occupational portrait of a women working at a sewing machine.
Unknown photographer, ca. 1853. Hand-colored Daguerreotype.
Courtesy of the Library of Congress, American Memory.

Until It Was Time (New York, 1911)

Gina Ferrara

A heap of rags, sheared remnants,
frayed rag time, Jelly Roll, the century
turning as threaded edges smoldered
the uncontainable colossal fire.
Industry churning
with greater ease than butter—
a convergence not of rivers, but soot and steam,
the ashen columns
ascending skyward in filthy beatitudes
charring the cumulus slowly adrift.
Whistles and shifts,
thirty-four minutes inflamed
those sisters and daughters,
mothers who unwound spools
to pull silken strands through slit-eyed needles,
thoughts of camels and the future,
the future of not having to sweat
by dim gaslight…the bolted doors
kept out any woman who slept late,
whose child was sick, who felt anemic,
a bevy of dialects, pinned hair up swept.
Heads bowed,
their English broken as crusts of cibata
or braided challah,
collars and sleeves sewed
in quick syllabic stitches—
shirt waists made with no sign of weakness
in shades of ecru
or ivory, until it was time
to jump or burn.

THREADS TO MEND THE WORLD

Malaika Favorite

I wore you down the catwalk of life.
I stitched my first dress by hand
Pricked my fingers until they resembled a pincushion.
Measured and re-measured the plaid of my days.

Nothing matched the mismatch dreams I had.
A kaleidoscope of failed intentions
Hanging off my skirt like a torn hem
In need of a safety pin.

I styled you when the cakewalk was the fashion.
My second dress was stitched on a sewing machine
pedal pushing stitches across my aspirations.
Singer sing me a spool of red thread

I am gauging my time by the garments I made
My last dress was a string of words
I am counting all the poems I have written
Lining up every word and measuring their length.

Like the spools of thread that held me together
I am hemming the world with ribbons of verse
Can one poem stitched into a flag
Stop a war or deter the path of a bullet?

VIII. About the Contributors

Nancy Alcalde was born and raised in a small town in Ohio. Her thirst for adventure and life led her to New York City, Los Angeles, and ultimately New Orleans, where she has resided for the last fifteen years.

Lee Barclay is the editor of *New Orleans: What Can't Be Lost—88 Stories and Traditions from the Sacred City*, an anthology in words and photographs in which culture bearers pay tribute to their home. A former community educator, crisis-intervention counselor, and legal advocate for sexual-violence survivors, Barclay now lives, writes, and edits in Faubourg St. John in New Orleans.

Rebecca Black's first book, *Cottonlandia*, won a 2005 Juniper Prize. She graduated from Tulane in 1997. A former NEA and Wallace Stegner Fellow, in 2011 she was a Distinguished Visiting Fulbright Professor at the Seamus Heaney Center for Poetry in Belfast, Northern Ireland. She is the 2016-2018 Poet Laureate of Albany, California.

Megan Burns is the publisher at Trembling Pillow Press and the author of three full-length poetry collections available from Lavender Ink. She also directs the Blood Jet Poetry Series in New Orleans.

Marda Burton is the co-author of *Galatoire's: Biography of a Bistro* and has also worked as a travel writer and journalist.

Rachel Carrico holds a Ph.D. in Critical Dance Studies from the University of California–Riverside and an M.A. in Performance Studies from NYU. She is currently a Faculty Fellow in the Dance Department at the University of Oregon, where she teaches dance history and is continuing her research on the aesthetic, political, and social histories of second lining.

Peter Cooley was born in the Midwest but has lived over half his life in New Orleans, where he is Senior Mellon Professor of the Humanities and Director of Creative Writing at Tulane University. He has published nine books of poetry, the most recent of which is *Night Bus to the Afterlife*. He is the Poet Laureate of Louisiana.

Judy Cooper's career in photography spans more than thirty years. In addition to working as the staff photographer at the New Orleans Museum of Art for fifteen of those years, she also did her own personal photography. Her work has been widely exhibited, from California to New York, and as far away as Kaunas, Lithuania.

Melody Davis is the author of five books of art criticism and poetry, most recently, *Women's Views: The Narrative Stereograph in Nineteenth-Century America* (University of New Hampshire Press, 2015) and *Holding the Curve*, poetry from Broadstone Books, 2013. She teaches at the Sage College of Albany.

Celeste Delafosse is a graduate of the New Orleans Center for the Arts and Tulane University's School of Social Work. Much of her working life has been focused on helping abused children. Most of her written work is for children, most recently a fantasy novel about dragons. She lives in Lafayette, Louisiana with her husband, zydeco musician Tony Delafosse, and their two boys.

Lenny Emmanuel's poetry has appeared in many literary and scientific publications. His most recent books are *Blue Rain* (2010), *Goodbye, America!* (2012), and *The Elements of Prose* (2013). From Savannah and Tybee Island, GA, he currently lives in Pass Christian, MS.

Malaika Favorite is a visual artist and a writer. Her poetry, fiction, and articles appear in numerous anthologies and journals, including *Pen International, Hurricane Blues, Drumvoices Revue, Uncommon Place, Xavier Review, The Maple Leaf Rag, Visions International, Louisiana Literature, Louisiana English Journal, Big Muddy*, and *Art Papers*. She is the winner of the 2005 Louisiana Literature Prize for Poetry. Her artwork is featured in many books including *African American Art and Artists* by Samella Lewis, *Black Art in Louisiana* by Bernardine B. Proctor, and the *St. James Guide to Black Artists* by Thomas Riggs.

Gina Ferrara is from New Orleans. Her books include *Ethereal Avalanche* (Trembling Pillow Press, 2009) and *Amber Porch Light* (CW Books, 2013). Her work has been published in places like *The*

Briar Cliff Review, Cultural Vistas and *The Poetry Ireland Review.* Since 2007, she has run the Poetry Buffet Reading series.

Jan Gilbert is a native New Orleanian, an interdisciplinary artist, curator, and educator. Her works have been shown widely in galleries, museums, cultural centers, and often as public art on city streets across the United States and abroad.

Lee Meitzen Grue is a poet and a writer, as well as longtime editor of the *New Laurel Review.*

Herreast Harrison holds degrees in Education and Museum Studies. She is the founder of the Guardian Institute, dedicated to the development of children through literacy, New Orleans's indigenous cultural arts, and West African and New World oral traditions.

Alice Henderson is a ceramic artist and painter who has exhibited her work in New Orleans, New York, San Francisco, Detroit, Baltimore, Denver, Baton Rouge, Austin, and Mexico. She taught Talented Visual Art for eighteen years in Orleans Parish at Ben Franklin High School, Hynes Charter School, and Esperanza Charter School.

Raymond "Moose" Jackson is a Detroit native and a resident of New Orleans since 2003. His work investigates sacred relationships with place. He received the 2009 Big Easy award for his play/poem "Loup Garou."

mary mac jones is a graduate of Tulane University who is originally from Memphis, TN. She is an aspiring screenwriter and filmmaker who has been published in the *Tulane Review.* Mary mac's interests include cartoons, dog-spotting, and nachos.

Karissa Kary is a writer, theater and event producer, and an Associate with the Tennessee Williams/New Orleans Literary Festival.

U.S.-born retired psychotherapist **Wendy Klein** is published in many magazines and anthologies. She has two collections from Cinnamon Press: *Cuba in the Blood* (2009) and *Anything in Turquoise* (2013), with a third, *Mood Indigo*, from Oversteps in 2016.

George Koschel has had short stories, poetry, and essays published in a number of literary journals and magazines, including *Coe Review*, *Ellipsis*, *glbtq online encyclopedia*, *NEgo*, and *RGD*. He also works as an assistant editor for the *New Laurel Review*. Besides writing, he is active as a longtime volunteer for NOAIDS.

Roselyn Lionhart is a community activist, musician, and spoken-word artist. In 2015, she was honored by the Mardi Gras Indian Hall of Fame for her work as a civil rights activist.

Sally Main is Senior Curator Emerita from the Newcomb Art Museum at Tulane University. She has over thirty-three years of museum and art administration experience, concentrating her research on the arts and crafts of the Newcomb Pottery Enterprise.

Bobbie Malone is the author of *Rabbi Max Heller: Reformer, Zionist, Southerner* (1997) and *Lois Lenski: Storycatcher* (2016). Bobbie has now retired from her tenure as Director of the Office of School Services at the Wisconsin Historical Society where, over more than fifteen years, she wrote or co-authored many publications for classrooms, including the award-winning fourth-grade textbook, *Wisconsin: Our State, Our Story* and *Thinking Like a Historian: Rethinking History Instruction*.

Martha McFerren is the author of five books, the most recent of which is *Archaeology at Midnight*. Her poems have appeared in publications such as the *Georgia Review*, *Southern Review*, and *Shenandoah*, among others, and in many anthologies. She is the recipient of an Artist Fellowship in Literature awarded by the Louisiana Arts Council, a Yaddo Fellowship, and a National Endowment for the Arts Creative Writing Fellowship.

Moonyeen McNeilage is an artist and writer who lives in Australia.

Jessica Mitchell is a graduate of Tulane University and holds a B.A. in English.

Marian D. Moore is employed by Leidos, Inc. at Entergy Services as a computer analyst. Her poetry has been published in *Drumvoices*,

The Louisiana Review, *Bridges*, and *ReformJudaism.org*. One work of fiction was published in the anthology *Crossroads: Tales of the Southern Literary Fantastic.*

Owen Murphy, a freelance photographer for over 25 years, specializes in photographing works of art for institutions, galleries and artists. He also co-founded the New Orleans Photo Alliance and was its first president.

Phyllis Parun, a New Orleans-born philosopher-artist-poet-essayist, has been a contributor to many literary journals and has exhibited in over forty art exhibitions. In 2011, she initiated the New Orleans Living Treasures Award recognizing community cultural pioneers.

Yuka Petz is an artist, designer and craftsman specializing in book design and bookbinding. She received her MFA in Book Arts/ Printmaking at the University of the Arts in Philadelphia and her BFA in Graphic Design from the Rhode Island School of Design.

Arthur Pfister, known as Professor ARTURO, is a poet and fiction writer, a Spoken Word artist, educator, performer, editor, and speechwriter. ARTURO, one of the original Broadside Poets of the 1960s, has collaborated on a medley of projects with a mélange of artists including painters, musicians, photographers, dancers, singers, fire eaters, waiters, cab drivers, and other members of the Great Miscellaneous. He recently published *MY NAME IS NEW ORLEANS: 40 Years of Poetry & Other Jazz* and *JAZZ STORIES*. A collection of his poems, *A Love Supreme*, was published in 2016 by the New York Quarterly Foundation.

Wayne Phillips has served as the Curator of Costumes & Textiles and Curator of Carnival Collections at the Louisiana State Museum since 1998. He is responsible for a collection of over 30,000 artifacts including Carnival costumes and accessories, original photographs, and paper ephemera.

Valentine Pierce is a spoken-word artist, graphic designer, and artisan who is always seeking new ways to explore her creativity.

clare e. potter is a Welsh language poet from Wales who has lived in Mississippi and New Orleans. She taught at Cardiff University, and is co-writing the life-story of Janet Vokes, a woman who bred a racehorse on a Welsh slag heap. Potter is also poet-in-residence at Llwyn Celyn, a medieval farmhouse in the Black Mountains. Her work has been published in *Poetry Wales, New Welsh Review, The Xavier Review, Cahoots* and *The Seminary Ridge Review.*

Pamela Rabalais-Vinci is Curator of the LSU Textile & Costume Museum and a faculty member in the Louisiana State University Department of Textiles, Apparel Design, and Merchandising. Her research interests include nineteenth- and twentieth-century dress, Louisiana Acadian textiles, and the 1941-1962 Acadian Handicraft Project.

Dinah Rogers is a photojournalist with over 30 years working on newspapers and websites.

Cynthia Topsey-Ellis is a community activist, a former Kellogg Foundation fellow, and a leader among the Garifuna people of Belize. From 1990 to 1992, she lived in New Orleans where she was a Visiting Scholar at the Newcomb College Center for Research on Women.

Susan Tucker is an archivist, author, and editor whose works include *Telling Memories Among Southern Women* (1988), *The Scrapbook in American Life* (2006), *New Orleans Cuisine* (2009), and *City of Remembering* (2016).

Janis Turk is an award-winning independent travel journalist and photographer whose new book, *Frommer's San Antonio & Austin Day by Day*, was recently released.

Jan Villarrubia's first poetry collection *Return to Bayou Lacombe* was recently published by Cinnamon Press in Wales. She has won numerous fellowships, grants, and awards for her plays. Among her full-length plays are *Turning of the Bones* (Great Stage Publishing), *Miz Lena's Backyard* (Dramatic Publishing), and *Odd Fellows Rest* (Xavier Review Press).

Donna Glee Williams is a writer, seminar leader, and creative coach. A sort of Swiss Army knife of the page, Donna Glee has seen her work published in anthologies, newsstand glossies, literary magazines, academic journals, reference books, big-city dailies, online venues, and spoken-word podcasts, as well as on stage and CD recordings. These days, her focus is on speculative fiction, aka fantasy and science fiction.

Beth Willinger, a sociologist and feminist scholar, has looked to the past as well as the present through her research on the history of the Christian Woman's Exchange, the history of Newcomb College, the impact of Hurricane Katrina on the women of New Orleans, and gender inequality in New Orleans and Louisiana.

Malcolm Willison is a manuscript editor and teacher who has been writing and publishing poetry for quite a long time in, and sometimes about, New Orleans, Key West, New York, and other places around the world.

IX. Acknowledgements

Thank you to all who helped with this anthology, especially our most wonderful contributors, and proofreaders Elizabeth Young Sweeney, Casey Wasserman, and Malcolm Willison. Thank you for talent and skill to book designer Yuka Petz. Thank you to the staff of the Louisiana State Museum, especially Melissa Smith and Michael Leathem; to the staff of the Louisiana Research Center at Tulane University's Howard-Tilton Library, especially Sean Benjamin; to the staff of the Newcomb Art Museum, especially Elizabeth Bahls; to the staff of the Historic New Orleans, especially Jennifer Navarre; and Chianta Dorsey and Christopher Harter of the Amistad Research Center. Thank you to private contributors of photographs especially Maureen Detweiler, Augusta Elmwood, Sally Reeves, and Suzanne Whann. Thank you also to professional photographers, those acknowledged in credits but also those who went beyond agreement to provide encouragement: Judy Cooper, Dinah Rogers, Owen Murphy, and book designer Yuka Petz. Thank you to all who long believed in this project, especially those of you who know well the busy lives all of us live, yet who made concessions to our tendency also to go slow.

Index

Illustrations and captions for illustrations are in **boldface** type. Proper names followed by page numbers in **boldface** denote authorship and first page of contributions.

Made in the USA
Monee, IL
10 July 2024